MACMILLAN SMALL BUSINE

The books in this series present their subject-matter comprehensively and in a sophisticated manner with more conceptual underpinning than has previously been provided.

The series is intended primarily for undergraduate and postgraduate students taking small business and related courses at universities and polytechnics. Books in the series will also be suitable for those working for professional examinations and for well-informed managers of small and growing businesses.

PUBLISHED

Paul Burns and Jim Dewhurst (eds): *Small Business and Entrepreneurship*
Paul Burns and Jim Dewhurst (eds): *Small Business in Europe*
Jim Dewhurst and Paul Burns: *Small Business: Planning Finance and Control*
Terry Hill: *Small Business: Productions Management*
Derek Waterworth: Small Business: Marketing for the Small Business

---

Series Standing Order

If you would like to receive future titles in this series as they are published, you can make use of our standing order facility. To place a standing order please contact your bookseller or, in case of difficulty, write to us at the address below with your name and address and the name of the series. Please state with which title you wish to begin your standing order. (If you live outside the UK we may not have the rights for your area, in which case we will forward your order to the publisher concerned.)

Standing Order Service, Macmillan Distribution Ltd, Houndmils, Basingstoke, Hampshire, RG21 2XS, England.

SMALL BUSINESS AND ENTREPRENEURSHIP

Edited by

Paul Burns and Jim Dewhurst

MACMILLAN

First published 1989
Reprinted 1990

Published by
MACMILLAN EDUCATION LTD
Houndmills, Basingstoke, Hampshire RG21 2XS
and London
Companies and representatives
throughout the world

Printed in Hong Kong

British Library Cataloguing in Publication Data
Small business and entrepreneurship. —
(Macmillan small business series).
1. Small business
I. Burns, Paul, *1949*– II. Dewhurst, Jim
338.6'42   HD2341
ISBN 0–333–42096–9 (hardcover)
ISBN 0–333–42097–7 (paperback)

Contents

List of Tables

List of Figures

Notes on the Contributors

Colin Barrow is Senior Lecturer in Small Business Development, Cranfield School of Management, UK. He joined Cranfield in 1984 having previously been at Stirling University and Thames Polytechnic. He has nine years' industrial experience, latterly as managing director of a small carpet company and is author of many books on small business including *The BBC Small Business Guide*, *The Pocket Entrepreneur*, *Route to Success* and many others.

Sue Birley is Sir Philip and Pauline Harris Professor in Entrepreneurship and Director of the Entrepreneurship Research Centre, Cranfield School of Management, UK. She joined Cranfield in 1985 from the University of Notre Dame, Indiana, USA, and was previously at London Business School. She is chairman of Newchurch and Company, Venture Consultants and has published extensively in the area of small business and entrepreneurship. She is the author of the well-known *Small Business Case Book*.

Paul Burns is National Westminster Bank Professor of Small Business Development, Cranfield School of Management, UK and Visiting Professor at the Open University, UK. He joined Cranfield in 1984 having previously been at Warwick University. He was founding director of the English Graduate Enterprise Programme and is Director of the Small Business Open Learning Centre at the Open University. A chartered accountant, he has worked with the Small Business Division of Arthur Andersen and Company. He is author and/or editor of *Small Business: Planning, Finance and Control*, *Small Business in Europe* and *Entrepreneur*.

James Curran is Reader in Industrial Sociology and Director of the Small Business Research Unit at Kingston Polytechnic, UK. He has been involved in research on the small business enterprise for well over a decade and has published widely on the subject. He is currently researching the impact of environmental influences, such as government policies and local labour markets, on small firms in the electronics and printing industries.

Jim Dewhurst was Senior Lecturer at the School of Industrial and Business Studies, University of Warwick, UK. He joined Warwick in 1969 having previously been at Cranfield School of Management and the Polytechnic of Central London. He is a chartered accountant and has extensive commercial experience including periods as company secretary and financial director, and is the author and/or editor of *Small Business: Planning, Finance and Control*, *Small Business in Europe*, *Business Mathematics* and *Cost-Benefit Analysis*.

Tony Lorenz is Managing Partner, Equity Capital for Industry Ventures (ECI), UK. He joined ECI in 1977 and became Managing Partner in 1986. After graduating from Trinity College, Dublin, he started his career with the Ford Motor Company and then spent five years in the corporate strategy division of PA International before joining Charter-house Group. A former chairman of the British Venture Capital Association and the founding chairman of the European Venture Capital Association, he is the author of *Venture Capital Today*.

William A. Sahlman is Associate Professor of Finance at Harvard Graduate School of Business Administration, USA. He has an AB degree in Economics from Princeton University, an MBA from Harvard and a PhD in Business Economics, also from Harvard. He is now executive director to a number of companies and is an adviser to Nathan/Tyler Productions, creators of 'In Search of Excellence – The Film'. He has written a number of articles including 'Capital Market Myopia' which was published as the lead article in the initial volume of the *Journal of Business Venturing*.

John Stanworth is Professor at the Polytechnic of Central London (formerly Regent Street Polytechnic), UK, and Director of their Small Business Unit. He has been involved in the field of small business for twenty years as a researcher, trainer and consultant. His prime research interests have centred around issues of entrepreneurial motivation, social relations in the small firm and, more recently, franchising. In the field of entrepreneurial training, his most notable achievement has been the design and direction of the London Enterprise Programme in association with the London Enterprise Agency.

Howard H. Stevenson is Sarofim-Rock Professor of Business Administration, Harvard Graduate School of Business Administration, USA. He returned to Harvard in 1982, having left in 1978 to serve as Vice President, Finance and Administration, of a large entrepreneurial firm in the paper industry. He is a director of numerous corporations, as well as a trustee for several private trusts and foundations, and has published extensively in the area of entrepreneurship, including *New Business Ventures and the Entrepreneur*.

Lister Vickery is Affiliate Professor, Entrepreneurship and Smaller International Enterprises, INSEAD (European Institute of Business Administration), Fontainebleau, France. He has extensive experience throughout Europe in the venture capital financing of young technology-based companies and is founder and chairman of one such French firm. He has worked for the International Finance Corporation, financing industrial projects in the developing countries of Asia and is the author of *Le Capital Risque*.

Acknowledgements

The authors and publishers wish to thank the following who have kindly given permission for the use of copyright material: Cranfield School of Management for the Body Shop Case; European Institute of Business Administration (INSEAD), the INSEAD Alumni Fund Chair, the partners in Kara Foods and Lister Vickery for the Kara Foods Case; The Harvard Business School for the Atlas Lighting Company Case, 9–384–235. Copyright © 1984 by the President and Fellows of Harvard College.

CHAPTER 1

Introduction

Paul Burns

1. Entrepreneurship and small business

The Western world is in the middle of a love affair with small business. This despite the fact that in Britain small business generates only 20 per cent of Gross National Product (GNP) and 40 per cent of employment. Why is small business so attractive? Is it that we are bored with the faceless bureaucracy of big business? Human nature being what it is, is it that we enjoy the story of the entrepreneur that so often lies behind the small business? Could it have something to do with the fact that whilst large businesses are slimming down their workforces, small businesses are expanding theirs? Or could it be that we all harbour within us a desire to set up our own business and to see it grow?

Economies of scale used to rule the industrial world. Big was cost-effective. Why have these basic economic tenets changed? If they haven't changed, then what is it that allows small firms not only to survive but also to prosper?

To a large extent the answer to these questions lies in the individuals behind the small firm: the entrepreneurs. The West is probably not so much having a love affair with small business as with these entrepreneurs. We are fascinated by entrepreneurs that start up small businesses and then make them grow. It is estimated that in the UK an average of two new millionaires are created each week from individuals who have an investment in a company floated on the stock market. In Britain they have been called 'the new rich'. They are the self-made men of today; their wealth has not been inherited. However, for these entrepreneurs, money is not a motivator but rather a pleasant by-product of being in charge of their own destiny. The motivation comes instead from a wish to earn a living in a way that suits them. They are motivated more by success than wealth. They all want to be their own boss, but more than that they want to be the boss of a successful, growing firm.

2. Small business defined

Small businesses are easier to describe than to define. The Bolton
Report,[1] as early as 1971, described a small business as follows:

- In economic terms, a small firm is one that has a relatively *small share
  of its market*.
- It is managed by its owners or part owners in a *personalised* way, and
  not through the medium of a formalised management structure.
- It is independent in the sense that it does not form part of a larger
  enterprise and that the owner/managers should be free from *outside
  control* in taking their principal decisions.

The characteristic of a small firm's share of the market is that it is not
large enough to enable it to influence the prices or national quantities of
goods sold to any significant extent. Personalised management is, perhaps, the most characteristic factor of all. It implies that the owner
actively participates in all aspects of the management of the business,
and in all major decision-making processes. There is little devolution or
delegation of authority. One person is involved when anything material
is concerned. Independence from outside control rules out those small
subsidiaries which, though in many ways fairly autonomous, nevertheless have to refer major decisions (for example, on capital investment)
to a higher authority. Of course, there are other characteristics of small
businesses that may be added to the list; perhaps the most obvious is the
severe limitation of resources faced by small firms, both in terms of
management and manpower as well as money.

The same Bolton Committee made heavy weather of a statistical
definition of small firms. Recognising that one single definition would
not cover industries as divergent as manufacturing and service, the
Committee used eight definitions for varying industry groups. These
range from under 200 employees for manufacturing firms, to over
£50 000 turnover for retailing, and up to five vehicles or less for road
transport. But any definition which is based on turnover, or indeed any
other measure of size expressed in financial terms, suffers from terrible
inherent disadvantages in times of inflation. The Department of Employment in the UK recently updated these statistical definitions. Small
retail businesses were defined as those having a turnover below £315 000
per annum and small firms in wholesale trades were defined as having an
annual turnover of less than £1 260 000. These definitions are shown in
Table 1.1

However, different government departments in the UK provide different definitions of small firms. The 1985 Companies Act distinguished
between small- and medium-sized businesses by defining three sets of
criteria: turnover, balance sheet totals and average weekly number of

Table 1.1 The small firms sector: statistical definitions

Business sector		Upper limit of the statistical definitions of small firms	
		Adopted by the Bolton Committee[a,c]	Revised to allow for inflation[b,c,d]
Manufacturing	no.	200	
Construction	of.	25	
Mining/ Quarrying	employees	25	
Retailing		50	315
Wholesale trades	Turnover	200	1260
Motor trade	£000	100	630
Miscellaneous Services		50	315
Road transport		5 vehicles	
Catering		All excluding multiples and brewery-managed public houses	

[a]Turnover at 1963 prices.
[b]Turnover at August 1983 prices.
[c]Turnover definitions have been revised — all other definitions are unaltered.
[d]The inflation adjusted figures have been estimated by applying the change in the general index of retail prices between the average for 1963 and August 1983, and rounding the result to the nearest £10,000. Note, however, that the retail price index (RPI) is more appropriate for adjusting the turnover of some industries than for others.

Source: Small Firms and Tourism Division, Department of Employment.

employees. To qualify for one category or another, two of the three statistical conditions outlined in Table 1.2 had to be fulfilled.

To make matters worse, statistical definitions of small firms vary widely from one country to another. Some use number of employees, some turnover, some capital employed 'variously defined', and some a combination of all three. Risking a broad generalisation, one may say, however, that in Europe small firms are those with less than 200 employees, and medium-sized firms are those with 200–500 employees. In the US, all firms employing up to 500 employees are regarded as small.

3. The book

This book is about small businesses, and the problems and the opportunities that they face. It is also about the entrepreneur, his character

Table 1.2   Small and medium-sized businesses (Companies Act 1985 criteria)

Business criteria / Business size	Upper limit of statistical conditions		
	Turnover (£m)	*Balance sheet total (£m)*	*Average weekly no. of employees*
Medium	5.75	2.8	250
Small	1.40	0.7	50

Source: Companies Act 1985

and how he manages a business. Not all small businesses are run by entrepreneurs and most small businesses are born to die or stagnate. In Britain, almost one third of all new businesses cease trading within the first three years of their life; of those that go beyond this stage most will never grow to any size but will plateau out to provide the owner/ manager with an acceptable living.

This book is concerned with small businesses, warts and all. It is concerned with new businesses, growing businesses, businesses that go nowhere and businesses that fail. It is concerned with the qualities needed to be a successful entrepreneur, not only in small firms but also in large; it is concerned with the style of management that entrepreneurs adopt; it is concerned with their management and employee relations; it is concerned with raising equity finance and the funding problems of growing businesses. It is also concerned with how large firms can develop small firms as part of their corporate strategy to encourage entrepreneurship in their management; and it is concerned with franchising, which is a way that enables many people to set up their own small firm without the need to be particularly entrepreneurial or to have any particular management flair.

The book is intended for use on courses about small business and entrepreneurs. It has developed out of MBA (Master of Business Administration) courses at Cranfield School of Management, UK. MBA scholars are fascinated by entrepreneurs and many come to business school harbouring a deep-seated desire to set up their own business. Sadly, few do so. However, the sheer diversity and complexity of the issues facing the entrepreneur in small business today are such that no one person can ever claim to be expert in all the areas. This book brings together a large number of contributors, all experts in their respective fields. It brings together academics and a practitioner, from the UK, from the USA and from France. These authors take an international view of the problems and opportunities facing small firms today and each chapter is followed by a case study which illustrates the points made in the chapter. The book will be suitable for those taking courses on small business and entrepreneurship in universities and polytechnics, both at undergraduate and postgraduate levels. However, it will also be of interest to entrepreneurs who take an interest in their own endeavours.

Chapter 2 is concerned with how businesses are started. Starting a business is a process which can take many years to evolve. This chapter starts by looking at the entrepreneur, his motivation and his background; it draws the distinction between an entrepreneur and the manager of a small business but suggests that the economic climate is an important factor in influencing the number of both entrepreneurs and small businessmen. It looks at the trigger that makes these people eventually set up their own businesses and the way they have to marshal a wide range of resources to get the business off the ground: Professor Birley calls it 'The resource merry-go-round'. She believes that strong informal networks are essential to help launch successful firms; these networks are ways of providing credibility and resources for the new business. For example, a previous employer may agree to be the first customer, a friend may allow the use of spare office space or a relative may be prepared to lend money with little real hope of return in the short- or even medium-term. However, even with the help of these informal networks, an entrepreneur faces many problems in setting up a new business.

Chapter 3 looks at some of the strategies that help small firms to grow as well as learning from the lessons of those that fail. Professor Burns emphasises that it is important to understand the economies of scale available within any market segment. He argues that successful small firms are based either upon a technological or a marketing innovation, or on a focused niche strategy with a differentiated product targeted at a clearly-defined market segment. Even following these strategies, any growing firm will face severe problems as it proceeds through different phases of its life cycle and he goes on to catalogue the changing emphases necessary to steer the business through these phases. From this are drawn the critical elements in the successful development of a business. Finally he gives us an insight into the process of failure; not only would this help to avoid the event but it also reinforces many of the lessons of success. However, understanding the process of failure, and even being able to avoid it, is not the same as being able to predict it and Professor Burns is not optimistic about our ability, as yet, to do that.

Chapter 4 once more looks at the entrepreneur. Mr Dewhurst is concerned with entrepreneurial motivation and he goes on to review methods of psychological testing for entrepreneurs. The case study attached to this chapter provides us with an example of one such test. Mr Dewhurst is concerned to balance the sometimes over-enthusiastic view of the entrepreneur by stressing some negative characteristics that cause problems within small firms. Finally, he looks at social attitudes to entrepreneurship in Europe and the environment that has contributed to their development, and concludes with some interesting observations on the role of hardship in generating the entrepreneurial spirit.

Chapter 5 looks at the process of entrepreneurship. Professors Stevenson and Sahlman boldly state that 'it does not appear useful to delimit the entrepreneur by defining those economic functions that are entrepreneurial and those that are not. Nor does it appear particularly helpful to decide which individuals are entrepreneurs and which are not'. They define entrepreneurship as 'the relentless pursuit of opportunity without regard to resources currently controlled'. For them, opportunity is the key that unlocks the view of the entrepreneurial process along six dimensions of strategy; strategic orientation; commitment to opportunity; commitment of resources; control of resources; the concept of management structure; and finally, the compensation or reward system. They contrast the role of the entrepreneur with that of the trustee/administrator and highlight the requirements for an entrepreneurial organisation of any size. This chapter therefore has lessons for large as well as small business.

Chapter 6 pursues the theme of the entrepreneur, this time in his relations with his workforce. Professor Stanworth and Dr Curran debunk the two typical stereotypes of employee relations in small firms: the first that small firms are indeed 'sweat shops'; the second that they are somehow 'utopian social settings involving highly satisfied and conflict free relationships'. They highlight the complexity of employee relations in the small firm across different industry sectors. Many of the characteristics that do emerge are indeed related to the characteristics of the typical owner/manager, but this is only one of a whole range of factors influencing employee relations which exhibit themselves in a correspondingly wide range of employee reactions to working in small firms. This chapter gives a balanced view of the 'pluses' and 'minuses' involved in working for a small firm.

Chapter 7 looks at the popular phemonenon of franchising. Taking up a franchise can be an easy way of setting up a new business for those of us who are less entrepreneurial and less willing to take risks. Certainly the franchise industry has witnessed a phenomenal growth: the question is, of course, who is making the money, the franchisees or the franchisors? Mr Barrow reviews the industry and describes what is involved in taking up a franchise, listing very clearly the advantages and disadvantages of taking this route into self employment. However, he also looks at the industry from the viewpoint of the franchisor, giving us examples of successful franchisors as well as an understanding of what is involved in developing the franchise chain.

Chapter 8 looks at equity financing in small firms. Professor Vickery reviews the sources of equity avilable, both informal and institutional, to small firms. He sets this in the context of the company's life cycle and the sources of funds available to it as it grows, and finally looks at 'packaging the deal' – that is, creating the financial structure which is so often looked upon by non-financiers as a sort of magic trick designed to make the numbers look more attractive than they really are. To do this he looks at a management buy-out, that of Ripolin UK in 1981. This chapter takes an international perspective on the provision of equity finance for small firms and provides data on international gearing levels.

Chapter 9 looks at the way small firms are spun-off from large firms. In particular it looks at three areas that are highly topical today: corporate venturing; management buy-outs; and management buy-ins. Corporate venturing is a way in which large or medium-sized businesses can partner small, or new, companies in growing or diversifying their own long-term business. Management buy-outs in the UK are now a well-established way by which large companies can divest themselves of business units to those units' own management teams. Management buy-outs are an extremely attractive, and low risk, way of setting up a new smaller business and have therefore attracted considerable interest among venture capitalists. Management buy-ins are the mirror of buy-outs and frequently involve a turnaround or recovery situation. With a buy-in, a new management finances the acquisition of a controlling position in an existing business. Mr Lorenz reviews these areas of big-business strategy and shows how the development of new small firms is as much an opportunity for large companies as it is for individual entrepreneurs.

Finally, in the Appendix to the book, we review the all-important business plan. Whether seeking a strategy for growth or the funds to make a business happen, the business plan is an essential ingredient in the recipe for success. The Appendix provides a specimen outline as well as some guidance on how it should be prepared and presented. Part of the coursework in most courses on entrepreneurship and small business involve the preparation or review of a business plan. Ideally, students should be asked to prepare a business plan on a business idea that they think has potential: preparing the plan forces them to be creative and entrepreneurial, and it also takes them beyond that stage and forces them to crystallise their ideas, write them down on paper, and show how they will be made to happen. It is not only creative, it is also an excellent management discipline: it integrates all the functional areas of management that, sadly, all too often are taught separately.

CHAPTER 2

The Start-up

Sue Birley

Starting a business is not an event, but a process which may take many years to evolve and come to fruition. Very few people are born entrepreneurs and very few new businesses are unique. Yet each year it is estimated that around 200 000 new firms are created each year in the UK. Whilst many do not survive beyond the first few difficult, formative years, many do continue to grow and provide a livelihood for both owners and employees. However, few of these grow to be the large firms of the future, or, indeed, beyond the ownership of the original founders. This is despite the widening availability of the new unlisted securities market (USM) and the over the counter (OTC) market, set up to trade in the shares of those firms of insufficient size to obtain a full quotation on the stock market. The study of 'start-up' is, therefore, concerned with two issues: first, the process by which an individual arrives at the decision to try to develop a business out of an idea; and second, the process of assembling the resources necessary to begin trading.

1. The entrepreneur

Earlier studies of the origins of the entrepreneur concentrated almost entirely upon their motivations. It was assumed that the entrepreneurial flair, the ability to take risks, and the desire to create a business, were inherent in the individual – he or she was born with them. This motivation was described by Schumpeter[1] as an 'innovative' drive, by McLelland[2] as a 'need for achievement', and measured by Rotter[3] as 'locus of control'. However, McLelland also showed that whilst these motivations were essential for the successful creation of business, they were not genetically bound. In his experiments, those groups which received his achievement motivation education demonstrated a larger supply of entrepreneurs than his control group which had not received the training. Thus evolved the idea that entrepreneurs were made rather than born; that lifetime experiences were just as important as genetic influences.

Cooper[4] provides the most comprehensive and useful framework for explaining the various factors which may contribute to the 'entrepreneurs decision'. He classified them into three groups:

1. 'The entrepreneur, including the many aspects of his background which affect his motivations, his perceptions, and his skills and knowledge.'
2. 'The organisation for which the entrepreneur had previously been working, whose characteristics influence the location and the nature of new firms, as well as the likelihood of spin-offs.'
3. 'Various environmental factors external to the individual and his organisation, which make the climate more or less favourable to the starting of a new firm.'

Cooper defined these three groups as Antecedent Influences; the Incubator Organisation; and Environmental Factors (see Table 2.1).

Despite this, little is known about the actual characteristics described by Cooper. The answer to the question on the lips, and in the minds, of every investor – 'How can we pick winners?' – remains elusive. Whilst the motivations of entrepreneurs have been studied extensively, there is, as yet, little known about the lifetime characteristics. Moreover,

Table 2.1   Influences on the entrepreneurial decision

Antecedent Influences

1. Genetic factors
2. Family influences
3. Educational choices
4. Previous career experiences

Incubator Organisation

1. Geographic location
2. Nature of skills and knowledge acquired
3. Contact with possible fellow founders
4. Motivation to stay with or leave organisation
5. Experience in a 'small business' setting

Environmental Factors

1. Economic conditions
2. Accessibility and availability of venture capital
3. Examples of entrepreneurial action
4. Opportunities for interim consulting
5. Availability of personnel and supporting services; accessibility of customers

much is culturally bound, being grounded almost exclusively in the United States.

Nevertheless, the limited data which is available regarding background tends to support the popular view that entrepreneurs are usually first children, from a family-firm background. This result is intuitively acceptable since such strong grounding in the business and ownership ethic at an early age is a useful and powerful driving force for children as they begin to choose future careers. However, this is not to say that all children from family firms choose business ownership as a future career, but rather that those who do choose self-employment tend to have had some involvement in a small or family business during their formative years. Indeed, many future inheritors of family firms eschew the apparently attractive future which awaits them for employment with some other, often large organisation where their progress is determined by their skill and training rather than by family relationships.[5]

The traditional view of the entrepreneur is as an uneducated, unskilled, poor immigrant, often with an ethnic background, who finds himself 'socially marginal',[6] and who, therefore, seeks upward social mobility. Whilst it is true that certain social groups have provided classic examples of this phenomenon – the Jews, American settlers, Asians in Britain – it is not true that this is sustained in the current economic climate. For example, conclusions regarding education have changed since the early studies by Collins, Moore and Unwalla,[7] which showed that the entrepreneur was badly educated: recent studies have found the entrepreneur to be better educated than the population in general,[8,9] and than his peers running the larger, blue-chip firms.[10] It must be noted, however, that the particular *content* of the education does not appear to be an important factor. Thus, Birley and Norburn found no connection between the type of degree awarded and the nature of the product/market of the new firms. Moreover, there is, as yet no evidence that those students in MBA programmes who chose small business or start-up electives are any more likely to be successful in running their own firm than their colleagues choosing other specialities to study.

Regarding age, there is general agreement that the typical entrepreneur starts his firm in his thirties. Whilst it would appear that this is a period of very high risk, when the individual is likely to be at his most financially stretched, it is also clear that this is the age when a strong base of business experience has been developed, when personal confidence is rising, and when frustration with the bureaucratic system begins to develop. Moreover, it is not surprising that this is also a time when many reach a personal crisis in their lives – the issues of 'Who am I?' 'What have I done with my life?' and so on are very powerful and positive motivators.

The data which examines incubator organisations is inconclusive.

Thus Teach, Tarpley and Schwartz[11] reported that 40 per cent of the respondents in their sample came from firms employing more than a thousand workers, and that only 41 per cent created firms in related industries. Birley and Norburn have reported that 'no particular pattern was observed in the employment experience of the high flying entrepreneurs' which they studied (see note 10). The mean number employed in the incubator firms was 6100; 43 per cent started firms in competition with their previous employer; whilst 37 per cent had no identifiable relationship.

2. Entrepreneur or small businessman?

If the thesis that entrepreneurs are made rather than born is accepted, then lifetime experiences must also mould the *nature* of the entrepreneurial decision, and the size and type of business eventually created. Researchers have sought to explain the variety of businesses created in terms of sub-classifications of motivation – not all those who choose to leave employment do so in order to create the IBM of tomorrow. Many, indeed most, have much more modest aims. Various models have been suggested. Stanworth and Curran delineate the 'artisan' who seeks intrinsic satisfaction; from the 'manager', who seeks recognition for managerial excellence; from the 'classic entrepreneur' who is profit-orientated (see Note 6). Similarly, Dunkleberg and Cooper[12] segment into the 'growth oriented', the 'independence oriented', and the 'craftsmen oriented'. Perhaps more simply, Carland, *et al.*[13] focus upon the essential factor of growth in distinguishing the small business venture from the entrepreneurial venture, and the 'small business owner' from the 'entrepreneur':

A **Small Business Venture** is any business that is independently owned and operated, not dominant in its field, and does not engage in any new marketing or innovative practices.

An **Entrepreneurial Venture** is one that engages in at least one of Schumpeter's four categories of behaviour: that is, the principal goals of an entrepreneurial venture are profitability and growth and the business is characterised by innovative strategic practices.

A **Small Business Owner** is an individual who establishes and manages a business for the principal purpose of furthering personal goals. The business must be the primary source of income and will consume the majority of one's time and resources. The owner perceives the business as an extension of his or her personality, intricately bound with family needs and desires.

An **Entrepreneur** is an individual who establishes and manages a business for the principal purpose of profit and growth. The entrepreneur is characterised principally by innovative behaviour and will employ strategic management practices in the business .

It is clear from the above that the study of the entrepreneur is not tidy, and that there are no easy formulas available to help in the difficult task of picking the winners – those entrepreneurs who can, and wish to, start the large firms of the future.

3.   Moving from passive to active

So far, this chapter has argued that the motivation to start a new firm, and the development of the associated product idea, take many years to incubate. The corollary to this is the fact that the supply of entrepreneurs is not a fixed quantity, but can be influenced by external factors. On a national level, the role of national culture, acceptable norms of behaviour and traditional family relationships clearly influence individual attitudes. Moreover, the availability of attractive role models such as Richard Branson (Virgin) or Stephen Jobs (Apple), and the much publicised success of the management buy-out, have made significant contributions to shaping national attitudes to entrepreneurial behaviour. However, beyond this, Cooper (see Note 4) suggests that the current economic climate is also an important factor in influencing the number of people who finally decide to move from either unemployment or employment to self-employment. Thus, the mere fact that many large firms have substantially reduced their employee base, and that management at all levels can no longer look to the large firm as a source of long-term security, has meant that many have sought a new form of security – that of self-reliance through the ownership of their own firm.

The factors described above determine the total supply of new firms, but what are the factors which *trigger* the particular decision at a particular time? Listed below are some which I have observed on a number of occasions, and personally experienced on a few.

The 'it works' syndrome

A product which has been worked on for many years, either as a hobby or at work, finally gells.

The 'eureka' syndrome

Perhaps the most exciting and satisfying – an idea completely out of the blue, but which is often simply a new way of packaging old products or ideas.

The 'if only' syndrome

'If only I could buy products in smaller packages' (Anita Roddick) . . .
'If only I could call a reliable service for emergencies . . .' (DynoRod!).

The 'high comfort level' syndrome

Constant encouragement from family and friends.

The 'friendly push' syndrome

The individual has constantly talked about an idea, and suddenly the
path is made clear. Resources are made available by a benevolent
employer in the form of, for example, premises or orders: friends and
family begin to disbelieve the intent, and the individual is finally forced
to make a decision one way or the other: entrepreneurship courses are
offered as a way of testing the idea and formulating a strategy for market
entry.

The 'misfit' syndrome

The fact that the person does not fit as an employee finally dawns upon
him. He is unhappy, does not get promotion, fights authority, always
believes that he could do the job better than those around him.

The 'unfriendly push' syndrome

Unemployment or enforced redundancy.

The 'no alternative' syndrome

This is usually brought about by physical disability or illness, rendering
the person unable to obtain regular employment, or to continue a
career.

The 'grey to white' syndrome

Many people 'moonlight' – sell products or services on the fringes of the
black economy whilst in full employment. For example, the amateur
antique dealer, the trainee accountant who does the books of a couple
of friends, the hairdresser who has private clients in the evenings.
Sometimes, however, the magnitude of the demand, and thus the
income, can force the individual from the fringes into full-time self-
employment.

Unfortunately, whilst these triggers clearly describe the process which many entrepreneurs go through as they move from the passive consideration of an idea to actively pursuing it, they cannot be used for forecasting either the potential start-up or the potential success. Thus, whilst the classic view of the entrepreneur is of a misfit and troublemaker within a large organisation, it does not follow that all misfits will eventually start businesses, nor that those who do will eventually prove to be successful.

4. The resource merry-go-round

Just as the process of reaching the decision to 'have a go' can be protracted, so is the process of actually assembling the resources necessary to commence trading. The entrepreneur begins with an idea for a product or a service out of which he wishes to create a business. Unfortunately, the process is not simple. Many different forms of business can be created to capitalise upon just one idea. For example:

- parts or all of the manufacture and marketing can be subcontracted, licensed or franchised.
- a joint venture can be set up with either a manufacturing or a marketing company.
- the business can include more than one part of the value added chain (the manufacturer of Kitty Litter in the USA also owned the raw material source; Laura Ashley is a manufacturing *and* retail organisation).
- various choices of distribution channel are available – for example, mail-order catalogues, retailers, wholesalers, agents, a direct sales force.
- assets can be leased, hired, bought or borrowed!

The choices made, and the resultant shape and size of the business which is eventually created, will be influenced by a combination of the following factors.

The entrepreneur's own 'concept of the business'

Very few people who start their own firm are able to be creative about its form. Most have very fixed ideas about the 'proper' shape of the business, much of which is derived from personal experience of the norms of other, similar businesses, but particularly of their immediate previous employment. However, whatever the entrepreneur's background, there is often a tendency to purchase assets early in the life of the firm rather than to lease or hire. Whilst this is not always advisable, since it is often better to retain as much flexibility as possible in the early

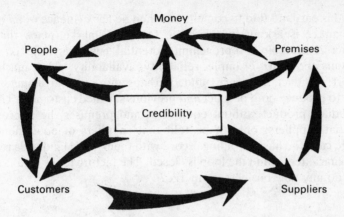

Figure 2.1   The credibility merry-go-round

life of the business, it is often the only way to ensure future borrowings – tangible asset backing is almost always sought by funding agencies.

The entrepreneur's motivations

There is nothing more frustrating to an investor who finds an idea which he considers to have great potential, only to discover that the entrepreneur merely wants to run a small workshop at the bottom of his garden, and to sell to a few friends and acquaintances. Many potentially large businesses have been stillborn at this very early stage.

The dictates of the market-place

The size of the potential demand, particularly in the development phase, will determine the nature of the resources assembled.

Perhaps the most important of all, however, is the entrepreneur's ability to ride successfully the resource merry-go-round[14] (see Figure 2.1).

In the final analysis, creating a business is about assembling resources – people, premises, equipment, customers, suppliers, money. Unfortunately, only very rich entrepreneurs are able to assemble an ideal shopping list, and to make swift and satisfactory purchases. Indeed, if this were the case, many more badly conceived and executed businesses would be born than is currently the case. The *process* of assembling the resources is critical.

The entrepreneur can mount the merry-go-round at any point. Let us imagine that he goes first to the bank, probably with an ill-thought-through proposal and very little documentation. He is sent away with a flea in his ear, and told to come back when he has evidence of an order. The banker is asking for evidence from the market-place that the product is credible. Approaching potential customers, he is asked questions about, for example, reliability, availability, price, marketing support, product insurance, and, perhaps more embarrassing, he is asked to produce both product *and* previous satisfied customers. Unable to produce product without equipment and premises, he approaches potential suppliers, only to be told that suppliers of equipment will require cash (he has no trading record with them), and landlords require bank guarantees – and the loop is closed. The picture looks bleak. How, then, do any new businesses emerge?

5.   The entrepreneurial network

In an article on 'New Venture Ideas' in the *Harvard Business Review* of July–August 1979, Vesper warns us not to overlook the 'experience factor' as a source of new venture ideas. He underlines the point:

> Instead of searching randomly, as many popularised entrepreneurship books seem to suggest, the entrepreneur should closely examine his or her own education, work experience, and hobbies as idea sources. The large majority of the entrepreneurs [which he] studied primarily used their own expertise rather than that of others.

This point is of fundamental importance. The 'experience factor' is not only of value in selecting new venture ideas, but also in providing a framework for evaluating their viability, for stepping off the credibility roundabout, and establishing the business. Credibility is established through personal contact and knowledge of the skills, motivation and past performance of the individual – the bankers call this the 'track record'. Since for an embryo firm there is no trading track record, investors must look to their previous relationship with the individual, whether it be commercial or personal. Thus, for example, a previous employer may agree to be the first customer, a friend may allow use of spare office space, or a relative may be prepared to lend money with little real hope of a return in the short or even medium term [in the UK, this is known as the 'Aunt Agatha Syndrome'].

This use of the existing contact network is a way of providing credibility, and thus comfort, to those organisations which are being asked to invest in the business by, for example, supplying raw materials on credit. It comprises two parts – the formal (banks, accountants, lawyers and so on), and the informal (family, friends, business contacts, for example) – both of which are equally important. However, in the study of start-ups in St Joseph County, Indiana, Birley[15] found that:

Informal contacts, mainly business contacts, are seen overall to be the most helpful in assembling the elements of the business.

Family and friends are the most useful where local issues were concerned, as with the seeking of location and employees.

The formal sources come to the fore when the elements of the firm are set and the entrepreneur is seeking to raise finance. It is hardly surprising, therefore, that the institution mentioned most of the time was the bank.

All other formal, declared sources of help, including the SBA [Small Business Administration], were mentioned on very few occasions.

Clearly, a strong informal or social network is essential for the successful launch of the firm. Aldrich and Zimmer[16]:

The approach we take . . . focuses upon entrepreneurship as embedded social context, channelled and facilitated or constrained and inhibited by people's position in social networks.

Further, they note that these social networks have an influence not only on the individual entrepreneurial decision, but also upon the total supply:

Voluntary associations, trade associations, public agencies, other social units increase the probability of people making connections with one another . . . The complex pattern of social organization described by Everett Rogers and Judith Larson in their book *Silicon Valley Fever* illustrates the synergistic effects of brokers, central meeting points – such as well known 'watering holes' and restaurants – and family and friendship networks that supported the high start-up rate in the Silicon Valley.

Unfortunately, despite the meteoric growth of Enterprise Agencies in the United Kingdom, and Small Business Development Centres in the United States, both of which were formed to provide advice and assistance for the new and small firm, these networks are not built up overnight. Aldrich and Zimmer continue:

Social networks build slowly, and thus it could be years before an area reaches a density threshold where reachability and hence entrepreneurship is facilitated. Formal studies are lacking, but it is our impression that the time to maturity for the Silicon Valley [in California] and the Route 128 complex [in Boston] was several decades. Accordingly, we expect the Research triangle of North Carolina to age another decade or so before any significant entrepreneurial activity occurs. At present, the spin-off and new start-up rate appears very low.

This casual empiricism would appear to apply in the United Kingdom also. Despite the recent publicity surrounding the 'Cambridge Phenomenon', it is some twenty years since the seeds of the project were originally sown.

6. Stumbling blocks

A new business entering a hostile environment is a delicate entity. Many embryo businesses fail to raise the necessary resources to commence full-time trading, and many new businesses fail in the first two or three years. The commonly received wisdom is that this is due to the unwillingness of the investing community, be it clearing banks, venture capital companies or financial funds, to put up seed capital. The response from these organisations is that there is plenty of money eagerly seeking good investment ideas, but that there are very few around. There is an element of truth in both of these. Unfortunately, entrepreneurs often approach investors too soon, and financial investors too often dismiss good ideas because they are presented without a formal business plan. It is not the purpose of this chapter to debate this issue, but merely to outline a number of the most common stumbling blocks along the way from an idea to a viable business.

The question as to whether the business will work must be approached from three separate, but interlinked, dimensions – the product; the package; and the person.

The product

Will it work?

The step from the workshop bench to commercial production of a product can be very large. The ability of the entrepreneur to 'bodge' when things go slightly wrong is important in the early design stages, but this is not an appropriate skill in a factory. Customers expect uniform quality and reliable performance for the products which they buy. Indeed, they expect the firm to provide some form of product indemnity. Thus there are three issues which the entrepreneur must consider:

1. Can the required skills be transferred to others at a reasonable cost?
2. What product indemnity is necessary, and what will be the cost of insuring the firm against claims.
3. What service support is needed in the case where repairs are necessary?

Whilst these questions are important for all firms – for example, liability insurance is an often ignored issue in service firms – they are particularly important for those firms with a complex manufacturing process.

How well is the entrepreneur protected?

Patents, copyright, registered trade names are all ways of affording some protection against predators. But too often entrepreneurs fail to protect themselves adequately. The most common argument against registering patents goes as follows: 'They are too expensive, they give my competitors too much information, and I couldn't afford to sue even if they did break the patent.'

Whilst this may be true in certain cases and, indeed, getting the product to market as fast as possible may be the best protection possible, the important point is that establishing *ownership* of the product or idea is of fundamental importance maintaining a competitive advantage. Too many entrepreneurs avoid the issue.

The package

Many ingredients are necessary in the translating of an idea into a viable business and it is the 'baking' – the packaging of resources and the strategy adopted – that determines future viability. Certain issues, however, are common.

Is there a genuine need?

The identification of market potential is fraught with difficulties, and this is even more so for a new business, even in those cases where the product itself may be well established. The relationship between price, product characteristics and market share is difficult to capture in a dynamic market environment, and to translate into forecasts of revenue. However, the most important issue is whether the entrepreneur knows and understands his market-place, and whether he has collected data which is appropriate to evaluating the viability of the business. Thus, expensive market research studies are often unnecessary in situations where the total market is large and established, and the entrepreneur is concerned to obtain a minute proportion of a local market. Conversely, a new, high-technology, expensive product which has few potential customers will require a detailed study of the market-place. In both cases, however, the entrepreneur should be concerned to ascertain whether his product will sell, and for this purpose there is no substitute for orders. Indeed, potential investors will be *most* impressed by such tangible evidence that the product is credible to customers.

What is the market entry strategy?

In the early days, the entrepreneur is attempting to establish the credibility of himself and his firm through the medium of his product. 'Product' in this case refers to the entire range of the marketing mix – product characteristics, price, promotion and place, or channels of distribution. Therefore, a market entry strategy which is flexible, and which allows for adaptation to customer reactions, is extremely important.

What is the best business format?

Unfortunately, the best business format may not fit the needs of the entrepreneur. Setting up a new manufacturing plant in a market dominated by large firms, both at the manufacturing point and, more importantly, at the distribution point, may well be courting disaster. On the other hand, a joint venture or a licence agreement with one of the firms could increase the chances of a successful launch quite substantially. It is often necessary, therefore, to separate the personal and commercial reasons for the choice of a particular strategy.

How long will it take

At the risk of appearing flippant, the answer to this question is usually 'twice as long as you think!' It may be the most important thing in the entrepreneur's life, but the same cannot be said of others. Moreover, this applies to both resources and sales. For example, lawyers can take an interminable time to negotiate leases; suppliers are not always reliable (after all, the entrepreneur is unlikely to be an important customer); printing cannot take place until the firm is registered for Value Added Tax – which takes time. However, perhaps the most underestimated factor in most start-ups is the time taken for the market-place to react to a new product. Cash flows can very quickly go severely awry, not because there is no demand, but because it takes, say, six months longer than anticipated to build up sales; six months during which employees and suppliers have to be paid.

What are the various legal forms of business?

Basically, there are four:

1. Sole proprietorship.
2. Partnership.
3. Incorporation or limited liability.
4. Co-operative or common ownership.

The main differences are twofold, the first concerning the nature of the taxation. In a sole proprietorship or a partnership, the law does not distinguish between the individual and the firm. Therefore, tax will be paid at the personal tax rates of the owners. Moreover, when a business is set up in the UK, any losses in the early years can be offset against the previous three years' taxable income. An incorporated firm is seen as a separate entity which therefore pays corporation tax.

The second difference concerns the nature of the liability. In theory, in a limited liability firm any debts which the firm incurs are limited to the assets of the firm. This is not the case for the other entities. However, this has been severely eroded by recent company and insolvency legislation. Further, the bank manager, landlord, and possibly suppliers, may demand personal guarantees before they will agree to trade with the new firm.

What do I do when things go wrong?

Things will almost certainly go wrong. Few entrepreneurs can forecast all possible problems, and even when they can, are able to provide adequate contingency plans. However, a successful entrepreneur will not only know his business sufficiently well to be aware of the most sensitive areas, but he or she also learns from mistakes. Moreover, it is no use trying to hide them from his investors. Few investors, whether they be the local clearing bank or a venture capital fund, expect the business plan to turn into exact reality, but they do expect to be kept informed. They most certainly do not like surprises.

Help!

Yes, there is help around. The traditional sources of advice and assistance for any firm come from professional relationships – the accountant, the bank, the lawyer, the customer or the supplier. However, each of these sources are likely to view the firm from a particular, technical bias; until recently, few professional advisers were able to give general commercial advice. Moreover, the type of advice, assistance and information which a new firm requires can be both time-consuming and cover a wide spectrum. Therefore, in recent years in both the United Kingdom and the United States, there has evolved a range of advice, assistance and education focused particularly on new firms and financed, at least in part, by the government. A diagrammatic representation of the sources of help available to the entrepreneur is seen in Figure 2.3.

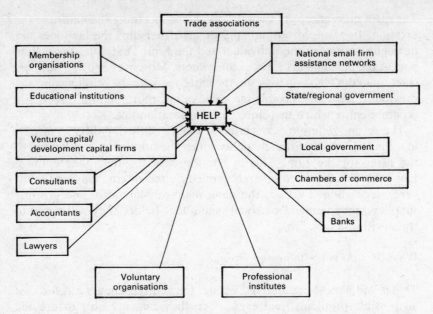

Figure 2.2   Formal sources of help for the entrepreneur

The people

We end where we began: small firms, new firms are about people – their goals, needs and skills are inextricably intertwined with those of the firm.

Are partners necessary?

This is probably the wrong question. The important question is whether the firm has the necessary combination of managerial and technical skills, and whether the people involved are wholly committed. They do not necessarily all have to own equity. Indeed, whilst the 'greedometer' can start running fairly early in the life of the firm, involving others can create severe problems in the future. A partnership is all too like a marriage, which many enter into with insufficient thought. There are two essential ingredients to a successful partnership.

1. **Clear Power**   The managerial roles of each of the partners should be clear and understood, particularly for those activities which fall outside their traditional skills. Thus, if one partner is responsible for selling, and one for manufacturing, cash control should not be allowed to fall between the two.
2. **Common Goals**   Few partners discuss their future needs and goals.

Yet this is often the eventual cause of substantial friction. For example, if one partner merely wishes to provide a comfortable lifestyle for himself and his family, whilst the other wishes to develop a large firm, there will be disagreements as to the level of reinvestment in the firm in the future.

Beyond this, however, is mutual respect, and the ability to resolve conflict. Too many assume that a cosy professional or personal relationship will survive the rigours of launching a firm. Often, it does not. Therefore, one document is essential at the formation of a partnership in establishing guidelines for the future – a legal partnership agreement which also incorporates a formula for dissolution.

Can anyone pick winners?

Yes, but not all the time. Moreover, it is neither easy nor totally scientific. Whilst it is always possible to evaluate the various elements of the product and the package, and thus narrow the bounds of risk, in the end it is a question of judgement. Does the entrepreneur have the necessary skills, greed, hunger, determination, stamina and energy to see it through? Do you . . .?!?

Case Study: Yodolo[17]

In July 1985, Guy McLelland approached Newchurch and Company, venture consultants based in the City of London who specialised in developing new ventures. Their brief was to collect market information, and to advise him on a European market entry strategy for Yodolo, a 'new frozen fruit wonder'.

The Yodolo product was the original of two American farmers, Lou and Bill Wade. The *Wichita Eagle Beacon* of Sunday 28 October 1984 summarised its history:

Tacoma, Washington – people stood three deep in the aisles to get a taste of Yodolo at the recent 1984 Pacific Northwest World Trade Expo in Tacoma.
. . . In 1975, William Wade, a businessman, decided that he would be happier as a farmer. To gain experience, he worked for a farming neighbour on weekends.

Eventually he found a farmer near retirement, who agreed to lease his farm to the Wades, who in turn would pay for the purchase as they worked the land. The deal was struck and Wade quit his job.

In the interim, before he took over the lease, he continued to work for a local farmer. One day, while unearthing and moving large boulders from a field with his bare hands, Wade strained his arms and shoulders. He sustained serious nerve damage to his wrists.

Although surgery was successful, his doctor told him to use his wrist as little as possible for the next five years. There went his dreams of farming. Also, he was denied any form of aid because of his doctor's mis-statement on a state compensation form when he described Wade's ability to work.

The husband and wife 'took turns with their levels of courage. When he was down, I was optimistic. When I was down, he was full of hope', she said.

An efficient homemaker, she shopped for nutritional food at low cost. A special on bananas prompted her to buy eight 40-pound boxes of the fruit to process in her food dryer. Unfortunately, the dryer's fan was defunct and the food would not dry completely.

There she was with '320 pounds of gooey, browning bananas', she recalled.

So she froze them. 'As the summer got hotter, the children began eating them like popsicles', she said.

Creative work ensued. She tried variations, blending fruit into toppings or purees, and rolling bit-size pieces of banana in peanut butter.

Eventually, William Wade joined in the experimentation. With each trial, he began to envision a family business devoted to selling the treats they were concocting.

At one point, the Wades took the banana puree to Refrigeration Specialities Inc. in Spokane to be whipped in the soft serve machine. . . . The result encouraged them to approach the Small Business Administration for guidance in starting their own business. The agency advised them to develop the product with one of their suppliers, which they did. While collaborating, the supplier tried to wrest Yodolo from the family's control, a pitfall they managed to elude.

Finally, the Wades started a limited partnership in 1981 with a venture capitalist and aided by local funding.

From the formation of the partnership, the primary thrust of Lou and Bill Wade's strategy was threefold:

1. To develop the technology to the point where the syrup could be stored at an ambient temperature for extended periods of time.
2. To search for natural ingredients which would stabilise it sufficiently to dispense through soft-serve machines.
3. To extend the range to multiple flavours.

Yodolo was finally launched on to the market in November 1984. It was a fruit flavoured, frozen dessert made largely from fruit juice in a wide variety of flavours, including Dutch Apple, Pineapple, Sweet Cherry, Mango Tango, Banana Plantation, Peach Blossom, Lemon Grove, Orange Country, Wildberries, Vanilla Coast, Concord Grape and Strawberry Patch. Although it had the taste and texture of ice-cream, it had less than half the calories per serving. Moreover, it contained no artificial preservatives or additives, and was totally free from fat, lactose, cholesterol or sugar.

The technology which the Wades had developed was radically different from any other frozen or chilled dessert. The liquid, ambient mix consisted of a fruit juice base to which were added a number of natural gums which acted as a complex stabiliser system. The relatively high acidity of this liquid product mix substantially added to the shelf life. When packaged aseptically, it could be stored at room temperature for up to 12 months. The liquid was converted into the final product by whipping, freezing and dispensing in a traditional ice-cream soft-serve machine.

Because the product was unique, it did not fit into any of the accepted classifications of food products covered by American food regulations. In particular, it avoided the extremely difficult regulations that apply to all products with a dairy component. Consequently it had been approved by the Food and Drug Administration, and a Certificate of Free Sale had been issued on 1 November 1983. An application had also been submitted to the Department of Agriculture for permission to market the product to government institutions. In addition, the Jewish Orthodox Union had classified it as Kosher, and it qualified as Hallal for Islamic religious purposes.

From its initial launch, the product was marketed through distributors to retail outlets owning soft-serve machines. These included restaurants, health food stores and ice-cream parlours as well as food stores. Appendices 1 and 2 are examples of marketing literature. The main competition was seen as ice-cream, yoghurt, and Toffuti, a soy bean curd. Appendix 3 is an extract from a publication by Yodolo comparing the attributes of the competition.

Consumer acceptance of Yodolo was rapid and enthusiastic (see Appendix 4 for an example of retailer response). In November 1984 the Wades were approached by representatives from a major Japanese food manufacturer who had sampled the product at a fair in Ohio and wished to negotiate a licence to manufacture in Japan (see Appendix 5 for an analysis of a consumer study conducted at the fair and presented in March 1985). Unsure how to proceed, the Wades sought help the US Department of Overseas Trade, who, in turn, referred them to Bogle and Gates, a firm of international commercial lawyers based in Seattle, Washington.

Guy McLelland was the lawyer responsible for negotiating the Japanese deal, and the more he saw of the product, the more he was convinced that there was massive potential throughout the world (see Appendix 6 for a resumé of Guy McLelland). Indeed, so convinced was he that he determined to launch the product himself in Europe. In March 1985, he left Bogle and Gates and negotiated a joint venture with Olympus Industries Inc., which had been incorporated from the limited partnership in December 1982. The new company, Yodolo Limited, was established with the shareholding being divided equally between Guy McLelland and Olympus Industries. The company owned the patent, trade mark, manufacturing and licensing rights relating to Yodolo for territories in Europe and the Middle East (see Appendix 7 for a complete list). By June 1985, when Guy McLelland approached Newchurch, he had already arranged for a Dutch company to manufacture the syrup which he intended to sell in exactly the same way as in the States – via distributors to retail outlets which traditionally dispensed ice-cream through soft-serve equipment.

Appendix A: Example of marketing literature

It's Not Ice Cream, Yogurt or Tofu.
Yodolo is a Natural, Low Calorie, Frozen Fruit Dessert

Yodolo is the newest dessert in the American marketplace. If you love the taste of fruit, you'll love Yodolo, because it's made from real fruit — the best Mother Nature can provide. For years you've enjoyed America's desserts such as pies, cakes, ice cream, gelatin, candy and cookies — and now you can add Yodolo to your list of favorite taste treats.

Take a look at what Yodolo offers you!

Yodolo is:
A New Dessert
Made from Real Fruit
Natural
Low in Calories
Nutritional
Healthy
Cholesterol Free
Sweetened Only From Pure Fruit Juices
Profits!

Yodolo is not:
Sweetened with Sugar or Artificial
    Sweeteners
A Dairy Product
Artificially Flavored or Colored
Preserved by Preservatives
A Substitute Ice Cream
Using Soy Bean Curd or
    Substitute Dairy ingredients

Yodolo Currently Comes in the Following Flavors:

Dutch Apple	Lemon Grove
Peach Blossom	Sweet Cherry
Concord Grape	Pineapple Paradise
Wildberry	Mango Tango
Orange Country	Kiwi Fruit
Strawberry Patch	Passion Fruit

Additional Flavors Soon to Follow:
Vanilla Coast
Guava Island
South Seas
    Pineapple-Orange
Banana Plantation
Lime Lite

Yodolo's taste and texture were tested with 84% of the response rating Yodolo excellent in comparison to fresh fruit, ice cream, and yogurt.

Yodolo works in most soft-serve equipment. If you own gravity fed equipment, you can expect a 60% to 70% overrun or about 65 3-oz. servings per gallon mix of Yodolo. If you have a pressurized machine, 70% to 75% overrun will yield approximately 75 3-oz. servings per gallon of Yodolo.

Labor & Handling
- Yodolo does not need special handling
- Yodolo comes in liquid form, needs no mixing
- Shelf life of 12 months at 80° or less
- No refrigeration until opened
- Aseptically packaged in a 2-gallon bag in a 2-gallon box
- Easier clean-up because it is a high acid product and non-dairy
- Simply open the spout and pour — that's it!!

For information Regarding Sales & Distribution of Yodolo, Contract:
Olympus Industries, Inc. · North 222 Wall St., Suite 320 · Spokane, WA 99201 · (509) 624–0227

U.S.D.A. Shield 8   ⓤ Pareve   F.D.A.

Figure 2.CS.1   Yodolo products' comparison

Appendix B

Table 2.CS.1 Yodolo products comparison

	YODOLO 100% All Natural (+) Fruit Dessert	TOFUTTI Soy Bean Curd (−) Flavourings	YOGHURT Milk, Flavours (−) Juice Based
Sugars added	(+) None	(−) Corn Sweetener, Honey	(−) Sucrose, Corn Sweetener
Calories (3 oz)	(+) 75	(+) 96	(−) 120
Dairy base	(+) No	(+) No	(−) Yes
Cholesterol	(+) No	(+) No	(−) Yes
Artificial colours and Flavors	(+) No	(+) No	(−) Yes
Preservatives	(+) No	(−) Yes	(−) Yes
Shelf life	(+) 12 months	(−) Dated	(−) Dated
Refrigeration	(+) No	(−) Yes	(−) Yes
Price	(+) Average	(−) High	(+) Average
Shipping	(+) Common carrier	(−) Refrigerated	(−) Refrigerated

Appendix C: Letter from Sebastian's Health and Nutrition Centre, Spokane, Washington, 5 October 1983

Sirs,

When we opened our new downtown store in May of this year, we included a restaurant bar on our plans. The menu centred around frozen yogurt. Approximately a month and a half after opening we were introduced to Yodolo. We agreed to try the product on an experimental basis. From the first day we served Yodolo we were amazed at the response. In the first two weeks we increased our daily sales by 40%, with the majority becoming repeat customers. Since then the sales of Yodolo have continued strong, while customer interest in frozen yogurt has declined to the point where we are phasing it out completely.

Yodolo is the only product we've ever sold which has an almost 100% favorable customer response. Now we literally could not stop selling Yodolo. Our customers wouldn't let us! For us Yodolo is a perfect product.

Sincerely,

Ted Hamilton
Owner Sebastian's

Appendix D: Extracts from a consumer study prepared for Yodolo, 7 March 1985, by the Market Data Communications Division of Harcourt Brace Jovanovich Publications, Inc.

Location of Survey: Home and Flower Show, Cleveland, Ohio.

Method of Data Collection: Survey forms were placed at the Harcourt Brace Jovanovich Publications where a self-administered survey was taken . . . In addition, survey-takers polled consumers as they taste-tested Yodolo at another location.

Response Rate: 387 forms were filled in . . . a cross-section of males, females, homemakers and singles in a wide age range from under 20 to over 50 with a mid-range of 20 to 36.

Results:

1. Rate the taste of Yodolo from 0 to 10 with 10 being the highest rating.

   44% rated the product 10
   17% rated the product 9
   21% rated the product 8
    9% rated the product 7

2. How does the taste of Yodolo compare with that of yoghurt?

   74% rated Yodolo better than yoghurt

21% rated it about the same
5% rated it not as good

3. How does Yodolo compare to the taste of soft ice-cream?

40% rated Yodolo better than soft ice-cream
38% rated it about the same
22% rated it not as good

4. How does the taste of Yodolo compare with that of Tofutti?

56% rated Yodolo better than Tofutti
34% about the same
10% not as good

5. Would they purchase Yodolo in the store?

98% Yes   8% No

6. Where would they expect Yodolo to be sold?

82% Supermarkets
26% Fast food restaurants
35% Ice-cream parlours
27% Dairy stores
23% Other (mainly health and nutrition stores)
NB Respondents were allowed to select more than one outlet.

7. How did they expect the price of Yodolo to compare with yoghurt, soft ice cream or Tofutti?

15% expected it to be priced less
65% about the same
20% more expensive

8. What did they like most about the taste of Yodolo?

Most frequent answers were – fresh fruit; natural flavour; and freshness.

9. What did they like least about the taste of Yodolo?

80% could find nothing they didn't like.
20% responses included – too cold; icy texture; lack of texture; need for richer taste; not sweet enough; not tangy enough.

Appendix E: Résumé of Arden (Guy) McClelland

Age: 41

Education and professional qualifications

1968   University of California, Los Angeles – BS in Business Administration

1972   University of Oregon School of Law – Doctor of Jurisprudence
1975–76 University of Paris – International and Comparative Law

Major career experience

1972–74 Hoberg, Finger, Brown and Abramson, San Francisco, California
1975–77 American College of Paris – Adjunct Professor 'International Business Law' and 'Business Law'
1975–77 Surrey and Morse, Paris – Resident Attorney
1977–81 McLelland Law Offices, Montana – Senior Partner
1982–85 Bogle and Gates, Seattle – Of Counsel, Co-Chairman, International Commercial Law Section

Appendix F: Territories covered by Yodolo Limited

Algeria	Luxembourg
Austria	Morocco
Bahrain	Netherlands
Belgium	Norway
Denmark	Oman
Egypt	Portugal
Finland	Qatar
France	Saudi Arabia
Greece	Southern Yemen
Iceland	Spain
Iraq	Sweden
Iran	Switzerland
Ireland	Syria
Israel	Turkey
Italy	United Arab Emirates
Jordan	United Kingdom
Kuwait	West Germany
Lebanon	Yemen
Libya	Yugoslavia

CHAPTER 3

Strategies for Success and Routes to Failure

Paul Burns

1. From birth to death

Most businesses are born to die or stagnate. It is no wonder that we are fascinated by those few that grow. It is also a natural instinct to pore over the remains of dead businesses to try to gather portents for the future.

There is a substantial turnover in numbers and types of businesses in all Western countries. However, whilst the number of deaths in the UK is fairly constant, the number of new firms being set up is rising. By 1984 the surplus of firms being set up over those dying was over twice that in 1980–36 000 compared to 16 000. That gave a net surplus between 1980–84 of 140 000 firms.

This is a pattern replicated in most of Western Europe[1] and the USA. Many countries report rising death statistics for businesses but almost all (with some notable exceptions such as Denmark) report birth rates that are rising more steeply. Thus, unlike Britain, many countries (such as the USA) report a higher rate of business turnover and Britain's birth and death statistics now compare favourably with those of most countries.

What seems a peculiarly British problem is getting businesses to grow, turning successes into companies of truly international scale. ICL, the British computer business which is almost five decades old, is now smaller than the Apple Corporation founded just over a decade ago. In 1960 the car manufacturer Jaguar was roughly the same size as Mercedes-Benz. Today, Daimler-Benz is some 15 times its size and of comparable size to ICI. Incidentally, ICI is now smaller than two of the top three West German chemical companies.

This problem shows itself in the relative size of Britain's small business sector. Whilst, in general, the small business sector employs between 60 per cent (France) and 83 per cent (Italy and Republic of Ireland) of the work-force, in Britain it employs only 37 per cent of the work force. Two out of three of those officially classified as self-employed in Britain do not employ anybody else, and this total has been growing rapidly in recent years.

Stanworth and Curran[2] have argued that because small-business owners place great value on independence, embarking on a high-growth strategy might lead them to feel their independence is threatened. Others[3] have argued that small-business owner-managers are aware of their lack of management ability to cope with growth and therefore simply reject it.

What is true in all countries[4] is that most small businesses grow only in the first few years after start-up and then stabilise to provide the owner-manager with an acceptable, independent life-style. At this stage the business provides sufficient sales to ensure survival, an adequate return on investment and acceptable standard of living. Most owner-managers seem satisfied at this 'comfort level' and their businesses do not grow beyond it. However, the 'comfort level' does seem to vary from country to country.

2.   Poring over the remains

Businesses can die in many different ways . . . and not always for regrettable reasons. Often entrepreneurs cease trading in one business to pursue another opportunity. Debts may be paid and employees found jobs in the new business. This dynamism is vital. It is evidence of the flexibility that can make small business so market-responsive. However, when the business dies because of insolvency leading to liquidation or bankruptcy, it is likely that creditors will be left unpaid, jobs will be lost and the businessman himself may lose money and prestige, causing hardship to his family. It is this failure that business analysts try so hard to predict and to prevent. Yet most business deaths do not involve bankruptcy or liquidation. Most businesses simply choose to stop trading, and the owners change to another activity. In both the USA and the UK only about 10 per cent of business deaths are due to insolvency.

Various studies give an insight into this process. One by Ganguly and Bannock[5] looks at VAT registrations and deregistrations in the UK over the period 1973–82, which it uses as a proxy for new firm births and deaths. The authors conclude:

1. 40–45 per cent of businesses will still be trading after 10 years.
2. Year in, year out about 9 per cent of businesses can be expected to die (deregister) – varying between 8 per cent and 15 per cent.

However, as might be expected, the early years are the riskiest and 60 per cent of deaths (deregistrations) take place in the first three years of existence. Thus, about one third of businesses cease trading within their first three years of life.

3. This profile of failure is not significantly different between sole traders/partnerships and companies.

4. There are few significant differences between individual sectors. However, the service sector, overall, tends to have a higher failure rate than manufacturing and construction and within that the retail sector has actually seen a fall in the number of the businesses in recent years. Unincorporated businesses tended to have a better survival record in production, construction, transport, wholesale and motor trades. Companies, on the other hand, were better in agriculture, retailing, professional and financial services and catering.

Other UK research by Stewart and Gallagher[6] using an alternative data base – the files of credit-rating agency Dun & Bradstreet – broadly supports these conclusions. This data base covers about one-seventh the number of firms in the VAT studies, but this still represents about 200 000 firms over the period 1971–83, and has the advantage that it can distinguish those firms that die or cease trading due to insolvency. It highlights the fact that insolvencies increase in times of recession. A surprising result is that for the smallest firms (1–19 employees) the proportion ceasing to trade (for any reason) actually falls during times of recession. Deaths fell from 7.3 per cent in 1971–81 to 6.3 per cent in 1981–82 and to 4 per cent in 1982–83 as the recession worsened. Whilst the death rate was higher for small firms than large firms in 1971–81, generally the reverse was true by 1982–83. Stewart and Gallagher suggest that this was, in the main, because there were fewer new business opportunities and shortages of capital in the recession of 1981–83, which forced entrepreneurs to continue in their current business.

This pattern is replicated in the USA where a study by Harris,[7] using a similar Dun & Bradstreet data base, supported these conclusions. However, Harris did conclude that small firms in the USA were more likely to cease trading (for any reason) than large firms, under all economic conditions.

3.   Anatomy of success

It would be naïve to think that opportunities for growth exist for all small businesses. Indeed, certain sectors of any advanced industrial society are almost exclusively the preserve of large businesses – for example, where significant economies of scale exist and can only be achieved by large plant size. Equally, it would be naïve to suggest that there is an unfailing formula for generating growth in a new business. Nevertheless, the elements of success may be broadly defined.

The entrepreneur

The entrepreneur is the key to the successful launch of any business. He is the person who perceives the market opportunity and then has the motivation, drive and ability to mobilise resources to meet it. However, it is difficult to create a picture of him. Barrow[8] catalogues certain typical characteristics:

- Self confident all-rounder . . . the person who can 'make the product, market it and count the money, but above all they have the confidence that lets them move comfortably through unchartered waters'.
- The ability to bounce back . . . the person who can cope with making mistakes and still has the confidence to try again.
- Innovative skills . . . not an 'inventor' in the traditional sense but one who is able to carve out a new niche in the market place, often invisible to others.
- Results-orientated . . . to make the business successful requires the drive that only comes from setting goals and targets and getting pleasure from achieving them.
- Professional risk-taker . . . to succeed means taking measured risks. Often the successful entrepreneur exhibits an incremental approach to risk taking, at each stage exposing himself to only a limited, measured amount of personal risk and moving from one stage to another as each decision is proved.
- Total commitment . . . hard work, energy and single-mindedness are essential elements in the entrepreneurial profile.

However, the entrepreneurial characteristics required to launch a business successfully are often not those required for growth and even more frequently not those required to manage it once it grows to any size. The role of the entrepreneur needs to change with the business as it develops and grows, but all too often he or she is not able to make the transition.

The product/service idea

The product/service idea is an element in the success of any business, but its importance is often overstated; an innovative entrepreneur can find ways of making existing products and services just that little more attractive to the customer. In 1970, David Dutton opened the first Pizzaland restaurant in London, copying ideas he had seen in the USA when he was at Harvard Business School. He opened some thirty Pizzalands before selling the business on to United Biscuits which expanded the chain further. Almost ten years later Bob Payton opened his first Chicago Pizza Pie Factory, also in London. That business now has a turnover in excess of £20 million per annum with additional restaurants in Barcelona and Paris. The product is different – deep pan pizza – and the atmosphere and enthusiasm of the restaurant staff are very different. There is no such thing as an ordinary pizza restaurant.

Nevertheless, the product must be right for the market and available at the time when the market wants it. The list of business failures abounds with products 'ahead of their time'. The key to any successful business is market responsiveness – understanding customers and their needs. And customers normally expect uniform quality and reliability of product across all elements of the marketing mix: product, price, promotion and channels of distribution.

Management

Understanding the customers and how the product or service can be made to fit their needs is a question of good management. Understanding the economics of the business's products or services and how they can be turned to the advantage of the business is a question of good management. Understanding which opportunities to pursue and equally which to avoid can also be a question of good management.

As the business grows the management style adopted by the entrepreneur needs to change, but equally the entrepreneur needs to plan its further development systematically and to apply management controls more effectively. Good management means directing all the resources of the business: design, production, quality control, finance, sales and customer service towards the aim of satisfying customer needs (see Figure 3.1) It is the mechanism by which the entrepreneur can turn the product/service idea into a successful business.

The final element in success is good luck – being in the right place at the right time. Every successful entrepreneur has good luck, although how much is chance and how much is hard work is another question.

4. Strategies for success

The average size of businesses varies from industry to industry. For example, the average size of a chemical firm is very large, whereas the

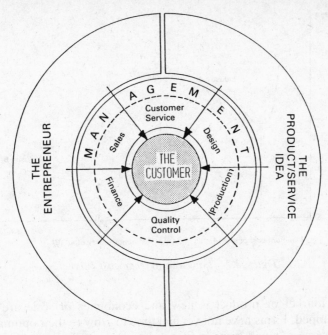

Figure 3.1   The elements of success

average size of a retail firm is relatively small. The fundamental reason for this is the extent to which economies of scale affect an industry; that is, how the total cost per unit produced changes as more units are produced. Generally, this can be expected to decline up to some point – for example, as an expensive piece of machinery is used more fully. However, beyond this point unit costs may start to increase – for example, as economies of scale of production become increasingly offset by rising distribution costs. The potential for economies of scale is often greatest in capital-intensive industries like chemicals. This is shown diagrammatically in Figure 3.2. Total costs include production, selling and distribution costs and are therefore dependent upon the state of technology, the size of the market and the location of potential customers. The unit cost for industry *A* turns up at a relatively low level of output, implying the optimal size of firm is relatively small in contrast to industry *B* where there are considerable economies of scale. Porter[9] calls these 'fragmented' industries, where economies of scale just do not exist and large firms cannot, therefore, dominate the industry.

As Dewhurst and Burns[10] have pointed out, small businesses will not be able to survive, in the long run, in an industry where economies of scale exist and are important. This bold statement must, of course, be explained, since we all know of examples where small firms have survived and prospered in industries where economies of scale exist. There are two major reasons for this:

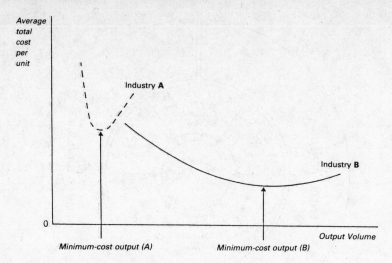

Figure 3.2   Long-run average cost curves

1. The market or product is new and economies of scale are being developed. Firms have not yet had time to grow to their optimal size. In this case, small firms must grow and aim to become large firms early in their life cycle simply to ensure their survival. These are the 'big bang' companies and they tend to be the glamorous ones that make the news headlines. However, obtaining market dominance is a high risk strategy and this road to high growth has many casualties on the way.

2. While economies of scale of production exist, the *market* for the product is limited, either in total or geographically, and the theoretical optimal size is not achievable. This happens particularly in highly specialised industries. But specialisation can be product- or market-based. Indeed, having a differentiated, specialist product or service often goes hand in hand with having a well-targeted market segment. This is called 'following a "niche" strategy'. It is important for small firms since it offers a better chance of selective, substainable growth than does the 'big bang' strategy.

An example of this is the microcomputer industry. Born in the late 1970s, with unknown demand for its products and no established producers, it has grown rapidly. However, the industry offers substantial economies of scale, particularly in research and development (R & D) for hardware and software. Consequently, the market has consolidated with many small firms going out of business. The survivors have been one of two types of firm. Firstly, firms like the Apple Corporation, which recognised that the industry would eventually be dominated by a few large firms offering low cost or premium quality products. Apple grew rapidly, grabbing market share worldwide so that it is now in a good position to compete with the big company entrants such as IBM. Secondly, the firms like Sun Computers which specialised in computer aided design and manufacturing equipment and targeted quite specific market segments. As often happens, it has been the middle-sized firm which has pursued neither strategy which has suffered in this industry.

There is a strong element of luck in the 'big bang' strategy, or put more scientifically, it is a high-risk strategy. Often firms only realise that it is the strategy they must adopt as the market or technology for the product or service develops. This is because the company needs to establish:

1. That the technology offers the economies of scale (and often cost curves can change dramatically over time).
2. That these economies are in some way important to the customer (through lower price or other advantages).
3. That they are achievable, given the market size.

Certainly, 'niche strategy' offers the better chance of success. It involves filling or creating gaps in the market that big firms find unsuitable for their large investment capacity. It involves specialising in customers or products, not methods of production. It emphasises the non-price elements of the marketing mix, such as quality, and satisfying a small, clearly-defined target market or segment which have these specialised needs. Frequently, small firms stress their inherent strengths in innovation, flexibility or personalised service.

One apparent problem with niche strategy is that it is based, by its very nature, on a limited market. However, what might be limited for a large company often offers wide opportunities to the small. Frequently, entrepreneurs pursuing niche strategies find further growth by diversification and this diversification is particularly effective if it pursues further niche opportunities.

The initial start-up of a business is often related to a 'disturbance event' in the owner-manager's life.[11] Sometimes growth of a business beyond the 'comfort level' is triggered by a similar 'disturbance event' such as a change in competition or customer tastes. Frequently these events pose distinct threats to the survival of a business and failure to react can lead to failure of the business. A key element after the 'disturbance event' is often the presence of a 'mentor' or 'credible example' who coaxes the business and the entrepreneur through this difficult phase.[12]

5.   The life cycle dynamic

The life cycle concept is a relatively simple idea which provides a useful framework for looking at the development of a small business. The idea is that every product or service, and therefore any business tied to just one product of service, faces a life cycle of five stages, as shown in Figure 3.3.

Stage 1:   Introduction
This is the stage where the product or service is introduced and encounters a certain amount of consumer ignorance and resistance. Sales are low and growing slowly and profits are low or negative.

Stage 2:   Take-off
This is the short period when the product or service becomes very popular. Sales and profits grow rapidly, attracting new entrants to the industry.

Stage 3:   Slowdown
After a while, the rapid growth slows down as competing products or services enter the market and it becomes saturated. Profits might actually dip at this stage.

Stage 4:   Maturity
Eventually the market becomes saturated and sales are static. Product sales may simply be for replacement. With some products or services this period may be relatively short, for others it can last for years. Often it can be extended by giving the product or service a facelift, as car manufacturers regularly do.

Stage 5:   Decline
After some time, sales will start to decline as substitute, improved products or services become more attractive and the old product becomes obsolete.

Different business have different life cycle curves. Our 'big bang' company will experience a rapid and dramatic take-off. It also faces the danger of an equally dramatic decline into bankruptcy. The 'niche' business will probably plateau at a lower level of sales but will have greater certainty of an elegant maturity.

   As the business takes off the owner-manager will have to recruit more people. His style of management probably needs to change with the life

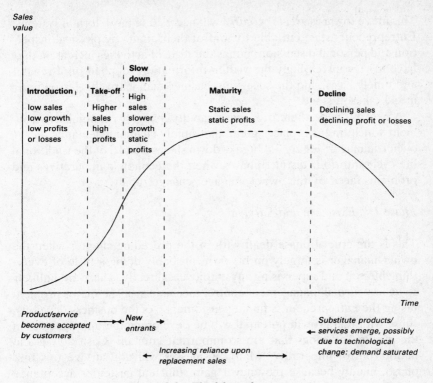

Sales
value

Introduction | Take-off | Slow down | Maturity | Decline

Introduction
low sales
low growth
low profits
or losses

Take-off
Higher
sales
high
profits

**Slow
down**
High
sales
slower
growth
static
profits

Maturity
Static sales
static profits

Decline
Declining sales
declining profit or losses

Time

Product/service
becomes accepted
by customers

New
entrants

Increasing reliance upon
replacement sales

Substitute products/
services emerge, possibly
due to technological
change: demand saturated

Figure 3.3   The life cycle curve

cycle of the business. The new, growing firm operates in an uncertain, unpredictable and often ambiguous environment. Whilst continuing as the risk-taker, always searching for new market opportunities, the entrepreneur needs to develop his team and delegate more and more. Delegating to those closest to the problem necessitates tolerating mistakes, supporting and protecting staff as they grow into their jobs, encouraging them to experiment and test the market, and rewarding their successful initiatives. Inevitably, there will be some confusion and ambiguity of tasks and a certain amount of internal competition, but organisational structures will need to be formalised as the business grows.

As the business approaches maturity the environment should become more stable and predictable and the emphasis will probably shift to control. The owner-manager may well become less of a risk-taker as he has more to lose. The emphasis will probably also shift to maintaining stability, fine-tuning and structuring the business more tightly: co-ordinating activities, eleminating overlap, careful analysis, and so on.

This move towards greater control will necessitate more formal systems. Entrepreneurs start out able to control their affairs by physical inspection and personal discussion, but as the scale of activities increases, they have to rely increasingly on written information supplied on a regular and timely basis, and the successful businessman learns his lesson early in the take-off stage.

A new businesss therefore faces a rapidly changing economic environment which, in turn, places great and rapidly changing demands on the owner-manager. Figure 3.4 breaks down stages 1 and 2 of the traditional life cycle into four distinct phases when the economic imperatives and problems faced by the owner manager change rapidly.

Phase 1:   Existence and Survival

This is the crucial phase dealt with in the preceding chapter when the owner-manager is largely on his own, probably doing a little of everything himself and supervising any employees directly. There are unlikely to be any formal management control mechanisms. The major problem facing the entrepreneur is finding customers. As the business develops, those with real growth potential will be developing the uniquenesses in the product offerings that are so important later on. Cash flow is the major control imperative. Many businesses will not survive this first phase, mainly because they never gain sufficient customer acceptance and they run out of start-up capital.

Phase 2:   Consolidation and Control

This is the phase when the owner-manager is proving that he can obtain repeat sales and that the business is really sufficiently profitable to provide the opportunity he is seeking. The business with real growth potential must be refining its unique selling proposition by this phase. Cash flow remains crucial but new budgets and targets will start to be set. Organisations remain simple. As in Phase 1, the onwer-manager *is* the business and control still tends to be informal. However, by this stage, any business that is not planning its cash flow is unlikely to survive.

Most businesses will not develop beyond this phase. Either the market potential for growth will not exist or the owner-manager will decide he does not want to see the business grow. If the business is to stay at this level then some basic financial, marketing and production control systems must come into being. As long as environmental changes do not destroy the market niche or inefficient management squander the resources, the business can probably stay at this phase indefinitely.

Figure 3.4 New business life cycle: introduction and take-off

	Introduction			Take-off
	Phase 1	*Phase 2*	*Phase 3*	*Phase 4*
OBJECTIVE	SURVIVAL	CONSOLIDATION & CONTROL	CONTROL & PLANNING	EXPANSION
MANAGEMENT STYLE AND ORGANISATION	• Owner *is* business • Owner does everything • Direct supervision of staff • Simple organisation • Informal systems • Opportunity driven	• Owner *is* still the business • Simple organisation • Informal systems • Some supervision and control • Cash flow planning	• Recruit staff • Delegate to staff • Encourage staff to develop and grow into jobs • Tighten controls on staff • Strategic planning	• Clearly defined staff roles • Further delegation • More decentralisation • Greater co-ordination and fine tuning of activities • Emergence of professional management • Operational and strategic planning
MARKETING PROBLEMS	• Getting customers • Developing unique selling proposition	• Generating repeat sales • Proving unique selling proposition	• Proving ability to combat competition • Further, steady market penetration	• Improve competitive situation • Major expansion (new market/products)
ACCOUNTING AND FINANCE PROBLEMS	• Cash flow • Testing projected margins and break-even	• Cash flow • Proving margins and break-even • Greater financial control	• Tighten financial control • Improve margins • Control costs	• Tighten financial control

FUNDING	• Owner's funds
	• 'Borrowed' resources
	  – leasing
	  – subcontract
	• Bank borrowing
		• Owner's funds
		• 'Borrowed' resources
		  – suppliers
		  – leasing
		  – subcontract
		• Greater bank borrowing
			• As before but search for expansion capital
			
			• Possible 1st phase venture capital
				• Venture capital for expansion

Phase 3:   Control and Planning

Those businesses that have growth potential which the owner-manager wishes to capitalise upon now come into a crucial phase of refining control and marshalling the resources needed for growth. The most important element in this is recruiting, developing and delegating to staff. Control systems have to be installed to monitor subsequent growth and this should provide the opportunity to improve margins by controlling costs and even gaining some modest economies of scale. In this phase the owner-manager needs to set down his strategic plans and look for the resources needed for the next phase. He must also prove that he can combat the competition that will inevitably emerge if the business is successful.

Phase 4:   Expansion

This is the exciting phase, when the business really does take off. However, to do so, there must be sufficient good staff in place, with their roles clearly defined and their activities properly co-ordinated. Many entrepreneurs are unable to do this and therefore premature expansion can lead to failure for the business. At this stage the business must be sufficiently strong so that it is able not only to combat competition, but also to improve its competitive situation. This is the phase where professional management starts to emerge. Indeed, any entrepreneurs who recognise their inability to cope with this phase will sell out to larger firms who will put in the professional staff to manage this important expansion.

It is very difficult to put a time-scale on these four phases since each business and market opportunity is so very different. However, each phase probably lasts at least one year. Having said that, in the UK, The Sock Shop came on to the unlisted securities market in 1987 after only five years – a listing that was more than fifty times oversubscribed.

When the business comes to the third stage of its development – slowdown – the emphasis is very much on consolidation and effective control. The business must have strong accounting controls which enables considerable fine tuning and the achievement of economies of scale. Churchill and Lewis[13] have proposed a similar growth model to this. They identify eight key factors which determine the success or failure of a business, four relating to the owner-manager and four relating to the company. These factors change in importance as the business develops, as shown in Figure 3.5.

The factors are:

Owner-manager

1. Owner's goals for himself and the business.
2. Owner's operational ability in key business areas.
3. Owner's managerial ability and willingness to delegate responsibility and to manage the activity of others.
4. Owner's strategic abilities.

Company

5. Financial resources, including cash and borrowing power.
6. Personnel resources (quality and quantity), particularly at management levels.
7. Systems resources, in terms of information, planning and control systems.
8. Business resources, including customer goodwill, market share, supplier relations, manufacturing and distribution process, technology and reputation, all of which give the company a position in its industry and market.

In fact, the life cycle concept tells only part of the story. Before a product or service is ever launched, money will have been spent undertaking market research, developing the product, installing new equipment and training staff. Figure 3.6 shows the probable cash flow cycle alongside the life cycle curve. It demonstrates the need for adequate funding prior to a product launch and indeed well into its take off stage. This cash flow pattern can frequently lead under-capitalised firms into situations of over-trading and illiquidity when they, paradoxically, have a successful product and a growing business.

A study by Ray and Hutchinson[14] of 'supergrowth' companies – companies which grew rapidly to a stock market quotation – compared to a matched sample of 'passive' small firms which did not grow to floatation underlines these conclusions. The results are summarised in Table 3.1. It is noticeable that the 'supergrowth' companies were considerably more focused in their objectives with a strong emphasis on forecasting financial data on a regular and timely basis; particularly cash flow, but also profit and sales. The changing style of management and organisational structure is also apparent as the companies move through their life cycle.

The approach of maturity will also lead to its own set of problems but products or services can have the mature phase of their life cycle extended by facelifts. However, at the end of the day, a business often has to diversify to maintain its growth. This is perhaps a more immediate problem for the business following a 'niche' strategy with a relatively limited market. Where to go next?

		INTRODUCTION		TAKE-OFF		
		Survival	Consolidation and control	Control of planning	Expansion	Slowdown
INDIVIDUAL	Owner's goals	***	*	***	***	**
	Owner's operational ability	***	***	**	**	*
	Owner's management ability	*	**	**	***	**
	Owner's strategic ability	*	**	***	***	***
BUSINESS	Financial resources	***	***	***	***	***
	Personnel resources	**	*	***	***	**
	Systems resources	***	**	**	***	*
	Business resources		***		**	

Figure 3.5   Key factors in the success or failure of a new business

*** Critical
** Important but manageable
* Modestly irrelevant

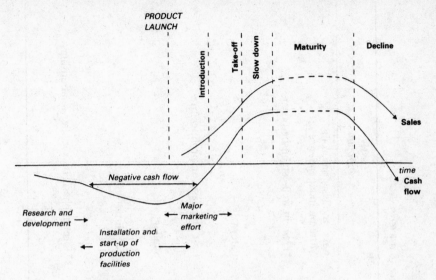

Figure 3.6   The life cycle curve and cash flows

6.   Product market strategies for further growth

In its search for further growth, a business has four options, illustrated in the product market matrix in Figure 3.7.

1. It can stay with its base product or service and its existing market and simply try to penetrate the market further. This is dealing very much with the familiar and is normally the lowest risk option, although the point will come when further penetration is not possible or economic.
2. It can develop related or new products for its existing market. For example, an off-licence might start to sell soft drinks or cigarettes. This is called *product development*.
3. It can develop related or new markets for its existing products. The off-licence might open a new branch in a nearby area of the town, or it might try selling directly to restaurants. This is called *market development*.
4. It might try moving into related or new markets with related or new products. The off-licence might try selling cigarettes directly to restaurants. Since this strategy involves unfamiliar products and unfamiliar markets it is high risk.

It is generally recognised that in comparing investment in related and unrelated areas, not only are the risks of the former lower, but also the returns are higher. Market and product development should, therefore, be incremental from the familiar to the unfamiliar. Further, it is claimed

48

Table 3.1 Supergrowth and passive company characteristics

	'Supergrowth' companies	'Passive' companies
OBJECTIVE	Maximise profits Increase sales	Less emphasis on profits More on independence
ORGANISATIONAL STRUCTURE	'Tree' structure Development of 'teams' 'Clover leaf' emerging	'Tree' in well-established firms
STYLE OF MANAGEMENT	Autocratic to start Consultation emerging	Paternal
STRUCTURE OF INTERNAL ACCOUNTING	Strong movement to profit centres	Less emphasis on profit centres
HISTORICAL DATA	Monthly or weekly profit/loss and balance sheet	Similar
FORECAST DATA	Strong on cash flow Trend to monthly forecasts	Very little
KEY VARIABLES	Cash flow Profitability Sales	More emphasis on supplier relationships

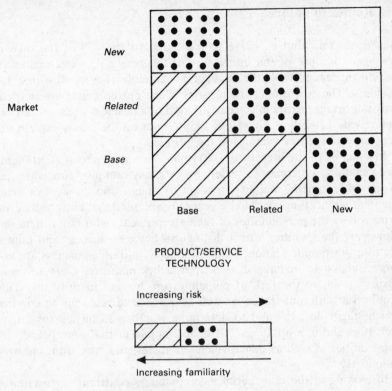

Figure 3.7   Product market matrix

that market developments are to be preferred to product developments 'because developing new customers is less risky than developing new products'.[15]

The strategies discussed above are called 'horizontal' strategies. Two further strategies for growth are open to the small firm. Firstly, 'backward vertical integration', when the firm becomes its own supplier of some basic raw materials or services and secondly, 'forward vertical integration', when the firm becomes its own distributor or retailer. Both strategies entail new product or service technologies and new customers and are, therefore, relatively risky.

It is generally accepted that vertical integration is not successful for small firms.[16] Perry suggests that vertical integration should only be a reaction to competitors' activities, for example to prevent them from controlling raw materials and services. He also points out that a period of consolidation should follow any growth surge, 'not because of organisational constraints but because of financial and entrepreneurial/managerial constraints'.

7.   Routes to failure

Businesses fail, that is, cease to trade against the will of the owner-manager, because of the interaction of the personal characteristics of the entrepreneur with the managerial situation he faces within his business. The personal characteristics of the entrepreneur are particularly important factors in the early period of a business's life – when the failure rate is highest. However, they do not on their own explain the actions of the entrepreneur and his business.

In a survey of the literature, Berryman[17] lists such personal problems as delegation, reluctance to seek help, excessive optimism, unawareness of the environment, inability to adapt to change and thinness of management talent. It appears to be generally accepted that entrepreneurial firms reflect the personalities of the entrepreneurs who build them up. However, the qualities which distinguish between success and failure are often disputed. The qualities required to initiate a business are not those needed to manage it as it approaches maturity. De Carlo and Lyons[18] point to the lack of guidelines on 'how to identify the skills required at different stages' as well as the lack of research 'to confirm which stages do exist and to determine whether all businesses do, in fact, pass through all stages'. It is also apparent that entrepreneurial personalities as well as management characteristics vary from industry to industry.[19]

In looking at the managerial incompetences contributing to failure, Berryman lists some twenty-five different deficiencies, grouped under the general headings of accounting deficiencies, marketing deficiencies, lack of adequate finance and other areas (such as excessive drawings, deficiences in accounting and managerial knowledge and advice as well as personal problems). Accounting problems are mentioned most frequently in the survey. All too many small businessmen rely on their auditors to produce out-of-date accounts on which to base their decisions. However, it has been pointed out that many of these problems are merely symptoms of incompetence rather than underlying causes, although they do highlight areas of action for advisers and trainers.

Larson and Clute's[20] empirical research is one of the pieces surveyed by Berryman. The personal characteristics and managerial deficiencies they say lead to failure are shown below:

Personal characteristics

- Exhibits exaggerated opinion of business competency based on knowledge of some skill.
- Limited formal education.

- Inflexible to change and not innovative.
- Uses own personal taste and opinion as standard to follow.
- Decision-making based on intuition, emotion and non-objective factors.
- Orientated to past, ignores future.
- Does little reading in literature associated with business.
- Resists advice from qualified sources but, paradoxically, accepts it from the least qualified.

Managerial deficiencies

- Cannot identify target market or target customers.
- Cannot delineate trading area.
- Cannot delegate.
- Believes advertising is an expense not an investment.
- Only rudimentary knowledge of pricing policy and strategy.
- Immature understanding of distribution channels.
- Does not plan.
- Cannot motivate.
- Believes problems not his making and a loan would solve everything.

The personal characteristics of the entrepreneur interact with the management defects inherent in the firm. However, the crisis that triggers the decline to failure is often brought about by some outside factor, as shown in Figure 3.8. Berryman talks simply of economic, and seasonal conditions, personal problems and fraud, but more generally the outside

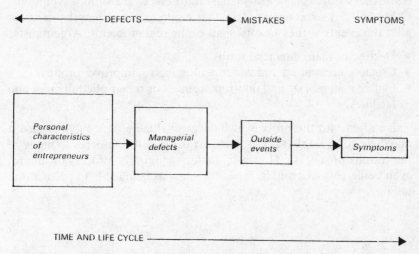

Figure 3.8 A framework for business failure

factors may be changes in the market, customer tastes, competition or distribution channels. It may also be bad business decisions made by the owner-manager.

Argenti[21] uses a slightly different model, talking simply about 'defects' and 'mistakes'.

Defects

- Autocratic, dominating chief executive heeding no advice.
- Chief executive also chairman.
- Skills on board unbalanced (for example, too many engineers).
- No strong financial directors.
- No participating board of directors.
- No depth of professional management.
- No budgeting system, particularly cash flow planning.
- No costing system.
- Failure to respond to change.

Mistakes

- High gearing
- Overtrading.
- The 'big project' which exceeds the business's resources.

The interaction of all these factors leads to symptoms of failure. Some researchers insist that most managerial defects are simply symptoms. Others refer to accounting data that emerges many months or years after the events as the outward signs of the real problems. Argenti lists:

- Decline of many financial ratios.
- Creative accounting and window-dressing to 'improve' profits
- Failing staff morale and non-replacement or repair of equipment and facilities.

This insight into the process of failure is valuable, not only because it may help to avoid that event, but also because it reinforces so many of the lessons of success. However, understanding the process of failure, even being able to avoid it, is not the same as being able to predict that failure.

8.   Predicting failure

It is a natural human instinct to want to predict the future but it is something we shall never be able to do with absolute certainty. However, if it is possible to predict failure (insolvency leading to bankruptcy or liquidation) with an acceptable degree of certainty then it might be possible to take corrective action in advance of the event. As bankruptcy rates rise so does the interest in failure prediction models.

Most failure prediction models are based on financial variables and as such they look only at symptoms of failure rather than underlying causes and give only a limited insight into the process of failure. Symptoms show up after the inherent mistakes have been made. Using financial variables, this time lag is likely to be further exaggerated since small firms are well known for their tardiness in producing accounts. Indeed, for some, this might be a contributory factor in their failure.

These financial models fall into two categories. Firstly, 'univariate models' which attempt to predict failure based upon the level and trend of a single financial ratio. The best-known of these was tested by Beaver[22] using data from seventy-nine US industrial companies. He compared the mean ratios of a group of failed companies with those of the companies that did not fail. The results are summarised in Table 3.2. The ratio which proved the best predictor was that of cash flow to total debt. As with all ratios, its predictive ability declined as the period prior to bankruptcy lengthened. Error rates were 13 per cent one year prior and 22 percent five year prior to bankruptcy. Some care needs to be taken when assessing these error rates, however. Ideally, error rates for both the original test sample (on which the model was developed) and a 'hold-out' sample should be given, as is the case with Beaver. Also, simply to say that 13 per cent of companies were misclassified as bankrupt or non-bankrupt is misleading. If I were to predict that no firm would ever go bankrupt then, given a large enough sample, my error rate would be under 1 per cent, given that under 1 per cent of firms go bankrupt in any one year. However, my error rate on failed firms (called a type 1 error) is 100 per cent and on non-failed firms (called a type 2 error) is 0 per cent. Analysts are naturally far more interested in type 1 errors and type 1 error rates are invariably higher than type 2 error rates.

The second category is 'multivariate models' which use multiple discriminant analysis to combine a number of ratios to produce a 'z-score'. The best known model is that of Altman[23] which combined five ratios, with different weightings, to produce a more comprehensive profile of a firm. These results are also summarised in Table 3.2 Whilst in the first year error rates are lower than those of Beaver's

Table 3.2 Bankruptcy prediction models

	BEAVER			ALTMAN			EDMISTER
RATIOS	Cash flow/total debt Net income/total assets Total debt/total assets Working capital/total assets Current ratio No credit interval			Working capital/total assets Retained earnings/total assets Earnings before interest and tax/total assets Market value equity/book value of total debt Sales/total assets			Funds flow/current liabilities Equity/sales Net working capital/sales Current liabilities/equity Inventory/sales Quick ratio
TYPE AND NO. FIRMS	79 industrials			33 manufacturers			42 SBA loan applicants
PERIOD	—			1946–65			1958–65
ERROR RATES (per cent)	Overall	Type 1	Type 2	Overall	Type 1	Type 2	Overall
*1 year	10 (13)	22	5	5	6	3	7%
2 year	18 (21)	34	8	18	28	6	
3 year	21 (23)	36	8	52			
4 year	24 (24)	47	3	71			
5 year	22 (22)	42	4	64			

* Years prior to failure. Figures in brackets represent test against hold-out sample.

model, accuracy falls off sharply with time, until three years prior to bankruptcy the model performs no better than a naîve random prediction model.

Multivariate models have been criticised for many reasons.[24] They would appear to be time and situation specific. Altman's model was based on data from fairly large manufacturing companies in the USA during the period 1946–65. When Ray and Hutchinson applied the model to their sample of UK 'supergrowth' companies, they discovered that nearly half of the companies would have been classified as bankrupt at some stage up to their flotation. The matched sample of 'passive' companies had a much lower proportion in this category.

Another model by Edmister[25] (also summarised in Table 3.2) looked specifically at small firms, using data from the US Small Business Administration. Overall, this model produced an error rate of 7 per cent one year prior to failure. However, Edmister had problems with data availability since he needed three years' data to develop his model and only 15 per cent of those firms in the SBA data base could meet that requirement. This led to problems of validation.

The lack and lateness of financial data for small businesses makes the use of these models seem questionable. To make matters worse, significant problems exist in establishing the reliability and consistency of the accounting data they use. Rising interest rates, a recessionary environment, the availability of credit and other macroeconomic factors are also likely to particularly affect small businesses. All in all, financial variables are unlikely to prove practical predictors of failure in small firms. However, research still continues.

9. Small can think big

The Prussian military strategist Karl von Clausewitz said: 'Have a good object in view'. In other words, think big! Small firms can and do grow. Entrepreneurs can and do make a fortune from the growth of their businesses. Some will be able to grow and adapt with the business, others will realise that they cannot change and hand the business on to 'professional managers'.

Much of government effort and public attention is directed towards new business startups, but creating conditions for second-stage expansion is also important for the economies of all countries. There are lessons to be learned from business failure, even if failure cannot be reliably predicted. More important, however, are the simple strategies for growth that have proved successful for so many firms. These involve a thorough understanding of the customer, the market-place and the economics of the product or service. The reality is, however, that most small firms will not follow these strategies; most small firms will not grow; most small firms are born to die or stagnate.

Case Study: The Body Shop International PLC[26]

Introduction

Towards the end of 1975, Anita Roddick set off to go shopping with her two small children in her local town, Littlehampton, in Sussex. As a young mother, this was something she did frequently. Littlehampton is on the south coast, a few miles west of Brighton and like most other small English towns, it has a range of shops and stores. That morning Anita Roddick needed to buy fruit and vegetables at the greengrocer and wanted to buy some cosmetics at Boots, the chemist. The children wanted her to stop at the sweet shop on the way.

As a direct result of an idea that came to her during that shopping expedition, Anita Roddick was, twelve years later, the Managing Director of The Body Shop International, a company worth over £70 million. Her husband, Gordon, was Executive Chairman.

> I know everyone wants to think that it is like an act of God. That you sit down and have a brilliant idea. Well, when you start your own business it does not work like that. I remember walking through Littlehampton with the kids, one in a pushchair and one walking beside me. We went into the sweet shop, then into the greengrocer and then to Boots. In both the sweet shop and the greengrocer I had choice. I could buy as much, or as little, as I wanted. I could buy half a pound of gob-stoppers or a kilo of apples, the quantities were up to me. In Boots I suddenly thought, 'What a shame that I can't buy as little as I like here too. Why am I stuck with only big sizes to choose from? If I'm trying something out and don't like it, I am too intimidated to return it, so I'm stuck with it.' That one thought, that single reaction was me voicing a need, a disappointment with things as they were. But if that's a need I have, lots of other women must have the same need, I thought. Why can't we buy smaller sizes – like in the greengrocers?

By the end of 1987, The Body Shop had 93 shops in the UK, from Aberdeen to Exeter, and over 180 in twenty-two countries around the world. The company was truly international, with shops as far a field as Canada, Australia, Dubai, Holland, Singapore and Sweden. By the end of the 1988 financial year the company hopes to have 220 overseas outlets and nearly 110 in the UK.

The Body Shops sold soaps, facial cleansers, toners and treatments, perfume oils, hair shampoos and treatments, hair colourings, skin creams, bath oils, lotions, sun preparations and other speciality products. They were all naturally-based with exotic-sounding names such as Goat's Milk with Honey Soap, Pineapple Facial Wash, White Grape Skin Tonic, Elderflower Eye Gel, Sea-weed and Birch Shampoo, Peppermint Foot Lotion and Raspberry Ripple Bathing Bubbles.

The background

Anita Lucia Roddick, nee Perella, was born in Littlehampton in 1942, the daughter of Italian immigrants. Her parents came from Monte Cassino and settled in Littlehampton to run the Clifton Café. Her father died when she was ten and the four children helped their mother to run the café. After leaving the local secondary school, she went to Bath College of Education where she took a three-year teacher training course. She started teaching, which she enjoyed, but wanted to try living abroad. She applied for a job with the United Nations in Geneva and was given a post at the Bureau of Travail Industriel.

As a young child, she had never had a holiday, so with the tax-free money she earned in Geneva, she decided to spend a year travelling round the world. She visited Polynesia, New Caledonia, Australia and Africa. In Tahiti she was interested by the local women who plastered themselves with what looked like lumps of lard. It was, in fact, cocoa butter; half the cocoa bean is used for chocolate and the other half is used as a local cosmetic. In Morocco she saw women washing their hair in mud. Thus her interest in the use of natural ingredients for cosmetic purposes was aroused.

She returned to England, tired of travelling, and met Gordon Roddick. He had graduated from the Royal Agricultural College of Cirencester in 1962 and had farmed overseas and in the UK before settling in Littlehampton. They were married in 1970. Although they originally had ideas about travelling overland to Australia and buying a pineapple plantation, the arrival of their two children made them put this idea aside. Instead, they bought and ran a restaurant in Littlehampton and later bought a small hotel.

Then, in 1975, the thought that came to Anita Roddick in the chemist's shop, combined with her interest in natural cosmetics, gave her the idea that was to be the basis of The Body Shop concept. In March 1976, Anita and Gordon Roddick opened their first tiny shop in Brighton. It had a leaking roof and ugly, unpainted walls. Anita Roddick decided that garden lattice, made of larch, would cover up the unsightly parts of the interior. They were painted green to reinforce the natural ingredients of the products. The shop had lots of pine shelving and a range of about a dozen inexpensive cosmetics, all herbal creams and shampoos, sold in simple packaging. In order to fill the spaces on the shelves, pot plants were placed between the products.

The money to open the shop had not come from any enterprise scheme or business development loan. Nor did the Roddicks have any success in convincing the banks they visited that Anita's idea was a good one. To raise any money from a bank, they had to put up their small hotel and restaurant in Littlehampton as collateral. Even then, all they could borrow was £4,000.

The early years

Anita chose the name 'The Body Shop' because she remembered thinking what a good name it was, when she had first seen it in the USA several years earlier. She had been struck by the fact that the thousands of garages across America call their car repair workshops 'the body shop': 'I was just taken by the name and, years later, it was absolutely right for what we were going to do.'

However right it was, it caused some problems when the shop first opened. It was in a tiny, cobbled backstreet in Brighton and was sandwiched between two undertakers' establishments. Both protested at the name of their new neighbour's shop and a planning appeal followed. However, Anita Roddick won Brighton Council's backing for the use of the name. But this episode was less embarrassing than the men, in rather dirty raincoats, who mistook it for a sex shop in its early months.

Not that these were the only trials and tribulations. Anita Roddick had found a cosmetic herbalist by looking through *Yellow Pages*. Unfortunately, the elderflower cream still had some flower husks in it and there were small pieces of cucumber in the cleansing cream. Even the ink which had been used to hand write the labels on the bottles started to run. Despite these problems, though, the shop took £130 on its first day.

About a month after the first shop opened, Gordon Roddick left for South America. He had long-established plans to ride a horse across the Americas, from Buenos Aires to New York; he expected to be away for two years. Before he left he gave Anita Roddick a yardstick by which to measure success: 'You've got to take over £300 per week to cover all your overheads and to be able to invest in more stock. If you don't take £300 a week, give it up and come over with the kids and join me in Lima!' there was never any need to take up the offer; from the reaction of the local press and the shop's early customers, it was clear that Anita Roddick's concept was going to work. Within a matter of months, she had taken the decision to open another shop, this time further west along the coast, in Chichester. Meanwhile, in South America events had not been going according to plan and Gordon Roddick returned prematurely to the UK. He too could tell that they had a success on their hands. In November 1976, The Body Shop was legally incorporated and the second shop opened.

At this stage, the Roddicks were faced by the problem of funding expansion. One of the biggest dangers was that the idea itself was transferable and success would only come from developing the brand name and reputation before others entered the market. Clearly, they did not have the cash themselves to invest in a rapidly expanding number of outlets, nor did they have the management infrastructure to cope with a large number of stores. It was Gordon Roddick who suggested the idea of franchising.

Franchising, as a method of setting up branded stores and shops in cities and towns across the country, had been growing fast in the USA during the 1960s. In the UK there were still relatively few such schemes in operation, although one of the most obvious was the chain of Wimpy fast food outlets. During the 1970s, however, franchising grew and new names such as Kall Kwik and Prontaprint started to appear in high streets up and down the country. If The Body Shop could expand as a franchise, the growth could be fast enough to secure the market that the Roddicks were developing.

In October 1977, the first Body Shop franchise was opened in Bognor Regis by Lee and Aidrie Bowles, a mother and daughter team. This was rapidly followed by a franchise in Hove and another in Blenheim Crescent, off Portobello Road in London. In the early part of the following year a small franchised outlet was opened in Brussels and in October 1978 the first substantial overseas franchise was opened in Stockholm.

The concept

Although Anita Roddick's decision to open her first shop had been sparked off by the need to buy cosmetics in variable quantities, the final concept brought together different strands of thought.

First, the decision was taken to focus closely on the ingredients themselves. Although the 1970s had seen a rise in health consciousness and a widening awareness of the value of natural ingredients in food, this decision was not part of the health food fad. Rather, it was the result of Anita Roddick's interest in natural ingredients as a result of her visit to different places around the world. She also felt a distaste for the synthetic, chemical compounds sold by the multinational cosmetic companies.

This same distaste extended to what she regarded as the falsely glamorous packages used by other cosmetic companies. Anita Roddick wanted plain and simple packaging for The Body Shop's products. She had always disliked the fact that, in her view, the men who ran the big cosmetic companies regarded women as easy prey for such flimsy substance as glossy packaging. Instead, the Body Shop products came in clinical plastic bottles with plain labels. In order to minimise costs still further, The Body Shop did virtually no advertising.

Because the company wanted to avoid the cost of advertising, the decor and design of the shops themselves assumed great importance. This was particularly the case because strong branding was important to the franchising operation. The distinctive logo and deep green decor became essential ingredients, as did pine shelving and 'the ambience of a sweet shop'. The attractive retailing environment was an integral part of providing the products with a shop to themselves, rather than being sold at point of sale in a health shop which was the fate of other natural ingredient products.

Most products were sold in five basic sizes; trial, small, medium, large and economy. With testers for use in the shops, shoppers could check whether they thought they liked the product before purchase. They could then try the small size and graduate to the larger sizes when they wanted to economise on price. The idea of offering refills originated in the early days of the first shop, when Anita Roddick ran out of containers. It subsequently proved a unique selling point.

The company claimed that it was unique in its method of selling the products: 'We use high quality ingredients in very modest containers. We keep prices at a very reasonable level by avoiding costly advertising, fancy packaging, and most important of all, by offering the refill service.'

Environmental consciousness

Anita Roddick had clear views on a number of issues. While she was a teacher, she had worked for Shelter, a charitable organisation which helped the homeless. As a result she always bore the less well-off sectors of society in mind when pricing her products. She also felt strongly about environmental issues.

The company's literature stressed that every part of the product was formulated by their herbalists and chemists with a purpose in mind. The therapeutic value of the ingredients was carefully considered in the selection process. Wherever possible, the company sought to get as close as possible to the natural source of each ingredient, with particular consideration being given to offering alternatives to other products 'which cause needless suffering to animals'. All the company's products were biodegradable 'to ensure that there is no danger to the environment in either their production or disposal'.

In terms of customer service, the company underlined that it was the only one in Europe which offered a refill service to shop customers on selected bottle products in order to 'minimise pollution of the environment and maximise cost effectiveness'. Finally, to reinforce the environmental consciousness of the company, the product catalogue made the point that the products were 'tested without cruelty to animals'.

Method of operation

As the company developed, a distinctive method of operation evolved which was to provide the basis for its future success.

Product development

From the start, product development was the special responsibility of Anita Roddick. Initially, she was heavily involved in developing the company's first products with the herbalist she had found in *Yellow Pages*. Subsequently, she worked closely with the herbalists and chemists employed by the company and with the growing number of suppliers as well as with a variety of independent consultants. As the company grew, she travelled extensively, visiting overseas outlets. She took the opportunity provided by this travel to add to her knowledge of indigenous natural ingredients. Wherever she went, she investigated local usage of available products, whether it was mustard oil in India or aloes in Mexico.

Manufacturing

From the start, subcontractors were used for most of the preparations. In 1982, when the company moved from Littlehampton, its new premises provided some manufacturing facility. When production started at the new Rustington premises, it was mainly restricted to shampoos, bath oils and other high volume items from the range. However, by 1984, when the company again planned to move to new premises, it was decided that more production could be done by the company itself. At that time, two subcontractors accounted for about 38 per cent of the products, one of them being Creighton Laboratories, a company which had worked with The Body Shop since 1976. It was company policy to have two or more subcontractors for each product, and the company held the formula for all its products. It was a point of some pride that 95 per cent of the company's products were made in UK. In 1984, a licence was granted to a Canadian manufacturer to improve supply to the North American market. Nevertheless, essential ingredients were still shipped from the UK.

Distribution

The main activity undertaken by the company was distribution. The company neither manufactured the majority of its products, nor did it own other than a small proportion of its outlets. Warehousing and distribution was the core activity and a sophisticated computerised stock control system was used to ensure that these operations were conducted with the maximum efficiency. The company used its own transport in the south-east region of the UK, but elsewhere subcontractors were used.

Marketing

Advertising and marketing costs formed only a small part of the company's expenditure. Heavy use was made of public relations to avoid the need for advertising, although local advertising was used when a new branch opened. The company made little or no use of market research because there was a high degree of customer contact as well as regular exchanges of information and ideas between the franchisees and central management. The company's own shops provided it with direct access to its customers and enabled it to maintain close contact with its purchasing public. Anita and Gordon Roddick regarded these shops as 'model' shops and used them to test new design ideas. Another reason for not needing market research was the low cost of launching a new product. Before a new product was launched, samples were sent to franchisees and managers of the company's own shops for personal testing. This proved to be a very successful way of testing the likely success of a product. After this, supplies of a new product could be made available at selected shops where the opportunity for customers to sample the product, prior to purchase, gave immediate feedback on consumer reaction.

Retail outlets

The average size of the shops grew as the range of products expanded. The early shops were often only 300–400 sq ft and in secondary sites. After the company went public in 1984, it became increasingly possible to find prime sites with 800–1000 sq ft in major retail centres.

The environment for each shop was carefully chosen. The shops had to attract people from the street, identify The Body Shop and offer an atmosphere that was relaxing and inviting. Products and information had to be displayed clearly and allow efficient customer flow. It was felt that if the shop failed on any of these counts, customers would feel dissatisfied and shopping would be less enjoyable. The shop facia was regarded as critically important in identifying The

Body Shop against the competition. The typeface, colour and symbol along with carefully considered proportions served to project the company's identity in the High Street.

The materials used in the shop interior were intended to reflect honesty of manufacture and presentation, with simple structures, open displays and no frills. Lighting was intended to be warm, friendly and welcoming. Information displays within the shops were designed to help customers to find what they were looking for, and to inform them of the origins of, and uses for, the products. The whole was designed to help the customer use the shop.

Franchise

In 1984, franchisees paid an initial franchise fee of £2000 and an annual operating fee of £800 which covered displays and delivery. This latter sum was subject to annual review, in line with the retail price index. There was a two-year waiting list of franchisees. Each franchise agreement ran for five years, although it could be terminated by the franchisee in any year. The agreement was renewable on similar terms at the end of the five year period, if the franchisee had met all his or her obligations under the agreement. The cost to the franchisee of equipping and stocking a new shop varied from £30000 to £70000. Many franchisees were able to obtain bank finance to assist in set up costs but, where necessary, the company itself would act as guarantor of the franchisee's liabilities under the leases on their shops. The company avoided buying property since it would tie up valuable capital needed to finance the growing business.

The siting, layout and design of each shop had to be approved by the company before it could open for business. In 1985, for example, five shops were relocated and redesigned to increase turnover and yields. Each shop had to carry the full range of Body Shop products. At least 75 per cent of the turnover was expected to comprise Body Shop products, although as the company's product range expanded it was expected that this proportion would grow. Franchisees were able to sell other items compatible with The Body Shop's marketing policies, but they could not sell competitive products and the company reserved the right to approve every item sold in each shop.

Franchisees received regular visits from company representatives who provided assistance with display, sales promotion and training. Information packs, newsletters and free promotional material were made available and franchisees had to return a monthly report on their sales. This enabled the company to monitor both trading results and the local sales performance of individual products. The company closely monitored the use of The Body Shop trade mark in all franchisees' literature, advertising and other uses.

By September 1984, many of the company's first franchisees were opening their third and fourth franchised shop. At that time, all the franchisees were women. A profile produced by the company at the time emphasised the importance of this: 'Since its inception, The Body Shop has always aimed to foster the ideas and abilities of women, in an industry which is aimed at women but which is traditionally run by men.'

As the company grew, so did the typical franchise outlet. Initially, they were small and tended to be tucked away on secondary sites. As they moved to prime High Street positions, franchisees had to develop a more sophisticated awareness of design, a more professional approach to management and a willingness to reinvest. The relationship between the company and its franchisees was seen as one of interdependence, with neither being able to succeed without the other.

Training

Sales assistants were often seen by customers as advisers. They would be asked about skin or hair care, product ingredients or which product they would recommend. The Body Shop Training School was established in 1985 and regular training was held at the Company's head office as well as the Great Marlborough Street shop in London. Courses included 'Appreciation of The Body Shop Philosophy', 'Product Information', 'Customer Presentation Techniques' and 'Ageing'. Experts were invited to come and speak on subjects as diverse as the myths of the cosmetics business and the value of newly-discovered ingredients. It was intended that staff should become aware of and responsive to the changing needs of society and, in particular, understand and support the 'unique role of The Body Shop as g powerful voice on environmental issues and the cosmetics industry'. Managers were seen as having additional needs and they attended specialist management courses on motivation and leadership.

Oversea franchise

For overseas franchises, the company's policy was to appoint a head franchisee for an individual country or group of countries. The head franchisee was then granted exclusive rights as the registered user of The Body Shop trade mark and as the distributor of Body Shop products. Again, the agreement was for a period of five years and could be terminated or renewed in the same way as the UK franchises. When the head franchisee had two or more shops of his or her own and a successful two-year record, he or she would be allowed to subfranchise. This was not always adhered to because the quality of head franchisee appointed by the company was high and the delays slowed the growth of the company's expansion in both number of outlets and volume of exports.

Efficient and well-motivated head franchisees were seen as the most successful method of securing rapid development for the company. Selection and monitoring of subfranchisees were left to head franchisees although, again, the company reserved the right to approve all subfranchisees and insisted on receiving regular financial information from the head franchisees. Standards of design and the maintenance of shops were similar to those which applied in the UK.

There were, however, some clear differences between domestic UK franchises and overseas franchises. No franchise fee or annual operating fee was charged by the company to its overseas franchisees. The reason for this was that profits were seen as less important in the short term than the exploitation of the concept in overseas markets. Profits would flow from product sales once shops were established. Other differences were that liquid products were generally exported in volume containers, to be bottled and labelled locally and that overseas franchisees did not need to stock the full range of Body Shop products.

The company's growth and development

By 1979, The Body Shop was turning over more than £250000 and making a pre-tax profit of 8 per cent. During 1980 and 1981 however, although turnover grew to £580000 and £828000 respectively, profitability fell; pre-tax profits in 1980 were 4.6 per cent and in 1981 dropped to 3.7 per cent. The reason for this was that the Roddicks were investing heavily for the future.

The number of company-owned shops and franchises continued to grow and by 1981, the number of overseas outlets was catching up with the number of UK shops.

	1976	1977	1978	1979	1980	1981
UK	2	4	8	9	15	22
Overseas	–	1	1	2	5	18

As the company grew, so did the need for management infrastructure. In 1981, Eric Helyer joined the company from Gala Cosmetics. He was appointed General Manager with responsibility for purchasing, production, warehousing and distribution. Gordon Roddick looked after finance and Anita Roddick concentrated on product development and the retail operation.

In March 1982, the company moved from its original premises in Littlehampton to new offices and warehouse facilities in Rustington, West Sussex. The new site had 17000 sq ft and included space for a head office, warehousing and a small manufacturing and packaging plant. At the same time, Keith Tiffany joined the company as Financial Controller and Company Secretary. He took over responsibility for finance, administration and the development of a computer-based warehousing system.

Although the company started to manufacture a small proportion of Body Shop products during 1983, in early 1984 it acquired and converted an additional 5000 sq ft of adjoining premises in order to increase its manufacturing capacity. At the time, 85 per cent of products were still made under subcontract and the company hoped to reduce this to 75 per cent with the addition of its new facilities. Even at this stage of its growth, the company only employed 75 full time staff.

In April 1984, The Body Shop went on to the Unlisted Securities Market (USM) in a placing by Capel Cure Myers. It was the first retailing franchise operation to be floated on the USM. In an interview with the *Financial Times*, Gordon Roddick gave his reasons for seeking a USM quote: 'We were attracted by the advantages of a high profile, especially because of our High Street image. It also improved our credibility. We became contenders for prime retailing positions with people who would have shown us the door a year before.' The publicity surrounding the company's entry to the USM boosted sales by between 25 per cent and 30 per cent.

Just over one million shares were offered to the public at 95p each. The company was therefore capitalised at £4.75 million. Anita and Gordon Roddick both sold shares, as did their first backer, Ian McGlinn. After the floatation, the Roddicks each owned 18.8 per cent of the business and Ian McGlinn owned 37.65 per cent. A further 7 per cent of the equity was reserved for the franchisees who ran the stores. The comparatively small number of shares issued, meant that despite a prospective price earnings ratio of 24, the shares opened at 160p, a premium of 65p. By the end of the first week's trading on the USM, the share price had nearly doubled to 195p and by early May was trading at over 200p. Almost immediately after the issue, rumours abounded that the company would be the subject of a take-over bid. Both Gallaher and British American Tobacco were rumoured to have expressed an interest. Since the Roddicks and Ian McGlinn between them controlled 75.2 per cent of the equity, it was relatively easy to reject the unwanted attention of bidders. The two prime candidates were seen as odd suitors for a health-conscious, ecologically-minded concern.

At the time of the floatation, the company had 43 shops in the UK and 56 outlets overseas and the product range was continually expanding. In 1983, bath products were introduced and sponges, combs, brushes and make-up accessories were merchandised under the Body Shop logo. The Christmas trade was enhanced by adding gift packs to the range of products. Altogether, the company produced and marketed 160 different preparations.

In 1985, Anita Roddick was voted the Veuve Cliquot 'Business Woman of the Year'.

As the company's international operations expanded, it became clear that expertise in this area was needed and Dr Johannes Oosterwijk was appointed as a non-executive Director to advise on the expansion of European operations. Plans were developed to improve distribution in Europe and in 1985 a new warehouse was established in the Netherlands to accelerate distribution to that county as well as France and Germany. The growth of the company's operations reached a point where it was estimated that each week a million customers visited the company's shops round the world.

When the company joined the USM, its financial year end had changed to September and the first results were eagerly awaited in January 1985. The £390000 profit forecast made in the prospectus at the time of admission turned out to be a considerable underestimate. Pre-tax profits for 1983–4 were £1.04m on a turnover of £4.91m. The company's shares were trading at 450p. The Body Shop was hailed throughout the financial press as one of the USM's greatest success stories.

In order to continue their expansion, Anita Roddick saw the need to educate the public about the type of products the company sold. In October 1985, a much publicised book, 'The Body Shop Book', was launched in time for the Christmas trade. The book sold well in the company's own shops, with 12000 hardback copies being sold in a relatively short period. However, a spokesman for W. H. Smith at the time commented, 'It hasn't matched up to our expectations. We put money behind it to promote it for Christmas because we thought it would be a big seller. But it wasn't. We really don't know why.'

In January 1986, Body Shop International moved from the USM to full listing on the Stock Exchange. It announced an 85 per cent increase in pre-tax profits to £1.93m, on turnover up from £4.91m to £9.36m. In order to increase the number of shares available on the market, a one-for-one scrip issue was made. In addition, because a minimum of 25 per cent of a company's shares must be available to the public for a full listing, Anita and Gordon Roddick sold a further 5 per cent of their shares. The share price in the market stood at 815p, which meant that the value of this placing of their shares was £2m. It also meant that in less than two years the company's market capitalisation had grown from £4.75m to over £40m. The number of outlets for the company's products had also been rising in line with profitability.

	1981	1982	1983	1984	1985	1986	6 months to 31.3.87
UK	22	32	43	49	72	76	84
Overseas	18	30	56	83	120	155	167
Total	40	62	99	132	192	231	251
Profit (£000s)	31	114	275	1043	1929	3451	3219

Continuing rapid expansion of The Body Shop chain meant that in July 1986, the company was able to move into new warehousing and manufacturing premises built on a greenfield site of four acres outside Littlehampton. It provided a factory building of 50000 sq ft, complete with technical facilities, and an office block of 10 000 sq ft for occupation in October 1986. This was enough capacity to service 500 outlets compared to the 190 outlets which was the maximum that could be serviced from the original Rustington premises. During the year, the senior management team was strengthened further by the appointment of a new Retail Operations Manager, Clive Henwood from W. H. Smith. In addition, new appointments were also made to middle management positions.

As the year progressed, two new product ranges were added. In September 1986, The Body Shop launched a range of cosmetics, called 'Colourings'. They were designed by make-up expert Barbara Daly, who specialised in make-up for the rich and famous, including the Princess of Wales. Barbara Daly and Anita Roddick had met in 1983 and become firm friends. Despite approaches by other large cosmetic companies, Daly had always refused to design a range of cosmetics until she met Anita Roddick.

The Colourings range was the first cosmetic range put together by women and was the first entirely new make-up range launched since Biba cosmetics were marketed in 1970. The cosmetics were formulated and manufactured without animal testing and natural products were used wherever possible.

In November, a new range of shaving cream, after-shave and talc was launched under the 'Mostly Men' brand name. Although it was expected that this range would be purchased by women for their boyfriends and husbands, the company was delighted to find that in the pre-Christmas period, it attracted men into The Body Shop to purchase the products for themselves. In a further development during 1986, the company opened two new shops of its own. They were in prime sites, one in Oxford Street in London and one in Terminal 2 at Heathrow Airport.

In January 1987, the company announced that profits for the year to September 1986 were up 79 per cent to £3.45m on a turnover of £17.39m. The ratio of net debt to shareholders funds was only 5 per cent. The number of outlets had risen to 83 in the UK and 153 overseas. During 1986/7, another 16 UK franchises and 30 overseas outlets were scheduled. The *Independent*, commenting on the figures, stated that 'In the UK, the practical ceiling is probably 300 and the company should be there in five or six years. But overseas the potential seems almost boundless, for Body Shop has a retailing concept that is genuinely international – something few other UK retailers could claim.' In February 1987, The Body Shop shares stood at 1225p. On 1st July 1987 Mr Stuast Rose was appointed Director to head up Corporate Strategy and Planning for the company's continued growth.

CHAPTER 4

The Entrepreneur

Jim Dewhurst

Because of the close relationship that exists between the entrepreneur and his business, the success or failure of the business is very much associated with two factors. These are the degree to which the aims of the business correspond with the real aims of the entrepreneur and, secondly, to what extent the real aims of the entrepreneur can actually – given his or her psychological make up – be achieved in practice. This chapter will develop these themes and in the course of this will arrive at some general indications of small business success or failure, and in particular why small business entrepreneurs in the UK are not widely seen – at any rate by the rest of the world – as being outstandingly successful.

1. Small business in the UK and Europe

It has long been held that small businesses in the UK have a vital part to play in its economy. The traditional wisdom is that small businesses can achieve this because of their flexibility, their innovative capacity and above all their high profitability. Yet it has been widely known (ever since the 1971 Bolton Report[1]) that the relative number of small businesses in the UK is smaller than that in any other comparable country. Until recently it was held that one of the reasons for this lack of input from the small business sector into our economy arose from the disadvantages that these businesses suffered in terms of government support, fiscal measures and general funding facilities. Ever since a report by the Economist Intelligence Unit (EIU) in 1983,[2] we know that this has not been true so far as the incidence of taxation and tax incentives are concerned.

Burns and Dewhurst[3] looked at small businesses in seven European countries, and in particular compared the situation of small business in France and West Germany with that in the UK. They concluded that 'the UK small businessman faces neither the burden of taxation nor the complexity of administration that many of his European neighbours face'. They also noted that the UK 'stands out as providing some of the best institutional facilities for equity capital for small businesses', and concluded that 'compared to his European neighbours the UK small businessman would seem to have little to complain about'. The EIU report, however, did rank the UK low in other matters. We shall consider these later.

One other tenet of the traditional lore concerning small businesses in Great Britain is also open to question: it has always been held that despite the disadvantages small businesses suffer in this country, their profitability record is high. Bolton, Wilson[4] and a number of other reports have shown that in terms of return of investment or return on total assets, small businesses generally have performed better than large.

Recent figures produced by the government in *Business Monitor* seem to show that whatever the position may have been in the past, the present tendency is for smaller businesses to do worse than larger in terms of profitability. In both 1981 and 1982 in manufacturing industries the return that large businesses made exceeded that of small business (provisional figures). Indeed, small businesses' return on invested capital has been only around 3 per cent.[5] Post-1982, satisfactory, figures, strangely, do not exist for comparison.

Thus, despite the fact that taxation and funding facilities for small businesses in the UK compare favourably with those available for their counterparts on the Continent, actual UK performance in terms of profitability recently dropped until it was well below that of large UK businesses. There is no evidence of a comparable recent poor performance by small businesses on the Continent. Why should this be? The government tries to help small businesses in this country in a variety of ways, and yet small businesses do not respond. One reason why this is so may be provided by looking at those factors in the EIU report other than funding and finance. Another clue as to a possible reason is provided when we recall that the close correspondence between the entrepreneur and his business is one of the characteristics of a small business. Can it be that the entrepreneur, or what he is trying to do with his business, is at fault? If this is the case we need at the very least to provide positive evidence that there are material differences between the UK entrepreneur and his counterpart on the continent and elsewhere overseas.

2. Entrepreneurial motivation

The Shorter Oxford English Dictionary defines an entrepreneur as 'a contractor acting as intermediary between capital and labour'. The

French economist Cantillon was the first person to introduce the term; he said that the entrepreneur was 'the agent who purchased the means of production for combination into marketable products'.

Early English classical economists such as Adam Smith, saw the entrepreneur as having a rather minor role in overall economic activity; they thought that he provided real capital, but did not play a leading or directing part. For such economists, one person, or indeed a group of persons, did not count much in the scheme of things: it was the broad pattern of supply and demand which effected change and only macro-economics mattered.

The first part of the nineteenth century saw, for the first time, the frequent use of the limited liability company as a means of business organisation. The second part was characterised by a growing separation of corporate ownership and management. This resulted in a re-examination of the position of the entrepreneur and greater emphasis on his role in the business. Much of the ensuing literature concentrates on the differences between the entrepreneur (the setter-up, the goal maker) and management which ran the business. Perhaps the main characteristic of truly small businesses is that this difference does not exist for them. Yet the role of the entrepreneur can hardly be discounted; no business ever started itself!

The goal to which the entrepreneur aspired was basically seen to be (or implied as being) profit maximisation. If we return again to the importance of the correspondence between the entrepreneur's own goals, and that of his or her business, we are faced with a problem. For nowhere in any of the psychological theories of the time, or indeed since, do we see profit maximisation as a *basic* motivation for individuals.

The social psychologists (mainly apostles of Sigmund Freud) saw drives 'as provided by the social environment in which man existed'. This, of course, differs from Freud's pan-sexualism with its implication that all other motivations and drives are derivatives of thwarted sexual desires. There are, of course, other groups – for example, self-theorists and the stimulus response theorists – but none of these considers profit maximisation, or indeed anything like it, as a good explanation of human, or business, behaviour.

In broad terms we have to conclude that if profit maximisation is indeed the goal of an entrepreneur then psychological theories, as such, are of little help to us. So how can we recognise, in practice, a good entrepreneur, how can we tell who is likely to be a successful one, or why he or she might fail, and – above all – why is the latter especially likely to occur in the UK?

3. Psychological testing for entrepreneurs

If psychological theory fails us in explaining the basic motives that drive an entrepreneur, will psychological practice help? Psychological tests come in two forms:

(i) Projective tests
(ii) Pencil and paper tests

Projective tests require that the individual writes – or, better still talks – candidly about something. For example, he or she may describe a picture or discuss a story. Which picture or story does not matter much; the assumption in this sort of work is that he projects his own inner feelings on to the description or discusssion. The technique is entirely analagous to that used in the Rorschach ink blot test. Broadly, the psychologist will be looking for the real attitude of the subject to those matters accepted as being of importance to the small business entrepreneur. Risk-taking, innovative thought, and decision-making capacity are typical. But such projective tests are expensive in terms of time and the use of trained staff and, moreover, the interpretation and explanation of the results is very much a subjective matter so they are, inevitably, of somewhat limited use.

Pencil and paper tests really exist in two types, though only one type is much used. The first type seeks to determine whether an individual is likely to have the qualities necessary to succeed in setting up and running a small business. The second type seeks to determine what kind of small business activity is likely to be suitable for him.

The underlying question which the first type tries to resolve is simply whether the individual is likely to be happier as an employee or as an employer. This requires a degree of self-analysis and such analysis is always a task from which one tends to shrink. In any case we all think we know all about ourselves, so why bother? In fact, when the test is carried out, and the answers looked at objectively, it is usual to find that an additional level of self-knowledge has been achieved.

Small business literature abounds with such tests. Indeed, it is probably true to say that no comprehensive small business book is produced today which does not include at least a simple test on these lines. The format varies, but the subjects include, *inter alia*, talents, skills, abilities, experience, interests and values, and attitudes to work, people, products and leisure.

The second type of paper and pencil test, though much less widely known, can be of much greater practical use. The aim of these tests is not only to assess the skills, aptitudes and experience necessary to set up and run a small business, but, more importantly, to determine whether that particular business satisfies the entrepreneur in terms of personal interests, social and economic conditions, job satisfaction, and so on. In other words, whether he will like it and whether the business is really 'him'.

For this test three columns are needed, one for the entrepreneur, one for the proposed business, and a third for the variance between the interests and desires of the entrepreneur and those offered by the prospective business. On the left of these columns are listed various interests and conditions: they will include such matters as place of work, hours worked, overtime work, and so on (see Table 4CS.5 on p. 92). Completing this sort of test and working out the variances is a long and complicated task, best done over several sessions. A high level of determination on the part of the entrepreneur is required, particularly when completing the column about his or her own interests, values and capacities in an entirely objective way. However, the benefits of such an analysis can be substantial. This simple format indicates to the budding entrepreneur, not what type of business he *fancies* he likes, but which type really suits his personal talents and abilities. In the Case Study at the end of this chapter we include a practical example of how this type of test can be used in deciding which of two alternative business proposals is the more suitable for a potential businessman. In the example, the alternatives considered by the entrepreneur are those of setting up a retail business selling small gifts, or taking up tutorial and lecturing work in retail management with a Cambridge correspondence college.

4.   The dark side of entrepreneurship

Tests may well tell a potential entrepreneur what type of business his talents and interests are most inclined towards, but they are less likely to be able to tell him whether he will succeed or fail as an entrepreneur and why. We have already noted some of the accepted characteristics of a successful entrepreneur: broadly, he is likely to be achievement-orientated and able to take responsibility for decisions; he is also likely to have high levels of energy, charisma and even seductiveness; he probably dislikes dull, repetitive, routine work. But what sort of man actually becomes an entrepreneur? What is his background likely to be?

It has been said by Derek du Toit,[6] an entrepreneur himself, that 'the entrepreneur who starts his own business generally does so because he is a difficult employee'. Since a small business is run by one man it seems certain that another characteristic of the man who wishes to run his own show is a need to be in control. The other side of this particular coin is that he probably finds it difficult to cope with alternating dominant and submissive roles. A manager in a large corporation, by contrast, has to play both these, when dealing with employees, and with colleagues more senior than himself. More specifically, he probably cannot play the submissive role very easily. So the picture we have of many hopeful entrepreneurs is of the man who is a failure in his managerial position in a large corporation because he hates being told what to do. He wants to be in a position where he tells other people – and no one tells him! But again, we have to ask if this background and these characteristics are likely to lead in the long run to success in a business controlled by one man.

Kets de Vries,[7] a psychoanalyst at INSEAD, has argued that a desire for control often leads to over-control; that is a desire to let no one else have any authority. This does not matter too much – indeed, it may well be a good thing – in a very small business when total control by the man who 'lives' at his business may be both practical and useful. The danger is that he will continue these habits when the business has grown to a size when they are totally inappropriate. In one fruit-juice bottling plant with about 200 employees, and a substantial number of senior marketing and production staff, the owner-manager could not relinquish tight control over minor matters. Letters and communications of any sort sent by members of staff had to be made with a 'pink copy'. This was the owner-manager's copy and every day he read through his copies of all correspondence, feeling that in this way he had everything still where he wanted it. The problem, as de Vries points out, is that in such organisations subordinates become infantilised. They are expected to behave as incompetent idiots, and that is the way they do behave. They tend to do very little, take no decisions and circulate very little information. The better ones do not stay. A buyer of such a company will find that he is not purchasing a good management team. Incidentally, the owner-manager developed an ulcer as a result of trying to cope with everything himself.

Entrepreneurs in such organisations typically, too, have quirks. Minor quirks hurt nobody so long as the business is small, but when the active co-operation and support of more people is required, they can be a great disadvantage. Frequently an entrepreneur in a growing organisation will become increasingly distrustful; he will begin to see all things as operating against him. Paradoxically, when the situation is bad, he may be at his best: he will feel that he has paid the price for success. Success, on the other hand, will reinforce distrust: he will go further along the road that he has already followed of only employing sycophants and business morale will inevitably deteriorate. One strange but not uncommon side effect of growing success in this type of entrepreneur needs mentioning. He may well have a desire for applause and recognition which needs to be institutionalised. He will wish to build a monument to himself. This may take the form of erecting a large office block with a large office for himself, or it may take less obvious forms. He may wish to support or endow local playing fields, swimming baths or parks. He may even wish to fund a chair (in his own name!) at a university.

One further problem may arise for the growing 'successful' business, which occurs when the entrepreneur wishes to cash in on his work, and decides to sell his business. Not infrequently, one of the terms of the deal is that he will stay on for a limited number of years 'at the helm'. This appears to be to everybody's benefit. The entrepreneur gets his money and retains his job satisfaction, since his work is unaltered; and the buyer gets the benefit of his expertise and connections. Customer loyalty will be unaffected. In fact, in such 'take-overs' all sorts of difficulties soon arise. The problems that we have mentioned: desire for control, personal quirks, distrust of subordinates and so on, all become magnified and this type of deal often does not work out well.

5. Social attitudes

In the previous section we looked at the negative aspects of entrepreneurship. Throughout we have been trying to find reasons for the failure of small businesses in general and particularly those in the UK. Do entrepreneurs in the UK have too many failings? Are too many *ci-devant* (but failed) corporate executives, now working out some of their failings in an alien arena? Are small businesses the last refuge of the low-rated individual? If this is at all true (and clearly we are stating the hypothesis in a very extreme form) then again we have to find reasons why this might be particularly common in the UK.

Earlier we noted that the EIU's *10 Country Study* gave high ratings for tax and funding for UK small businesses. The summary of conclusions in this report states 'The *overall* rankings by the Assessment Group of EC countries in order of their favourability to profit maximisation by existing small business was as follows:

1. West Germany
2. Greece
3. France
4. Netherlands
5. Denmark
6. Belgium
7. Luxemburg
8. Irish Republic
9. UK
10. Italy.

The details of these rankings of small and medium enterprise environmental factors are shown in Table 4.1.

In almost all matters other than taxation and funding, the UK is reported as doing poorly. In discriminant legislation and treatment (this heading includes organisation and services to small businesses, monopolies and merger legislation, disclosure provisions for company accounts, procurement, and information, training and counselling) the UK comes last. It also comes last in premises and labour (this heading includes educational levels) and in most other sections it does pretty badly. Why should this be? Is it the entrepreneurs themselves who are at fault or is it partly that the UK provides such a poor 'social' environment for small businesses? Is it perhaps a matter of deep-rooted negative feelings about business in general and small business in particular which only in this country finds such an extreme expression?

The attitudes within the UK to work in any industrial business by any other than the 'working' class, has been devastatingly attacked by many (but mainly non-UK!) writers. Martin Wiener[8] in his review of English society in the nineteenth and twentieth centuries argues that in the nineteenth century 'the low status given to a career in trade and industry did serve a purpose – the Empire needed a large, confident and fairly conventional class of administrators, whereas the economy seemed to be taking care of itself'. A century later the situation had changed dramatically. By then the colonies and the Commonwealth needed comparatively little attention. The economy, by contrast, lagged. The need was for the best effort in industrial production, but attitudes were then, as now, unbelievably slow to change. James Callaghan, when he was Prime Minister in 1976, complained that 'many of our best trained students have no desire to join industry'. MBA students from UK business schools would have been happy at that time to have joined a respectable city institution (such as a stockbroker, a firm of chartered accountants or a merchant bank) or possibly a blue chip business such as Imperal Chemical Industries (ICI) or Rolls Royce. But even if they did join the industrial *crème de la crème*, it was only in the functional areas of finance, personnel, marketing or administration. Production was, and still is, a dirty word. But the position is entirely different elsewhere; in both France and Germany a production manager or engineer is addressed by the courtesy title of 'Engineer'. This is a mark of respect and is seen as such. But in the UK, whilst doctors, rectors and professors are called by their titles and respected for their work, production people are neither called by a title nor respected for what they do.

In the UK this attitude of distaste for industry in general, and manufacturing industry in particular, spreads into all disciplines. In research we find a split between pure research (which is academically and socially acceptable), and applied research. One is seen as clean; the other dirty. The purest, cleanest research is probably 'pure' mathematics (again the same emotionally charged adjective) as compared with

Table 4.1 Small and medium-sized enterprises: environmental factors

Factor	Weight	Belgium	Denmark	France	West Germany	Greece	Irish Republic	Italy	Luxemburg	Netherlands	UK
Labour											
Labour costs	50	10	6	5	7	1	2	4	8	9	3
Employment legislation	50	6	6	8	4	7	2	3	8	7	5
Education levels	50	4	1	6	5	3	9	7	10	2	8
Trend in unit costs	65	2	3	5	6	8	9	8	2	4	10
Premises											
Premises	115	2	4	8	6	2	9	8	4	4	10
Taxation											
Total tax as % GDP	15	8	8	7	4	2	7	4	2	8	4
Local taxation	10	4	1	6	2	7	9	6	4	9	8
Personal taxation	40	9	10	1	3	2	7	4	6	9	6
Rates of corporation tax	5	3	6	10	4	9	1	8	2	7	5
Incidence of corporation tax	35	6	4	6	6	9	6	8	9	2	2
Carry forward/back	30	7	7	7	4	10	1	7	7	3	2

Capital gains	5	2	7	1	10	5	8	5	7	9	3
Value added tax	10	7	4	8	5	6	5	9	3	6	3
Capital/credit											
Tax incentives	50	3	3	3	8	8	8	8	8	8	1
Credit guarantees	75	6	6	6	2	6	10	10	6	2	6
Subsidised loans	75	5	5	5	5	2	2	9	4	9	9
Discriminant legislation											
Government organisation	30	2	9	5	2	9	5	9	5	5	5
Monopolies and mergers	50	6	3	2	2	6	10	6	6	6	10
Disclosure rules	50	7	10	4	2	7	2	7	4	7	9
Procurement	50	9	6	3	2	6	6	9	9	2	6
Information, training	35	7	7	2	2	7	7	7	7	2	7
Economic activity											
Nos of SMEs	30	7	3	6	9	1	3	3	8	5	9
Trends in share of activity	20	8	7	5	7	6	4	8	2	7	3
Population change	5	9	3	4	6	10	2	9	6	1	6
Active population	10	6	1	5	3	9	10	7	4	8	2
GDP change	20	7	8	4	6	4	1	4	9	4	10
Consumer prices	20	5	5	7	2	10	8	9	5	2	5

applied mathematics. Above the door of well-known institution there is engraved the hope that pure mathematics 'never has been and never shall be of any use to anyone'. For supporters of this view, it must have been sad when the beautiful abstract conditional probability work of an eighteenth-century clergyman by the name of Bayes was two centuries later found to be of practical use in business decision-making. When George Boole created the complex mathematical structure since called Boolean algebra, he little thought that it would form the basis for work in switching circuits and logic gates for that most practical of all aids – the electronic computer. What once was clean now is not!

In the UK, industry has only proved attractive to the well-to-do when the pull of money or family tradition has been very powerful. Most frequently it has been the profession of last resort, to fall back on when success in other, reputable, occupations has not been possible. The only other possible alternative in such situations was teaching. Many researchers in this area, such as Rosemary Stewart or Roy Lewis, have confirmed this from their field work.

But if industry (and manufacturing industry especially) in the UK is one of the last resorts of the unsuccessful, what about small businesses? If we continue with our example of the employment of MBA students as providing a good indicator of job desirability at a reasonably high level, the conclusions are shattering. Until very recently, small business was a total non-subject not only at any university but even in business schools. No courses were held and no students even considered working in this area. It is true that in the last few years the situation has begun to change dramatically; now we have well-attended small business option courses both at MBA and undergraduate levels. Courses for those wishing to set up their own small business are now run at some universities, for example the Manpower Services Commission-funded Graduate Enterprise Programme, Firmstart Programme and (for existing managers) the Management Extension Programme.

The attitude to small businesses in the UK is indeed very different now from what it was only a few years ago, but in this country all we are doing is trying to correct our huge existing negative bias against such organisations. In the USA there has long been a tradition of a much more positive vision. The man who starts from scratch and becomes a millionaire (preferably before reaching the magic age of thirty) is held in the highest public esteem. He is a sort of latter-day folk hero. Again, we have to contrast this with the situation in the UK. A large number of potential business entrepreneurs are undoubtedly corporation 'cast offs', and in our present economic climate there are many of these. To the outside observer it has seemed for many years that most large corporations have had some staff posts which appeared to be for quite useless purposes. In fact they were for useless people: people who had fallen by the wayside, but which a benevolent company did not wish to cast aside. When corporations eventually do cut back, where do these people go? Many, it is clear, go into small businesses.

6. Hardship, self-reliance and discipline

One final example of the effects of this negative attitude to small businesses in our society will suffice. In the nineteenth century, making money in business was, as we have seen, always the work of the unfavoured few. So who were the people who filled the vacancies that the establishment declined? Some we already know about, but in many cases it was well-educated and well-informed people who were members of races and sects which were not highly regarded by society at large.

The Jews, for example, amongst others, helped to fill this vacuum, and we have a parallel today in the small business situation. Ethnic minority groups, such as Asians, prepared to work long hours in business such as retail shops and with a full family commitment, are amongst the most prolific and successful. But they are there because the opportunities are not available to them elsewhere. They are there because they are prepared to accept the tough conditions which, it is clear, often do occur in this socially unacceptable area of business management. There are parallels to this situation throughout the world. The 'Malaysian' Chinese in Malaya, Indonesia and other countries in South East Asia provide one example. In Malaya these 'many genera-tion' Chinese expatriates are present in large numbers. They do not constitute a majority of the population, so that voting control and political power has always been with the indigenous Malays. Neverthe-less, the control over business (still mainly small business) and over almost all professional work by this ethnic minority group is still – despite strenuous efforts by the ruling Malaysian government party – nearly absolute. The Chinese work long hours, they accept hard condi-tions and they thrive on it.

Malcolm Harper[9] mentions many such examples: 'The Indians in East Africa, the Armenians in Egypt, the Lebanese in West Africa, the Kikuyu in Masailand, the Mahajans all over India except in their desert homeland of Rajasthan, the Tamils in Sri Lanka, the Palestinians in Arabia and the British almost everywhere except in Britain; all have shown that dislocation and hardship can lead to enterprise.' He argues that: 'The very experience of living in a difficult environment, and of planning, financing and executing a move and then surviving in a new and often hostile environment requires qualities of self-restraint, absti-nence, hard work and voluntary postponement of gratification which are normally far more severe than those demanded by the lifestyle of those who remain at home, or of the indigenous people of the place in which these refugees relocate.'

Perhaps, in the UK, we should encourage small business training schemes which are themselves tough and which emphasise the characteristics of toughness and discipline required to succeed in this area. Perhaps we tend to featherbed 'start-ups', to encourage new businesses with financial support in the early months which subtly deprives the entrepreneur of the need to fight hard for survival in a hostile business environment. If this, too, is true, we have some clear guidelines on how to encourage small business entrepreneurship in the UK: we need to make small business entrepreneurs realise that self-reliance, hard work and discipline are necessary factors for success. The other side of the coin is that, as we have argued, we need to change the attitude of our society to small business. We have to encourage the vision – so common on the Continent – of a hardworking small-business community which is respected and admired in its own right. We have to encourage the right people to move into this area. Not until society sees success in small business as the sort of achievement which they would expect and admire from determined, hard-working, well-motivated, intelligent people, will these people become entrepreneurs.

Case Study: John Jederman

John Jederman (JJ), aged 47, is married with two children aged 17 and 19. The elder child has left home; the younger has a place at Essex University. JJ has a cottage at St Neots, 18 miles from Cambridge. He has a CNAA degree in Business Studies. For the last three years he has been a temporary lecturer in marketing at the local polytechnic in the Commercial Studies department. Cut-backs at the polytechnic have meant that they can no longer employ him. Prior to his job at the polytechnic he was employed for nearly ten years in a small toy manufacturing business run by an owner-manager. JJ worked in the sales department and with an assistant covered the whole of England and Wales. For the last three years he had also assumed some responsibility for manufacturing and design and the owner-manager regarded him as his 'second in command', so JJ was most upset when his employer announced, somewhat abruptly, that he was getting on in years and wished to retire, was selling the business, and that all the staff would be dismissed. JJ tried to purchase the business himself, but was unable either to raise enough money, or to persuade his employer to keep the business going.

Before his employment with the toy manufacturer, JJ had a short-term commission in the Army's Supply and Transport branch (then the RASC). Nearing the end of his service, he had been assessed for his leadership and personal qualities, and a comprehensive report made out. This report was based on 'in-depth' interviews with a battery of army psychologists, and also on reports from his senior officers. Some parts of the report (a copy of which was given to JJ) were concerned only with army matters and have been omitted; the relevant parts to this Case Study are shown in Appendix A below.

JJ is now considering two propositions. They are:

1. To set up a new company, 'Funlines', to innovate and market low-priced impulse gift lines. His detailed proposal, shown in the form of a business plan, is outlined in Appendix B on page 83.
2. To take up an offer of writing, lecturing and tutorial work in retail management and business studies at the Cantab Correspondence and Tutorial College, based near Cambridge. This would involve him in:
   (a) writing notes for HNC, ONC, GCSE and also new degree courses in retail and marketing management, and business studies generally.
   (b) lecturing at the correspondence college two days and some evenings a week.
   (c) tutorial and assignment checking work for students.

A copy of the contract offered him is shown in Appendix C on page 91.

John Jederman now sees himself as being at the parting of ways. Whichever course he pursues has to be successful or, at the least, secure and satisfactory, since, with his fiftieth birthday approaching, he will soon be too old to change. Once committed, he will be on board a single track tram!

JJ decided to spend some time in testing his personal desires, interests and needs, as he sees them, in a variety of complex forms, against those provided by each of the alternative forms of employment. He is aware that his attempt to quantify these factors could be criticised as being 'very subjective', and he is aware too that the main benefit arises from the increase in self-awareness that must come from working through this exercise. His wife has already made her opinion quite clear. Based on her experience of him in his previous two jobs she comes down firmly on the side of the correspondence college post. Tutoring, writing and lecturing are all forms or work which are congenial to him, she says. JJ wonders if her view may be subjective too, influenced perhaps by the big disparity in the amount of time he will spend at home with each job.

On the all-important question of salaries, JJ is unable to make any clear distinction between the two jobs; both appear to offer about £15000 per annum, or a little more. He realises, however, that so far as risk is concerned there is a substantial difference. This factor is included in the test.

JJ completed the test (Table 4.CS.5); he was as honest with himself as he could be, and he was mildly surprised at the result. Prior to taking the test he had been quite certain, in his own mind, that his strong preference was for setting up the 'Funlines' business.

Appendix A: Extracts from report on Lieutenant J. Jederman

Leadership and initiative

That this officer has latent leadership qualities is not in dispute. We have only to refer to an occasion when his unit was on loan to the Malaysian government and engaged on bringing up sensitive supplies to government troops in Negri

Sembilan. A small group of aborigines, drunk on a local brew made from palm trees, successfuly raided his supplies. Lieut. Jederman on his own initiative, walked to the aborigines' camp, talked to the leader, quietened him down and returned with the supplies.

However, we have to add that in our opinion it was the situation which itself brought out the action from Jederman. In other circumstances – for instance, when his unit was relaxed and at rest – it seems that Jederman reverted to a passive role and indeed control of the unit appeared to pass to Jederman's Sergeant, NCOs and Other Ranks.

This position is paralleled in other situations where initiative needs to be shown. If there is a clear need for initiative, Jederman will supply it. If no initiative is manifestly demanded, Jederman is not forthcoming. He is not good at foreseeing likely trouble, and taking a firm line in advance.

Dominant/Submissive Roles

Jederman takes orders easily provided he has confidence in his commanding officer. Weak or uncertain leadership from above throws him into some confusion. He likes clear directives and clearly delineated areas of authority. Again, paradoxically, once it is evident to him that he must act on his own, he does so very effectively. It is on the borderline that he has problems.

Junior NCOs generally regard Jederman as fair, and easy to work with. There is some evidence that they may on occasion exploit his good nature, but the extent to which they are allowed to do this is limited. On the occasion . . (here follows another long military example of his 'easy-going' attitude).

Personal Qualities

Jederman is easy to get on with, friendly, generally of a sunny disposition, liked and respected by his peers. Occasionally he goes through bleak periods. In such circumstances he tends to retreat into his own company, though he will talk over his problems with his friends. He always does seem to have one particular friend with whom he spends most of his available time.

Intelligence

Jederman scores highly on both quantitative and (to a slightly lesser extent) on non-quantitative, lateral thinking-type tests. His raw IQ score is high, around 146.

Ambition

Jederman is ambitious and seems prepared to put himself out to gain the necessary qualifications and experience in order to go higher. We rather doubt, however, if Jederman has the necessary qualities of ruthlessness to reach the very top. He can be ruthless and very determined when placed in a situation where this is clearly demanded. In other situations he takes a more passive role. In the final analysis he probably lacks much of the killer instinct. It is this which makes us question whether he is suitable for promotion much beyond the ranks immediately above him. (It was this comment, more than anything else, which made Jederman decide that – although a permanent commission has been offered to him with promotion to the rank of Captain – he would be better not to accept, and that he should take his chance in 'civvy street').

Appendix B: 'Funlines' proposed business plan

Introduction

This plan has been compiled by the founder of the proposed business.

It relates to a proposal to establish a business involved in the innovation and marketing of low priced gift lines.

The purposes of the plan are:

(i) To determine and demonstrate the viability of the proposed business.
(ii) To enable the business to present a case for financial support to bankers.
(iii) To act as a basis for control in the proposed business.

Statement of goals

(i) *First year of operation*
To generate sufficient profits to enable me to maintain the standard of living I currently enjoy with a salary of circa £15 000 per annum and to provide a return on initial investment of 40 per cent. As demonstrated in Appendix I (Profit and Loss Account) this would require a turnover of £200 000 and pre-tax profits of £17 000 would be generated.
(ii) *Second/third years of operation*
By retaining profits within the business to increase turnover by the end of year three to £300 000 per annum with the subsequent increase in profit and return on investment.

Environmental Factors

The major market is seasonal and therefore depends on reasonable weather during the summer months with the subsequent high/low level of tourism.

As will be discussed later, competition within the industry comes chiefly from importers and it is felt that there are three main trends which have developed over the last two to three years:

(i) It would appear that we now have to accept an exchange rate of around £1 sterling/$1.50 (US dollars) and almost all relevant sources of supply for importers trade in US dollars. Furthermore, all international sea freight rates are charged in US dollars and they obviously form a major proportion of the landed cost of imported merchandise. In addition, UK Customs and Excise duties are charged on a percentage basis of £ sterling landed cost and due to the two factors mentioned have effectively increased in cash terms.
(ii) The major sources of supply are in the Far East and are very dependent on

the US market, which has been and is currently very depressed. Due to the subsequent drop in revenue, the Far Eastern manufacturers will not spend money on developing new ideas and the market 'cries-out' for something different.

(iii) Imported goods have been subject to quota arrangements with HM Customs and Excise but are now subject to EEC quotas. Hong Kong has therefore lost its special rights as a colony and its goods are now subject to duty. Similarly, South Korea has lost its 'Third World' classification and its goods are subject to duty. These two countries would be in the top three sources of supply for the importer.

Existing market

The traditional avenues of trading, that is, manufacturer or importer/ wholesaler/retailer have been almost totally eroded in the gift trade and the importer generally deals solely with the retailer.

The customer is usually to be found in a holiday centre, which may be a coastal or recreational centre, and he wants a quick turnaround from the product. His normal mark-up would be around 100 per cent on cost.

Competitive analysis

The competition would come almost totally from importers who are buying their products mainly from Far Eastern sources. They are in size between £1 million to £8 million per annum turnover and are geographically spread around England, the location of the major ones being shown in Table 4.CS.1.

They market mainly through trade shows held between early December and late February when they take initial orders, and then during the season through a network of self-employed agents or representatives. As can be seen from Table 4.CS.1, they operate on a product range varying from 1000 to 4000 items.

The representatives of customers at the trade shows vary from professional buyers to owners to managers, depending on the type of outlet.

The pricing strategy of the competition is generally to add 50 per cent to 55 per cent to landed cost, although this can reduce for very large buyers.

Table 4.CS.1   Locations of major importers

Location	Turnover	Number of Product lines	Number of Representatives
Newcastle on Tyne	£6m	2000	10
Leeds	£8m	4000	20
Southend on Sea	£3m	4000	15
Harlow, Essex	£5m	3000	15
Scarborough	£1m	1500	6
Leeds	£2m	1000	4
Weston-Super-Mare	£1m	1000	3

The competition

(i) Their strengths:
Significant financial muscle;
Bulk buying, so low unit costs;
Established representatives/agents;
History/tradition.

(ii) Their weaknesses:
Lead times on imports;
Total dependence on imports;
Currency fluctuations;
Dependence on Far Eastern ideas;
Import tariffs, quotas;
High overhead content.

The marketing plan

(i) The target market

The products fall within the cheaper end of the gifts category and are therefore always liable to change, improvement and whims of fashion, and are generally in an impulse-buying situation. It is common at the cheap end of the gift trade for products to have a three-year product cycle. The products have been targeted on the child/adolescent segment and the buying motives are self-consumption and gifts for others.

The market worth for any particular range of products is virtually impossible to evaluate although the total gift market must be considered extensive. The magnitude of this proposed operation is therefore unlikely to upset the present market. Probably the most important factor in the market is the seasonal nature of demand.

The UK market may be segmented geographically as follows:

(a) England
(b) Ireland
(c) Scotland
(d) Wales

I have decided to ignore the Scottish and Irish markets and concentrate on the English and Welsh outlets, of which I already have some knowledge.

The market may then be segmented as:

(a) Coastal
(b) Inland
       (i) Major tourist attractions, i.e. zoos, etc.
      (ii) General gift boutiques/greetings shops.

The coastal market, whilst being spread over the period June, July and August is, in fact, highly concentrated in the six-week period of the school summer holidays.

The inland tourist attractions, whilst still being seasonal, have a six-month trading period.

The general inland gift shop covers a twelve-month trading period with the occasional peak, for example, at Christmas.

The market may then be segmented by customer:

(a) Credit-worthiness
(b) Location
(c) Size

> (i) Large national multiples, for example, John Menzies, W. H. Smith, etc.
> (ii) Larger centralised outlets, for example, West Midlands Safari Park.
> (iii) Smaller single gift shops.

I have decided that due to the limited resources available financially, payment by my customers is paramount and I will therefore aim at those with the ability to pay quickly. The location will be primarily inland to extend the operating season and fall into the medium-size retail outlets.

(ii) Marketing mix

(a) Product
The gift trade in this country tends to follow trends that are innovated and established in the USA. The nature of the product necessitates being first in the market and therefore the US market must be studied very closely for developments.

The product will be six lines designed for a children's market and retailing for a maximum of 99p. Inside this limit the psychological price barriers are 25p, 50p and 75p.

The product offers a differential advantage over competitors' products in quality, display at point of sale, exclusivity and servicing of customers.

(b) Price
The retail prices are as discussed above at 25p, 50p, 75p and 99p. The normal retail mark-up is 100 per cent on cost and I must, therefore, aim my products at 12p, 25p, 35p and 50p.

Normal trade terms will be net 30 days, but in line with the proposed policy relating to financial limitations it is proposed to give a substantial discount, say 10 per cent, for payment within seven days. This discount can satisfactorily be included and 'lost' in the initial mark-up.

(c) Place
It is my intention to deliver the initial orders personally to improve customer contact and service. Repeat orders, because of lower quantities and lightweight products, will be mailed.

It will be unnecessary to carry stock initially as orders will only be placed to match orders previously taken by me. After the initial product input, estimates will be made as to the likely repeat level. An extremely reliable source of information on this score will be the zoos and safari parks where reasonable trading levels are reached two months before the coastal trade begins. Their results will be researched and forward orders placed as appropriate.

(d) Promotion

A number of intended initial customers are already well known to me, and in that sense little promotion is necessary and can be done by telephone or letter.

It is my intention to hire a suitable showmobile during the initial selling period to introduce my products to the customer. This, I believe, is preferable to trade shows because of the limited market I am aiming at, and it increases convenience to customers. Once the product is introduced to the customer orders for replacement stocks can be from the catalogue, by letter or by telephone.

(iii) Controls

Because of the seasonal nature of the business it is felt that the twelve months fall into six distinct categories with three different types of control. The six categories are *summer selling*, *summer deliveries*, *summer repeats*, *winter selling*, *winter deliveries* and *winter repeats*. Because the goods are initially sold on display stands the control would be numbers of stands sold and then in the delivery period, number of stands delivered. The control during the two repeat periods must be level of percentage repeats by product line.

(iv) Costs

The costs of the first year's marketing operation will be time, travelling and subsistence. These will be incurred annually during January, February, June, July and August each year. The costs in the first year have been estimated at £8000 for motor vehicles and £3000 for subsistence.

The manufacturing plan

(i) Product development

All manufacturing will be sub-contracted out due to the variety of products being sold. A manufacturer for each type of product will be located and the product developed in conjunction with him.

(ii) Facilities

An acquaintance owns and operates a warehousing/despatch service in Burton-on-Trent and my intention, at least in the short term, is to use this service to enable me to have more time to devote to the marketing of the product. The only facilities necessary, therefore, will be an office and this will be located at my home in order to have the necessary back-up from my wife.

(iii) Organisation

With manufacturing and warehousing sub-contracted, only marketing, product development and administration will have to be handled. I will personally handle product development and marketing, leaving my wife to deal with administration matters.

(iv) Costs

Due to the pricing structure of this proposal and of my customers, manufacturing costs must be a maximum of 25 per cent of retail price. Any product failing to meet this specification will not be considered.

Warehousing, as previously discussed, will be sub-contracted also, at a cost of 5 per cent of turnover. Insurance cover for stock only and delivery of goods will be at my expense.

All office facilities are already available at my home and therefore the only real cost will be the extra telephone expenses incurred.

The financial plan

(i) Capital

The directors of the Company will be:
(a)   The founder as Managing Director
(b)   The founder's wife as Director and Company Secretary
It is estimated that the two directors will each invest £2500 in Ordinary Share Capital. It is projected that a further funding of £32 000 will be required in the first year. See cash flow forecast (Appendix II attached).

(ii) Cash flow

The cash flow forecast attached shows the total funding necessary. Because of the different types of funding available, interest has been excluded. Funding is at a maximum mid-year. This pattern would be repeated in subsequent years.

(iii) Break-even analysis

A break-even chart of the first year of operation is included (Appendix III). This is based on the assumption that costs of goods, stands warehousing, cash discount and postage are variable costs and that all other costs are fixed.

Because of the relatively high fixed overhead content of costs the break-even point is rather high. However, little cash has to be injected initially until orders are forthcoming from customers.

(iv) Profit and loss forecast

A first year profit and loss account is attached (Appendix I). This shows that even at this relatively low level of turnover a satisfactory return on investment is made in the first year. It is felt that the level of turnover is easily attainable and that the volume is restricted only by the need to limit financial borrowings.

(v) Financial projections

The costs in this project are relatively simple to project and control. The key to success and to control is the sales turnover. Careful gauging and monitoring of turnover will be carried out on a daily basis.

Key fundamentals to the business

(a) Sources of new ideas both in the introductory stages of the business and later to stimulate customers and expand the customer base.
(b) Location of reliable competitive suppliers with whom a continuing mutually profitable arrangement can be developed.
(c) Operational plan to utilise the existing customer base.
(d) To utilise fully the financial resources available without putting the business at risk.

(e) To continue to improve the profit as forecast in year one by the measures in (a) and (d) above and increase the return on initial investment to 100 per cent per annum by year three.

The research and development plan

(i) Product development must be an ongoing task with regular introduction of new lines. It is intended to maintain the same restrictions in price range as this is the market/product field with which I am familiar. All developments will be made with this in mind. The search for new product ideas may involve visits to centres of innovation for gifts such as the US and Italy.

(ii) As increased funds become available the market must be expanded to cover a larger percentage of the prospective customers known to me. The larger customers mentioned in the market segmentation may then be attacked.

(iii) Net Development

The net development must be to aim at a higher market share in the area of the market defined as the target market without putting the company at risk either financially or in terms of resources.

Appendix I

Table 4.CS.2   Year 1: Profit and loss account

		(£000s)	
Sales		200	
Less discounts allowed		20	
			180
Less cost of sales			
Goods	90		
Stands	10	100	
	—		
			80
Variable expenses			
Warehousing	10		
Postage	4	14	
	—		
			66
Fixed expenses			
Salaries and wages	23		
Leasing	5		
Motor vehicle costs	8		
Telephones	2		
Printing and stationery	2		
Subsistence	3		
Artwork	4		
Sundries	2	49	
	—		
Net profit			17

Appendix II

Table 4.CS.3   Year 1: Cash flow

	Jan	Feb	Mar	Apr	May	Jun	Jul	Aug	Sep	Oct	Nov	Dec	Total
Sales	–	–	20	55	35	20	30	25	9	2	2	2	200
Receipts (Net of discount)	–	–	5	30	30	25	40	30	25	12	5	3	205
Outgoings													
Purchases (incl. VAT)	–	–	15	25	20	15	30	5	3	2	–	–	115
Stand costs	–	–	3	3	2	–	–	1	1	–	–	–	10
Warehousing	–	–	1	3	2	1	2	1	–	–	–	–	10
Variable costs	–	–	–	–	1	1	1	1	–	–	–	–	4
Fixed costs	8	4	4	4	4	4	5	4	3	3	3	3	49
VAT	–	–	–	–	–	7	–	–	3	3	3	3	10
Monthly totals	8	4	23	35	29	28	38	12	10	5	3	3	198
Monthly movement	(8)	(4)	(18)	(5)	1	(3)	2	18	15	7	2	–	7
Cumulative	(8)	(12)	(30)	(35)	(34)	(37)	(35)	(17)	(2)	5	7	7	7

Appendix III

Table 4.CS.4   *Year 1: Break-even analysis*

	£000s
Sales turnover	200
Fixed costs	49
Variable costs	134
Net profit	17

Contribution per £1 sales: $\dfrac{66}{200} \times \dfrac{100}{1} = .33$

Break-even point: $\dfrac{£49\ 000}{33p} \times = £148\ 000$

Appendix C: Contract between Cantab Correspondence and Tutorial College (hereinafter CCTC) and John Jederman

1. CCTC will pay John Jederman a yearly salary of £15 000, payable monthly in arrears, together with certain additional fees and commission payments for writing course material as shown in items 2 to 7 inclusive below.

2. CCTC will pay £1500 for the preparation of new degree course material in retail and marketing management. This is an advance on commission which will be at the rate of 5 per cent on sales of the two courses from now onwards. It is agreed that the advance on commission shall be paid within the period of 30 days after receipt of the material for the course.

3. Annual Statement of Fees and Commissions. During the month of December in each year, CCTC will submit a statement containing the following information in relation to the twelve months ending on the preceding 30th September.

   (i) The fees (net VAT) received by CCTC during the twelve months from students taking the courses for which you have written the material.

   (ii) The percentage of those fees due.

   (iii) The advances, if any, made in the course of the previous twelve months.

With each such statement CCTC will remit the amount shown on the statement.

4. Duration of Agreement for Commission Payments. The agreement for Commission Payments will continue for the duration of the course. The course shall be deemed to come to an end when CCTC, on reasonable, substantive grounds (for example course no longer required because of major syllabus change withdrawal of subject, replacement course needed to meet radical changes in the syllabus, course inadequate for current examination requirements, etc.) decides that the course is no longer to be marketed by CCTC.

Appendix D

Table 4.CS.5 Psychological test results

FACTOR	JJ's VIEWS AND CORRESPONDING WEIGHT		FUNLINES — JJ's ASSESSMENT AND CORRESPONDING WEIGHT		JOINT WEIGHT	CCTC — JJ's ASSESSMENT AND CORRESPONDING WEIGHT		JOINT WEIGHT
Pay								
Risk	Unhappy at risk	6	High	−8	**−48**	Moderate	−4	**−24**
Capacity to earn more	Required to be available	4	Many	+5	**+20**	Some	+3	**+12**
Fringe benefits	Appreciated	3	A few	+1	**+3**	Not available	0	**0**
Conditions of work								
Human contact	Essential, but happy with periods on his own	5	Variable	+2	**+10**	Sometimes lonely	−2	**−10**
Monotonous/variable	Likes variety	3	Little	−2	**−6**	Some variety	+1	**+3**
Travel								
At work	No 'nights away'	2	Some nights away	−2	**−4**	None	0	**0**
To work	Unhappy with too much	2	A lot	−5	**−10**	Some	−2	**−4**
Hours of work	Dislike of 'office' hours	3	None	0	**0**	Some routine	−4	**−12**
Weekends	Required to be free	3	Not always free	−2	**−6**	Always free	0	**0**
Holidays	Important	4	Wintertime only	−1	**−4**	Any time	0	**0**
Job Satisfaction, etc.								
Job satisfaction	Very important	10	Good	+4	**+40**	Fairly good	+3	**+30**
Integrity	Important	8	Some	−2	**−16**	Satisfactory	0	**0**
Humanity/toughness	Dislike of hard dealing	5	Toughness	−4	**−20**	Satisfactory	0	**0**
TOTAL					**−41**			**−5**

Note The 'Joint Weight' is the product of the weight of the particular Factor and JJ's Assessment of the Corresponding Weight for Funlines or CCTC.

5. Course Maintenance. Following publication of the new course(s) and (subject to the rights of termination set out above) it is required that you:

   (i) rewrite and update the lessons, tests and specimen answers of your course(s) whenever modifications are required by changes in the law or practice or by alterations in the applicable syllabus or in the regulations of the examining bodies.

   (ii) rewrite for CCTC every December, or earlier if necessary, any modifications which you believe should be made to the lessons, tests and specimen answers of your course(s) in readiness for the following academic year.

6. Annual Report/Rewriting/Revision Fee. For the services to be provided under Paragraph 5 of this agreement CCTC will pay an annual retaining fee of £500. This payment is additional to any commission due under item 2.

7. Copyright. It is agreed that copyright in the course materials be vested in CCTC

8. Holidays with pay. Three weeks are allowed per year in addition to statutory bank holidays.

9. Sickness or injury pay entitlement. The salary of a member of the staff less any national insurance benefits to which he/she is entitled will continue to be paid in full for a period of up to 3 months due to illness or injury in any period of twelve months. Beyond that, payments or part payments shall be at the discretion of CCTC.

10. Superannuation arrangements. Monthly-paid members of staff are required to join the CCTC pension fund.

11. Period of notice. Three months, to expire at the end of the calendar year.

12. Retirement. Members of the teaching staff will retire at the end of the calendar year in which they reach the age of 65 years, with the option to retire at any time after the age of 60.

13. Residence. Members of staff are required to live within a reasonable distance of their place of work.

CHAPTER 5

The Entrepreneurial Process

Howard H. Stevenson and
William A. Sahlman

The word 'entrepreneurship' has entered the managerial vocabulary as the 1980s' equivalent of 'professionalism', the managerial buzzword of the 1970s. Many managers are trying to understand the concept of entrepreneurship, and how their own organisation can be made more 'entrepreneurial'. As might be expected, a phalanx of consultants and advisers have entered the market to help managers accomplish the goal of instilling entrepreneurship into their companies.

Our purpose in this chapter is to attempt to shed light on the concept of entrepreneurship and to understand the extraordinary level of interest in the topic. We will define entrepreneurship as a management process, and will suggest why we believe encouraging entrepreneurial behaviour is critical to the long-term vitality of the international economy. Most importantly, we will see that the practice of entrepreneurship is as important, if not more important, to companies as they mature as it is to start-ups. Finally, we will examine some of the requirements for preserving entrepreneurship as companies grow and experience success.

1. Interest in entrepreneurship

It would be difficult to overstate the degree to which there has been an increase in the level of interest in the topic of entrepreneurship. Every day, somewhere in the world, the news media relate new stories abour the exploits of the new hero or heroine – the entrepreneur. Indeed, in the USA, a large number of new media forms have been created to focus on this topic alone: examples include *Inc.*, *Venture* and *Black Enterprise*. The subject has even grown to a sufficient stature that magazines like *Fortune* and the *Harvard Business Review* routinely devote significant sections to the subject. To illustrate, a recent *Fortune* cover story was entitled 'America's Greatest Entrepreneur', and described Ken Olsen, founder and chairman of Digital Equipment.

The world of big business has also given strong signals that, whatever entrepreneurship may be, more of it is needed: Jack Welch, the president of General Electric, has announced an entrepreneurial mission for the multibillion dollar giant he leads; Exxon, the world's largest company, created (but later disbanded) a new venture group; IBM created the 'Entry Systems Division' that was responsible for launching the personal computer; Fred Smith, founder of Federal Express, has identified a major role he plays in the company as a preserver of the entrepreneurial spirit; and Lew Lehr, retired chairman of 3M, has discussed how he encourages entrepreneurial behaviour throughout his company. Still other large firms, like Sohio, Analog Devices and Monsanto, have created venture capital investment vehicles to enable them 'to support entrepreneurship outside of the traditional structures'.

Economists have also begun to acknowledge the importance of the entrepreneurial function. Such distinguished economists as Kenneth Arrow and Will Baumol have focused their attention on the subject of entrepreneurship. Not since Joseph Schumpeter have so many talented theoreticians devoted so much effort to understanding the entrepreneurial process.

In addition to more theoretical essays, a number of economists have begun to gather and assess data on the contribution of entrepreneurial activities to the economy. Beginning with the seminal work of David Birch at Massachusetts Institute of Technology (MIT), analysts have discovered that small and entrepreneurial firms play a major role in economic growth and innovation.

These studies have not gone unnoticed by politicians. A survey by Touche Ross, the US accounting firm, revealed that 82 per cent of the mayors of more than half the US cities of 250 000 and upwards population believed small business to be more important in job creation than large firms.

Another striking phenomenon is the emergence of interest in entrepreneurship at universities. The number of courses offered in entrepreneurship has increased eightfold over the last nine years, according to a survey of US educational institutions carried out by Karl Vesper. The content of the courses has changed and additional research has been done. Harvard University's president, Derek Bok, noted this trend when he said:

> The [Harvard] Business School is beginning to see its role is not just training general managers but also to train and provide a preparation for people

starting their own business . . . It's a kind of a new freedom to go out and take some risks and run your own show . . . It's a kind of a new frontier for people of some boldness and creativity.

Yet another strong indicator of increased interest in entrepreneurship is provided by the unprecedented increase in recent years of new business formation. Basically, the number of annual new business incorporations has doubled in the last ten years, from annual rates of about 300 000 to over 600 000. While not all of the new business starts identified in such data could be classified as entrepreneurial ventures, the evidence is very strong that the incidence of entrepreneurship has increased dramatically in recent years.

These trends are mirrored in the venture capital markets. The decade 1975–84 saw explosive growth in the amount of capital committed to venture capital firms in the USA. There was a concurrent dramatic increase in the amount of money raised in the public capital markets by young companies. Table 5.1 documents these trends.

Although the magnitude of initial public offerings and venture capital assets is small in relation to total investment capital of the USA, the trends indicate increasing economic importance and these trends are being mirrored in other countries throughout the world.

2.   Why is interest so high?

So, interest in entrepreneurship seems to be broad-based and higher than ever: the remaining question is, why? The present surge appears to derive from several major changes in the economy and in society. First, as noted earlier, there has been an unprecedented increase in the level of activity in areas such as new business incorporation. The number of success stories has grown by leaps and bounds: examples include Steven Jobs of Apple, Bill McGowan of MCI Communications, Mitchell Kapor of Lotus Development, Bob Swanson of Genentech, Jim Treybig of Tadem, and Mrs Field of Mrs Field's Cookies.

Second, only recently have the data that testify to the economic importance of entrepreneurship become widely disseminated. Before these data were made available and analysed, the perception in the USA was that big business was the dominant economic force in the country. However, in recent years, those sectors of the economy dominated by large firms have fallen on hard times. This dramatic decline in the fortunes of the Fortune 500 has caused everyone to reassess the situation and has lent credibility to studies showing the importance of the entrepreneurial sector.

As this has occurred, additional attention has been given to the

Table 5.1 Venture capital industry funds ($000)

Year	Net new private capital committed to venture capital firms ($)	size of total pool ($)	Estimated disbursements to portfolio companies
1984	4 200	16 300	3 000
1983	4 500	12 100	2 800
1982	1 800	7 600	1 800
1981	1 300	5 800	1 400
1980	700	4 500	1 100
1979	300	3 800	1 000
1978	600	3 500	550
1977	39	2 500–3 000	400
1976	50	2 500–3 000	300
1975	10	2 500–3 000	250
1974	57	2 500–3 000	350
1973	56	2 500–3 000	450
1972	62	2 500–3 000	425
1971	95	2 500–3 000	410
1970	97	2 500–3 000	350
1969	171	2 500–3 000	450

Notes: Net new private capital = total new private capital less withdrawals. All numbers measured at cost.
Source: Venture Economics, Inc., Wellesley, Massachusetts.

ideologic foundations of the entrepreneurial economy and entrepreneurship has come to be seen as a dominant factor in determining success in the international competitive battle.

Finally, there is the overwhelming evidence that for groups comparable in background and education, those who are self-employed entrepreneurs find more satisfaction in their jobs. A major sociological change has occurred in the USA that has given individuals the desire and opportunity to take control of their destinies.

Economic importance of entrepreneurship

In the 1960s, the word entrepreneur was often used to describe individuals who had profited from a situation at the expense of others and little substantive distinction was drawn between a promoter and an entrepreneur.

The stunning increase in the incidence of new business formation that began in the mid-1970s resulted in a gradual but perceptible change in the use of word entrepreneur and the degree to which such activities were viewed positively. Because of the extraordinary successes and contributions of individuals such as Steve Jobs and Steve Wozniak at Apple Computer, both the media and the public began to take notice.

The mid-1970s were characterised by major changes in technology and also by major changes in other areas; for example, in government regulation. Out of such changes were born some tremendous success stories. In the area of deregulation, for example, Don Burr was able to found a new airline, People Express, and guide that company to a position of prominence in the industry. The fact that Burr has failed subsequently to ensure the success of People Express can in no way detract from the company's accomplishments of the early 1980s and the attendant change it forced on the entire airline industry. Entrepreneurs like Don Burr have been responsible for changes in the US economy that have affected millions of consumers.

In part because of the increase in positive publicity attributed to successful entrepreneurial ventures, a number of economists began to study the effect of such activities on the economy. David Birch, at the time an economist at MIT, first revealed that small companies were disproportionately responsible for job creation in the USA and subsequent work has supported Birch's conclusions.[1] For example, in 1986 the US government's report, *The State of Small Business*, showed that 'small business-dominated industries added jobs at a rate almost twice that of industries dominated by larger firms: 11.4% compared to 5.3% from November 1982 through October 1984'. That same report emphasised that '67% of all new jobs in this country are created by small business and that small firms account for 38% of the Gross National Product'.

The message from the government study and from David Birch's original work, as well as that of others, is that the engines of change are small and select, and we must gain a better understanding of those small but effective economic units. This conclusion has been replicated in many other countries. The economists have learned that the predictions of J. K. Galbraith in *The New Industrial State* regarding the demise of the entrepreneur were indeed premature.

Thus, there seems to be very strong evidence that small firms play a major positive role in the creation of new jobs in the economy. A related issue that has received a great deal of attention has been the degree to which small firms are responsible for innovation. The same US government study cited earlier stated that, for various periods between 1972 and 1982, 'small business responded more quickly to market opportunities and created more than their proportionate share of new jobs as part of that response'.

The National Science Foundation found that small companies produce four times more innovation per research dollar than do bigger companies. Others examining the same study quote a figure of twenty-four times the number of innovations per dollar of research. Still others find that smaller firms are 2.5 times more innovative per employee than larger firms.

It is also instructive to look at data on value creation as a measure of the productivity of small firms. To illustrate, there is a great deal of evidence on returns to investors in venture capital situations. Over the period between 1965 and 1982, the median return on funds invested by professional venture capitalists was in excess of 25 per cent per annum. Equally importantly, no professionally managed firm reported a loss over the life of the relevant partnership. These data suggest that those companies funded by venture capital, although admittedly few in number, have been enormously successful in creating value, far more so than the large company sector.

Such findings have given rise to concern that many of the largest firms are not innovative, and are not generating efficient and effective new technology: they are not even generating competitive products on a world scale. The biggest companies in steel, automobile, non-ferrous metals, farm equipment and consumer electronics have lost one competitive battle after another and major sectors of many economies are suffering.

No matter what set of statistics is chosen, there is clear agreement among scholars and practitioners alike that smaller firms follow the economic logic of Schumpeter: 'You do not ask the owner of the stage line to build a railroad'. The smaller firms do not face the constraints imposed by large investment in existing technology: thus, they are both free and compelled to innovate.

This is not to say that large firms are not critical to development, to cost-based efficiency and to dealing with truly world-scale production and marketing processes. Nevertheless, it is clear that smaller firms developed many important inventions, including zerography, air conditioning, the Polaroid process, cellophane, insulin, penicillin, helicopters and ballpoint pens.

Smaller firms have the necessity and the capability to innovate. Although many opportunities are eventually successfully pursued by the larger firms, it appears to be smaller firms that, more often than not, attempt and succeed in leapfrogging existing technology.

Psychological and personal rewards of entrepreneurship

When attempting to understand the increase in the level of interest in, and the incidence of, entrepreneurial activities, it is important to study the psychological and social aspects of the phenomenon. There are basically two ways to attack this aspect of the subject: in the first, an attempt is made to understand the factors that drive individuals to pursue entrepreneurial activities (the 'push' side); in the second, the factors that induce entrepreneurial behaviour are identified (the 'pull' side). The data presented below in Tables 5.2, 5.3, 5.4 shed light on both aspects of the issue.

Paula Duffy and Howard Stevenson recently studied over 6000 graduates of Harvard University's Graduate School of Business Administration. Among the questions addressed was the degree to which their job satisfied their personal values, the nature of those values, and the degree to which they had achieved financial success. In each of these measures, the entrepreneurially self-employed stood out as being significantly more rewarded by their career than their classmates who had pursued administrative careers working for others.

The degree to which the self-employed found greater satisfaction in their jobs was striking. Table 5.2 shows this comparison.

Table 5.2   Job satisfying personal values

	Self-employed (%)	Work for others (%)
To a great extent	53.6	34.6
To a significant extent	33.3	42.2
To some extent	9.4	15.4
Not significantly	3.6	7.8

Table 5.3 provides evidence on the underlying value priorities of the sample group.

Table 5.3   *The four most important job values*

	Self-employed (%)	Not self-employed (%)
Economic	39.2	31.6
Other job features	29.9	40.2
External rewards	10.8	11.6
Life-style values	19.9	16.5

Perhaps one of the greatest distinctions was the degree to which those who were self-employed had achieved financial success. The distinction between the two groups with similar training and background was remarkable (see Table 5.4).

Table 5.4   *Financial net worth fifteen or more years following graduation*
(percentages)

	<$50 000	$ 50 000–249 000	$250 000–499 999	$500 000–999 999	$1 000 000–2 499 999	$2 599 000
SE	11	11.2	17.7	14.6	29.2	24.8
Non SE	1.9	20.1	24.3	22.8	19.1	11.8

(SE = Self-employed; Non SE = Non self-employed)

One can certainly not assert the generality of the findings taken from such a unique sample base although the evidence from the *Forbes 400* survey (Vol. 140) would indicate that the road to wealth in the USA is either inheritance or self-employment.

These data have not gone unnoticed outside the ranks of Harvard Business School graduates: the number of self-employed in the USA has grown by over 20 per cent between 1970 and 1980 according to official census data. An additional 1.5 million individuals became self-employed during that decade.

Thus, the entrepreneurial revolution that has been observed the last decade has resulted in a very large number of individuals who are simultaneously wealthier and more satisfied with their jobs. To some degree, they were 'pulled' in to entrepreneurial behaviour by this attractive reward structure – or perhaps they were 'pushed' out of their previous career in large companies because they were dissatisfied. Whatever the explanation, it is difficult to refute the evidence that a major trend is under way.

3. Defining entrepreneurship

To summarise, there has been a striking increase in the level of attention paid to the subject of entrepreneurship. This increase in interest seems to have stemmed from some major economic and social changes in the American economy as analysts have discovered that small firms contribute mightily to economic growth and vitality. Moreover, many have chosen entrepreneurial careers because doing so offers greater economic and psychological rewards than does the large company route. However, yet to be resolved is determining what the nature of the underlying beast – entrepreneurship – is. How is it defined? We have been purposely vague up to this point, at times using implicit definitions such as 'small business' or 'founder-led' or 'innovative', but our objective in this section is to explore the definition issue in greater depth.

Entrepreneurship was once compared by Peter Kilby to the Heffalump:

> It is a large and important animal which has been hunted by many individuals using various ingenious trapping devices . . . All who claim to have caught sight of him report that he is enormous, but they disagree on his particularities. Not having explored his current habitat with sufficient care, some hunters have used as bait their own favorite dishes and have then tried to persuade people that what they caught was a Heffalump. However, very few are convinced, and the search goes on (Kilby, *Hunting the Heffalump: Entrepreneurship and Economic Development*, 1971).

At the risk of adding to the confusion, it may be helpful to review the historic definitions applied to the subject. There are several schools of thought regarding entrepreneurship and these may be divided roughly into those that identify the word with an economic function: those that identify it with an individual; and those that view entrepreneurship in behavioural terms.

The economic functional analysis of entrepreneurship focuses upon the economic role rather than the individual who performs such a role. The emphasis upon economic role was the historical wellspring of interest. Richard Cantillon said that entrepreneurship entails bearing the risk of buying at certain prices and selling at uncertain prices. This risk-bearing function was the definition used by Cantillon when he first coined the word 'entrepreneurship' in the early eighteenth century.

Jean-Baptiste Say broadened the definition to include the concept of bringing together the factors of production. This definition led others to question whether there was any unique entrepreneurial function or whether it was simply a form of management. Schumpeter's work in 1911 added the concept of innovation to the definition of entrepreneurship: he allowed for many kinds of innovation including process innovation, market innovation, product innovation, factor innovation, and even organisational innovation. His seminal work emphasised the role of the entrepreneur in creating and responding to economic discontinuities. Although his work on business cycles assumed equilibrium as the normal state, he recognised that the fundamental source of disequilibrium was the entrepreneur. More recently, observers of the phenomenon of entrepreneurship have suggested that entrepreneurship involves creation of new enterprises and that the entrepreneur is the founder.

While many analysts have focused on the economic function of entrepreneurship, still others have turned their attention to research on the personal characteristics of entrepreneurs. Considerable effort has gone into understanding the psychological and sociological wellsprings of entrepreneurship – as Kent refers to it, 'supply-side entrepreneurship'. These studies have noted some common characteristics among entrepreneurs with respect to need for achievement, perceived locus of control, orientation toward intuitive rather than sensate thinking, and risk-taking propensity. In addition, many have commented upon the common, but not universal, thread of childhood deprivation, minority group membership and early adolescent economic experiences as typifying the entrepreneur.

What are we to make of the attempts to identify entrepreneurship by economic function or by personal characteristics? Does either approach shed light on a subject of obvious interest?

Consider, for example, the degree to which entrepreneurship is synonymous with 'bearing risk', 'innovation', or even founding a company. We believe attempts to pigeon-hole entrepreneurship do not contribute very much to our understanding. Each of the terms described above focuses upon some aspect of some entrepreneurs, but if one has to be the founder to be an entrepreneur, then neither Thomas Watson of IBM nor Rey Kroc of McDonald's will qualify; yet few would seriously argue that these individuals were not entrepreneurs.

Although risk-bearing is an important element of entrepreneurial behaviour, it is clear that many entrepreneurs bear risk grudgingly and only after they have made valiant attempts to get the capital sources and resource providers to bear the risk. As one extremely successful entrepreneur said; 'My idea of risk and reward is for me to get the reward and others to take the risks'.

Creativity is clearly not a prerequisite for entrepreneurship. Many successful entrepreneurs have been good at copying others and they qualify as innovators and creators only by stretching the definition beyond elastic limits.

With respect to the 'supply side' school of entrepreneurship, many questions can be raised. At the heart of the matter is whether the psychological and social traits are either necessary or sufficient for the development of entrepreneurship. Character traits are at best modalities and not universalities, since many successful and unsuccessful entrepreneurs do not share the characteristics identified. Further, historical studies do not show the same character traits in earlier entrepreneurs. Also, the studies of the life paths of entrepreneurs often show decreasing 'entrepreneurship' following success. Such evidence at least raises a question whether the nature of entrepreneurship is immutably imbedded in the personality from early stages of childhood development. Finally, while many authors have purported to find statistically significant common characteristics of entrepreneurs, the ability to attribute causality to these factors is seriously in doubt.

4. Entrepreneurship as a behavioural phenomenon

In managerial terms, it does not appear useful to delimit the entrepreneur by defining those economic functions that are 'entrepreneurial' and those that are not, nor does it appear particularly helpful to decide which individuals are entrepreneurs and which are not. The first exercise appears to be rather more semantic than practical. The second appears to be fruitless in that individuals in our society may attempt entrepreneurship and often succeed even if they do not fit the standards of academic judges as to their entrepreneurial personality or sociological background.

We believe that entrepreneurship is most fruitfully defined as the relentless pursuit of opportunity without regard to resources currently controlled. Moreover, we believe there is an underlying process in entrepreneurship that starts with the identification of opportunity and ends with harvesting the fruits of one's labours. We argue that certain outcomes are desirable for individuals, for organisations and for society and defining entrepreneurship in terms of these outcomes can help to provide mechanisms for inducing the desired behavior. Experience shows that entrepreneurship as an economic function is not a single point but rather a range of behaviour. We have identified six critical dimensions that distinguish entrepreneurial behaviour from more administratively orientated behaviour. These six dimensions are the following: strategic orientation, the commitment to opportunity, the resource commitment process, the concept of control over resources, the concept of management, and compensation policy.

We are discarding the notion that entrepreneurship is an all-or-nothing trait and we shall examine the behavioural dimensions in terms of a range of behaviour between extremes. At one extreme is the *promoter* type of manager who feels confident of his or her ability to seize opportunity regardless of the resources under current control. At the opposite extreme is the *trustee* type of manager who fosters efficient management by emphasising the effective utilisation of existing resources. There is an important role for both in our economy, and the discussion that follows is not meant to be judgmental.

Before elaborating on the differences between entrepreneurial and administrative behaviour, a digression on what we mean by 'opportunity' is in order.

The nature of opportunity

Opportunity is the key element of entrepreneurship and has several important elements: first, it is a relativistic concept, that is, opportunities for individuals vary depending on age, previous accomplishments and financial resources and even the social milieu in which the individual is functioning. Perhaps the reason that many studies have found entrepreneurship to arise frequently among the disadvantaged or among certain minorities has been that they have been systematically excluded from the personal opportunities that lay in traditional hierarchies, through either a lack of 'the proper background' or from outright prejudice. The reason for some individuals becoming 'entrepreneurial' after adversity is that their previous stream of opportunities has played out or become blocked. The reason that individuals become 'less entrepreneurial' following success simply may well be that they have defined their personal opportunities along non-business dimensions of power, prestige or leisure, or they simply begin to focus on preservation of their existing resource base.

The implications of this concept of opportunity are clear. A possible situation becomes an opportunity when the results of the action are deemed to be desirable and feasible. It is also clear that particular skills, talents and attitudes toward risk influence the perception as to whether an outcome is feasible. Training, knowledge and self-confidence contribute to such perceptions.

Strategic orientation

The entrepreneur–promoter is orientated towards the pursuit of opportunity, whereas the administrator–trustee is preoccupied with the resources currently controlled. Table 5.5 shows this orientation and the pressures that drive managers towards a particular orientation. As can be seen, much of the force to the trusteeship orientation arises out of organisation demands. The opportunity focus is a function of the changing environment.

Commitment to opportunity

Where the promoter is committed to action, doubt remains about the durability of the commitment. The trustee is slow to act, but the commitment is durable. There are obvious advantages in coping with a rapidly changing environment when the commitment can be made quickly and dropped just as quickly. See Table 5.5.

Commitment of resources

The entrepreneur is known for doing more with less. Many entrepreneurs start the pursuit of an opportunity with no resources other than the confidence that they have identified a 'real opportunity'. The administrator–trustees have as their major preoccupation and as the source of their personal rewards the effective administration of the resources that they currently control. The result is a very different process by which resources get committed to the pursuit of an identified opportunity. For the entrepreneur, it, perforce, is multi-staged as necessary resources are acquired from others. The entrepreneur–promoter is thus perceived as a gambler and tentative. The trustee is often simply responding to the source of the rewards offered. Table 5.5 shows this dimension.

Control of resources

The entrepreneur–promoter is often horrified at 'overheads' and the encumbrances that resources used in the business imply. The trustee–administrator is often compensated on the basis of the amount of assets under his or her management and the number of people employed. These are totally different attitudes and responsive to very differing measurement schemes. See Table 5.5.

Concept of management structure

The orientation towards opportunity often brings with it the desire of the entrepreneur–promoter to keep in touch with all the key players and to be able personally to sell the concepts and involvement, and to provide personal payoffs. The trustee–administrator often views organisations more formally, where responsibilities and authority should be well defined. The decision to use and to rent resources implies the necessity to manage in a different way. See Table 5.5.

Compensation reward systems

Entrepreneurial organisations base compensation on value creation and on team performance, while administrative organisations base compensation on individual responsibility levels (for example, assets or resources under control) and on performance relative to short-term accounting targets (for example, profits or return on assets) and rely heavily on promotion as a means of reward. Table 5.5 shows these differences and lists some of the factors underlying each solution to the issue of how to measure and reward employees.

All these characteristics have been gathered on to one chart, Table 5.5. When examining this chart it should be kept in mind that the authors do not intend to be judgmental in differentiating between entrepreneurial and administrative behaviours. Each behaviour mode has its place, and the degree to which a particular management style or process is appropriate will depend heavily on the company, the people who work there, and the demands of the external environment. There are often equally strong reasons to be on the entrepreneurial side as on the administrative side. What is necessary is for management to know that there are choices and to act intelligently in making those choices.

Nor should the reader infer that entrepreneurship is important and trusteeship is not. In fact, the goal of entrepreneurship is often the creation of value and wealth, and success in the pursuit of the entrepreneurial goal thus leads to the need for effective trusteeship.

In developing a behavioural theory of entrepreneurship, it becomes clear that entrepreneurship is more than an individual and different from a well-defined economic function or set of functions: it is a cohesive pattern of behaviour. The reason why the authors believe that entrepreneurial behaviour is critical now, particularly in larger companies, is simply that the world has changed and the nature of the change suggests that managers must generally gravitate to the left of the scale introduced earlier.

Having stated that the new competitive world demands more entrepreneurial behaviour on the part of managers, there are major hurdles. We will discuss some of these hurdles in the next section, and then offer suggestions for preserving entrepreneurial behaviour in the larger company.

5. The transition from entrepreneurial to trustee/administrative management

The transition from the start-up phase to a more mature phase is often accompanied by a decreasing ability and willingness to identify and

Table 5.5 Key business dimensions

Pressures toward this side	Promoter	Key business dimension	Trustee	Pressures toward this side
Diminishing opportunity streams Rapidly changing: Technology Consumer economics Social values	Driven by perception of opportunity	Entrepreneurial domain ⟷ Administrative domain STRATEGIC ORIENTATION	Driven by resources currently controlled	Social contracts Performance measurement criteria Planning systems and cycle
Action orientation Short decision windows Risk management Limited decision constituencies	Revolutionary with short duration	Entrepreneurial domain ⟷ Administrative domain COMMITMENT TO OPPORTUNITY	Evolutionary of long duration	Acknowledgement of multiple constituencies Negotiation of strategy Risk reduction Management of fit
Lack of predictable resource needs Lack of long-term control Social need for more opportunity per resource unit International pressure for more efficient resource use	Multi-staged with minimal exposure at each stage	Entrepreneurial domain ⟷ Administrative domain COMMITMENT OF RESOURCES	Single-staged with complete commitment upon decision	Personal risk reduction Incentive compensation Managerial turnover Capital allocation systems Formal planning systems

Pressures toward this side	Entrepreneurial domain	← Dimension →	Administrative domain	Pressures toward this side
Increased resource specialization; Long resource life compared to need; Risk of obsolence; Risk inherent in any new venture; Inflexibility of permanent commitment to resources	Episodic use or rent of required resources	CONTROL OF RESOURCES	Ownership or employment of required resources	Power, status and financial rewards; Co-ordination; Efficiency measures; Inertia and cost of change; Industry structures
Co-ordination of key non-controlled resources; Challenge to legitimacy of owner's control; Employee's desire for independence	Flat with multiple informal networks	MANAGEMENT STRUCTURE	Formalised hierarchy	Need for clearly defined authority and responsibility; Organisational culture; Reward systems; Management theory
Individual expectations; Competition; Increased perception of personal wealth creation possibilities	Value-based; Team-based; Unlimited	COMPENSATION/REWARD POLICY	Resource-based; Driven by short-term data; Promotion; Limited amount	Societal norms; IRS regulations; Impacted information; Search for simple solutions for complex problems; Demands of public shareholders

pursue opportunities. In large measure, this change is the direct result of the success experienced in the past. Managers want to protect what they have created, and the desire to protect is what precludes pursuit of new opportunity.

By contrast, firms which have remained entrepreneurial even after they have achieved success seem to have three characteristics: opportunities are broadly perceived; individuals within the organisation desire to pursue them; and the individuals believe that it is possible to succeed in the pursuit of opportunity. Thus, opportunity in such firms is seen as visible, desirable and feasible.

It is a basic belief of the authors that normal individuals pursue personal opportunity. The definition of opportunity is a function of their own upbringing, their perception of possibilities available within their societal surroundings and their own sense of 'right', 'justice' and 'need fulfilment'.

The perception of opportunity is thus highly relative. What is a desired future state depends largely on current circumstances and the forecast of likely future circumstances if nothing were to be changed. Those for whom the current state is ideal, or nearly so, will not be seeking change as much as those for whom the current state is totally unsatisfactory. Those for whom the society or organisation throws up 'impossible' barriers will not seek opportunity either. The 'impossible barriers' can be of two kinds: prescriptive barriers that prevent action, or consequential barriers created by endowing failure with such consequences that rational human beings will not make the attempt. Table 5.6 illustrates the situation.

If the goal in a company is to maintain entrepreneurship, there are many elements of success that act to prevent achievement of that goal. We must understand each of the forces and then attempt to examine the mechanisms by which organisations have successfully resisted those forces.

6.   From entrepreneur to satisfied manager

Success most directly affects top management's desire to precipitate change, especially as it might affect them personally. Many of the classical studies of entrepreneurs and the 'entrepreneurial personality' have shown that entrepreneurs are highly likely to have come from excluded or disadvantaged groups. Almost by definition, as success is achieved, the entrepreneur prefers the present state to the one that he or she experienced in the past. The status quo – in terms of power, status and financial rewards – is good; and often, the prospect of 'normal growth' is sufficient to provide all desired rewards.

Table 5.6 Managers' opportunities

| | Future goals | |
	Change	Status Quo
Possible	Entrepreneur	Satisfied manager
Perceived capability		
Blocked	Frustrated manager	Classic bureaucrat

In fact, for many, the prospect of growth, change and additional financial success have almost frightening consequences: growth and change often imply commitment and involvement and this commitment and involvement might be required at precisely the time when life-style considerations might have the individual define as his or her opportunity for additional leisure, involvements in politics or charitable activities, or simply managing the resources that have already been accumulated.

Growth and change often also imply risk. The risk can either be financial or simply ego-based. The financial risk is obvious, but for many successful entrepreneurs, their self-image is one of 'infallibility'. New actions or activities put that self-image at risk at what is often a psychologically vulnerable point in their lives. As physical health and vigour decline, even marginally, and as challenges to authority rise, the self-image can best be sustained by sticking to an area where personal confidence is highest and where 'nothing more needs to be proved'.

The consequence is that movement from entrepreneurship to trustee-ship can be both natural and rational. The very success that was the basis of entrepreneurship has sown the seeds for a harvest of satisfaction. In a sense, the goal was achieved. The organisational implications are obvious: the leader desires the status quo, and the system, structure and culture will be developed to achieve that goal.

7. Entrepreneurship and the bureaucrat

It is often thought that the entrepreneur and the classic bureaucrat are poles apart, and in the sense the authors intend, it is true. Whereas the entrepreneur desires change and sees the change as possible, the classic bureaucrat neither desires change nor sees the possibility of change. In many cases, however, the authors would argue that the bureaucrat is the creation of the successful entrepreneur.

Often, the successful entrepreneur views others within his or her organisation as simple extensions of self, both out of a need for control and as a consequence of narcissism. The function of others in the company is to carry out orders, and information and control systems are designed to provide command and control feedback. The individual within the organisation does not believe that initiative is valued or desired. The clear message is that orders are issued from the top. The organisation may be in the midst of rapid and far-reaching change, but the change will *not* be a result of the initiative from below. Thus, there is no need for the individual below to seek means of improving the operation because it will be wasted effort.

The result is further reinforced by the perception of who will bear the cost of change. Management's view of the human factor as 'a specialised tool' has caused individuals to be replaced rather than retained as strategies changed. Even as 'progress' arrives in the form of automation and improved methods, the perception is that 'more is expected for the same reward' or that 'more productivity means fewer people'. It should be no surprise that such changes are resisted.

Often, management has ignored the fact that individuals are extremely perceptive regarding their own self-interest: the collective memory of organisations is long and detailed and actions taken in the past that have negatively affected lower-level employees are long remembered. The perception is that most positive rewards can easily be removed when the need is felt, and that which is in hand is the only certainty.

The ego and the drive to succeed and to surmount difficulties that is inherent in the entrepreneur is thus the catalyst that creates the classic bureaucrat within his or her organisation.

8.   The entrepreneur and the frustrated manager

Unfortunately, the entrepreneur often creates not only the bureaucrat but also the frustrated manager. In the organisations run by successful entrepreneurs, the same command and control mentality that stymies the lower-level bureaucrat often faces the manager in the middle also, but the response may be slightly different. The manager who sees the need for change and desires it can be blocked and, upon sensing the blockage, he or she can respond by seeing personal opportunity in serving the status quo as the goal. Then, personal power status and financial reward can be achieved even at the expense of serving only the short-term and the obvious. It is perhaps this fact that has led to so much criticism of current management practice. The individual manager may well recognise the need and desirability for the organisation to change, but the organisational 'fact of life' is that, in the words of Sam Rayburn, a famous US politician, 'to get along, you go along'.

The same frustration is often relieved in a form that is positive for society, but damaging to the existing firm: the manager leaves, and the investment in training, experience and judgement is lost. The most important loss, however, is the future source of ideas, impetus for change and creative dissatisfaction that the frustrated manager brings to the organisation.

It is unfortunate that the success of the entrepreneur and the methods by which that success is often achieved are the source of the responses in organisations that lead to bureaucracy and stagnation. The rest of this chapter will discuss what companies have done and can do to maintain the spirit of entrepreneurship throughout the organisation and not just at the chief executive level.

9. The requirements for an entrepreneurial organisation

The individual entrepreneur is a person who perceives opportunity, finds the pursuit of opportunity desirable in the context of his or her life situation, and believes that success is possible, and these three elements are those that distinguish the individual entrepreneur from the vast majority of the populace. In the individual, these three aspects have certain manifestations.

The ability to perceive opportunity is often founded upon deep personal knowledge and experience in products and markets. The entrepreneur not only has to have a better idea, but he or she must recognise that it is better in some way that can deliver value to the ultimate customer. Success comes from perceiving the reality accurately, including not only the product, but also the manufacturing and delivery systems and the resulting economics.

The desire to pursue opportunity on the part of an individual is often the result of a complex balancing of risk and reward. We would submit that the reason that so many disadvantaged and 'marginal' individuals have had entrepreneurial instincts has been that *any* success was a reward compared to the initial starting position. Conversely, the risk could not be high since there was little money or social status at stake. What was at stake for the individuals at the margin often was reputation and credibility within the local community that provided whatever support and finances that were available. The reward inherent in individual entrepreneurship is only one part of the motivation package; the lack of permanently damaging risk is equally, if not more, important.

The USA has been fortunate that even for the individuals who have 'succeeded', individual entrepreneurship has not been foreclosed by a perception that failure meant total risk of social position and denied the possibility of rejoining institutional organisations or even starting over as an individual entrepreneur. This has been very different from the perception observed by the authors in many European countries, where one failure tends to impose permanent social and business ostracism.

The well-trained professional in the USA has been an amazing source of independent entrepreneurial energy compared to the importance of this resource in other countries. We must ask why the 30 per cent of the graduates of Harvard Business School who have become successfully self-employed have not continued to make their contributions through the organisational frameworks to which their training originally took them.

The individual entrepreneur has to have the perception that success is possible. No sane individual starts out on an economic mission where failure is perceived to be the most probable outcome. We can all argue with the accuracy of the entrepreneurial perception. In general, however, the individual entrepreneur believes that success is possible because of the uniqueness of the idea, the strength of the product, self-perception of quickness and hard work, or some other fact known mainly to the entrepreneur which will guarantee success. It is this belief that success is possible and, in fact, owed, that often keeps the entrepreneur going when others are critical and rejecting of his or her proposals.

These same three factors must be built into the organisational life if the entrepreneurial success of the founding individual is to be perpetuated. The facts are, however, that these factors cannot be perpetuated by cloning the founder or by developing a mechanistic set of rules that ensure extensions of the brilliant thoughts of the leader. They require the building of an adaptive organisation.

10. Increasing the perception of opportunity

In order to make certain that the organisation perceives opportunity, certain requirements must be met in structuring the jobs of individuals. The four most important ones are: creating jobs with real time market input; making individuals responsible for broadly-defined objectives; recognising success will come only through balancing functional needs; and institutionalising change as an organisational goal. In one form or another, these characteristics underlie the success strategies of osganisations that have maintained their entrepreneurial flavour.

Creating jobs with real time market input

This may simply be a restatement of the admonition in T. Peters and R. Waterman, *In Search of Excellence Lessons from America's Best Run Companies*, to be close to the customer. Companies that are great seem to structure themselves so that each function and each level knows what the market is demanding and uses those market demands to structure their own sets of goals and objectives. The high tech firms that survive have to do this, but more importantly, the low tech firms (automobiles, steel, and so on) often do not. Management could labour under the illusion supported by carefully drafted reports that the customer was placing unrealistic demands on the company. The great companies never let the top management, the middle management or the lowest level employee forget that the customer pays the bill.

Create responsibility for broadly defined objectives

When organisations start, the entrepreneur is responsible for everything. Complex trade-offs are necessary between service, cost, profit, specialisation and breadth, and somehow these trade-offs, even if unarticulated, are made and the decisions are implemented. Decisions, once taken, are reviewed frequently in the light of the feedback from the market outlined above. As companies grow, the conventional wisdom is to specialise, to delegate and to differentiate. Often, as the goals of the subunits become more measurable, the opportunities are lost in the organisational interstices. Time trade-offs are made inappropriately, with the long-term being sacrificed to the short-term. Return on assets dominates future growth options, and the quality/service goal is subordinated to other more concrete and measurable goals. Any sense of ownership or authorship is lost.

Balancing functional needs

At the early stages of an entrepreneurial company, the unity of command of the entrepreneur allows a dynamic equilibrium among competing functional claims. Integration is inherent. In the early stage, R&D is king. Later, marketing consumes the bulk of the human and financial resources, or manufacturing assumes dominance and the needs of each function can be sacrificed to the benefit of the whole organisation. Later, as the functional units become separated, each has both an individual legitimate claim and an agenda for its own future. More critically, these agendas are often in conflict: maximisation along the

manufacturing dimension requires reduction in model features and stabilisation of production runs; maximisation of sales requires almost the
opposite. One or the other function assumes dominance so that the
subunit goals are achieved while the organisation's opportunity overall
is lost. Successful firms have maintained an ability to co-ordinate activities among the functions, to prevent the dominance of any individual
function and to assure that each will have strong continuing advocacy in
order to assure the long-run capacity of the organisation to meet all
needs.

Change must be recognised as desirable

This becomes tautological. If an opportunity is defined as including a
change, then only those organisations that desire change will recognise
opportunity. Where satisfaction and preservation of the status quo have
become the norm, then it is highly unlikely that opportunity will be
perceived, much less acted upon. Excellence must mean a restless
dissatisfaction with the current state and success often breeds compla-
cency. As discussed earlier success often turns an individual's thoughts
to other areas of endeavour. For the company wishing to continue to be
entrepreneurial, it must convince everyone that change is the company's
overriding goal.

11. Building the desire to pursue opportunity

One of the most remarkable discoveries made by successful managers is
that the people who work for them understand themselves and also the
systems that the company has put in place. We have all experienced the
ability of the worker on the factory floor or the salesperson to identify
that behaviour which will yield the greatest personal return for effort
expended. We have also seen how the better players in the organisational game are where the positive action is and far away from the
scenes of disaster when they strike. If individuals understand their
self-interest, then a critical task for management wishing to perpetuate
entrepreneurship within an organisation is to continue to make the
pursuit of opportunity consistent with the self-interest of the individual.

Some organisations, like Memorex for example, have attempted to
create highly leveraged rewards for certain individuals within their
organisation, but these plans have often failed because ultimately the
vertical and horizontal inequities that result are unexplainable and
unsustainable. The managers who seem to be able to continue to build
an entrepreneurial organisation have focused on three elements in

building their culture: pursuit of opportunity is rewarded, the risk of failure for the individual is reduced and flexibility in execution is accepted.

Pursuit of opportunity must be rewarded

The cult of the bottom line has taken hold of American management: success can be judged only after the fact. The search for objectivity demands that 'bottom line results' be the measure of success. Management that desires new projects to be supported have to recognise that the very act of initiation requires investment, commitment and, in too many companies, courage. Companies such as 3M and IBM, as well as many lesser-known companies, recognise that they have to have a high number of start-ups in order to get the requisite number of successes. Venture capitalists recognise that they will lose money on almost 50 per cent of the companies they back and good capital budgeting systems allow many more starts than can or should be fully funded. The tentative initiative is encouraged and rewarded with the full expectation that only a few will meet the test of the final 'bottom line'.

The consequence is that people are given a sense of satisfaction for merely having tried: there is explicit recognition of the fact that many, if not most, major successes arise from unconventional sources and the ultimate fate of the company may ride with someone whose ideas require patience, protection and a little faith. It would be hard to imagine a request for funding to develop a pad of papers that don't stick well to anything and that will sell at six times the equivalent cost of other competing pads. Yet, it is precisely such a product – 'Post-its', that have brought a highly profitable $250 million in sales to 3M. Many other equally bizarre ideas have ended in the dustbin at that company, yet the fact that everyone is encouraged to try means that some will succeed.

Risk of failure must be reduced for the individual

The entrepreneur often has a clear personal focus on the availability of extraordinary reward, but as companies grow in complexity, the possibility of a huge reward for everyone often fades.

If the rewards become highly differentiated, then management is in a dilemma. The same factors that increase the rewards for one individual may well provoke sensations of injustice among others. The pattern of observed behaviour is that justice predominates. The rewards within most hierarchical organisations are largely based upon position and seniority, with only modest differentiation by performance. It is a curious anomaly that short-term rewards are most highly leveraged for those individuals whose performance has little direct effect on short-term results: namely, top management.

Many successful companies have engaged the reward/risk dilemma by reducing the consequences for failure to the individual. We see this in many of the successful high tech firms. In J.T. Kidder's *The Soul of a New Machine*, the 'losing' team is not lost to the company; their attempt is recognised and rewarded. The Japanese system also recognises the team aspect of success and failure and does not focus either major reward or retribution on the team captain.

This is appropriate since the company is seeking to have many initiatives, but the individual deals with only one at a time. Thus, the company can afford a certain number of failures. If a system is set up so that the individual cannot afford any, then it is highly unlikely that any initiatives will be tried that are of the kind that can have significant potential. If, in fact, the risk to the individual is his or her career and the risk to the company is minimal, there is a clear irrationality in the risk distribution system. Unfortunately for many companies, the statement is often heard that, 'Any failure will finish you here. Promotions go to the people with the totally unblemished records.'

Change cannot be tantamount to failure

In addition to the tyranny of the 'bottom line', another managerial myth has taken firm root: that myth is that 'good plans do not need changes'. Many companies expend tremendous effort in developing three- and five-year plans for capital, personnel, market share and expenses. The feeling, right or wrong, among management is that 'deviation from these plans reflects badly on our managerial skills'. In times of stable growth, that response is reasonable, even if it is not productive, but in times such as we are currently experiencing, it can be disastrous. Economic, technological, political and social changes require responsive or pro-active behaviour. It is hard to imagine plans in any industry that could have endured and led to prosperity in the period 1980–85. Those companies that adapted quickly to changed circumstances, that adopted appropriate new technologies, that recognised customer changes, and that forsook their corporate egos, did best. Changing times often convert strengths to weaknesses, and the wholehearted commitment to an unswerving path is often foolish in the face of the rapid oscillations that are currently being experienced.

12.   Making people believe that they can succeed

Opportunity for the company will not be pursued entrepreneurially unless the individuals within the organisation believe that it is personal opportunity for themselves. It is clear that in the small entrepreneurial organisation there is an identity of interest between the individual entrepreneur and the corporate form in which the opportunity is pursued. As companies grow, two critical events occur: there is a separation of the reward structure: and there is a developing feeling of 'can't do!' Often, the very persistence and control that made the individual entrepreneur successful is the force that destroys entrepreneurship as the company grows. Many studies have referred to the problem as a lack of delegation of authority from the top manager, but the problems are often more complicated than that: there are often impediments built into the organisation just through the process of professionalisation and these make individuals believe, often correctly, that initiative cannot gain support. There are four common features in organisations that often make people believe that they *can* succeed: there is short-term slack in the resource allocation system; the resources allocation system is multi-staged; sharing of resources is the norm within the organisation; and one negative opinion does not kill an idea.

Short-term slack makes resources available for new initiatives

Studies by P.R. Lawrence and D. Dyer, published in *Renewing American Industry*, and numerous case examples, as well as our own practical experience, suggest that one of the most important ways to encourage initiative is to allow people to experiment and to try initiatives without insisting on premature public exposure of the attempt and by allowing 'bootlegging'. The individual often has good but unprovable ideas and the opportunity to explore those ideas without personal ego and reputational risk is critical. Small amounts of slack allow the engineering feasibility, the market concepts and even the production processes to be tested without the full organisational glare.

Multi-staged resource allocation required

The controller often reacts immediately to the proposal just enunciated: the 'purpose of the control system is to see that resources are not wasted', and the issue then becomes whether failed experiments are wasted. The experience of many companies shows that learning from the failures is often more valuable than that from marginal or submarginal successes. The technology, the market feedback and the joint economics of production are often critical to future strategic successes.

The issue then becomes how to have the necessary 'control' in order to meet the responsibilities for the trusteeship of the resources. One pattern of successful companies is to introduce multi-staged resource allocation procedures. The first stages are very loose with a great deal of trust. The acquiring of considerable resources for major projects requires the normal hard-nosed capital budgeting requests seen in many companies: some studies have identified as many as seven stages in the capital budgeting process at 3M. The early stages are very simple, and it is expected that all but the most patently foolish ideas will get a shot (and even some that at first blush appear to be foolish), but before substantial commitment of corporate assets are made, there is careful and rigorous examination of projections, assumptions and technology.

The question may be asked 'What makes the difference in this process?' The answer appears to be that people believe that their ideas will receive a test backed by real resources. They believe that it is the success potential of the idea being tested and not their skill within the political processes of the firm. The ideas that finally do not receive support can be seen by one and all not to have met a competitive challenge for the allocation of the resources. The individual can continue to devote time and energy backed by hope and thus feel that his or her ideas have the chance to succeed.

Make the sharing of resources the norm

The only way the above two activities can work is by developing a norm of sharing resources. If every idea has to have its own uniquely assigned resources, two problems arise. First, there is tremendous duplication of expensive resources. Second, the assignment of resources creates an internal momentum that often makes it difficult, if not impossible, to terminate a project and the human resources become skilled advocates of the status quo.

One of the major problems for growing companies is that as they meet the challenge of delegating authority, they allow separate fiefdoms to develop. Each fiefdom's baron understands that power, status and financial reward will come from acquiring control over tangible assets and building the employment base. As every top manager knows, overheads ratchet upward inexorably, so the battle then gets fought to 'hold down overheads' since 'fixed costs aren't and variable costs don't!' Developing the sharing norm requires credit to be given for accomplishment using the resources of others and for allowing the resources to be used. It requires an understanding that the corporate mission is more important than the subunit mission. Most of all, it requires management to have a sense of justice and fair play.

This norm can be reinforced by simple control techniques of measuring the cross-use of assigned resources and it must be ingrained into management's psyche by the constant reinforcement of the team spirit. The implications for top management are tough. They lose some control of the capital budgeting process, since ideas can be supported both directly through channels and indirectly through the 'loaning of slack' from organisational peers. The cost of loss of control might well be considered in the light of the benefit of less resource intensity and in the increased rate of initiatives that seem to result in companies using this system.

Through the norm of sharing, new technologies, market data, economic knowledge and customer input can be fed into projects. If, as originally stated, the process of identifying opportunity requires close touch with all the external forces shaping the competitive environment, then using the internal expertise is both efficient and effective.

One 'no' cannot block the project

The individual entrepreneur starts out with a vision but often encounters numerous non-believers along the way. They say 'no' but the 'no's' have little effect because the individual can attempt to gain support from alternative sources. As the company succeeds, however, the source of the resources for the individuals within the company becomes the company itself: the structure that is set up to control resources becomes monolithic – the individual has to get 'approval from the boss'. Thus, the entrepreneurial chance to convince one of many providers of resources gets thwarted and the game becomes one of finding out what the boss wants and delivering it.

Even those companies that escape the monolithic dictatorship often fall into another trap: a trap which is either participative, consensual decision-making or a complex decision process. The emphasis on giving everyone a say requires that the proponent of change convinces everyone. The problems with this kind of system are obvious. First, change is often not in every person's self-interest. Frequently, there are winners and losers. Losers, or potential losers, can always find a reason for 'more study', a little more certainty or, even with the best of good will, have differing perceptions of the risks and rewards for the overall company. Thus, a negative vote is cast. Second, such a system can generate spurious 'no's'. The problems of miscommunication, of differing momentary priorities and of illogical consequential connections can cause people of good will and intelligence to block action.

Companies that successfully grow and maintain their entrepreneurial spirit do not let the conservative protectors of the status quo block action; they shift the burden of proof at the early stages of an initiative to those who would wish to block it. In some companies, it goes so far as to create a situation where managers have the right to a certain amount of small initiatives out of corporate funds and the manager's boss can block such an expenditure only with the concurrence of his or her own corporate superior. Needless to say, few initiatives are seen to be so bad as to be worth a reversal from on high.

Responsibility ultimately must be placed on the individual employees for pursuit of opportunity. They will never feel and execute that responsibility if the system provides ready excuses because of lack of control over resources for the initiative. The people in the firing line have the best information and if top management in a growing firm restricts the initiatives to themselves, then the scope of the corporate mission is ultimately severely limited.

The goal of maintaining entrepreneurship requires that opportunity be identified and pursued. Small steps, strategic experiments and organisational learning are critical. The lessons from companies that have successfully managed growth are clear: initiative must be encouraged; the individual must believe that it is in his or her self-interest to take the first step; and the individual must believe that success is possible within the organisational context.

13. Summary

Entrepreneurship is not inconsistent with size: growth is one measure of success for the entrepreneur. Many successful large firms still practise entrepreneurship, and the managers within feel empowered to pursue opportunity. The individual manager is the key: he or she must view the pursuit of opportunity as being both desirable and feasible. The lessons that are learned by following the success of companies that have remained entrepreneurial through their growth phases are critical. They encompass the skills that good general managers must possess, but they also require an understanding that the individual can and will pursue opportunity. The organisation sets the rules for achieving personal success, and the individual then plays the game.

If a company wishes to remain entrepreneurial, it must tie the individual's view of personal opportunity to the company's needs. This includes developing the ability to perceive opportunity, increasing the desirability of pursuing opportunity and building the confidence within the individual manager that the pursuit of opportunity can succeed.

In order to implement these three goals, careful attention must be paid to the following six questions:

1. What is the appropriate concept of control to encourage entrepreneurship?
2. How can the emphasis on responsibility be increased at all levels within the organisation, and how can the emphasis on authority be decreased?
3. How can the organisation better deal with the failures that will inevitably occur?
4. What can be done to insure that teams are created and maintained?
5. How can individuals be encouraged to maintain and develop their functional skills as well as general management skills?
6. How can the organisation structure be designed to adapt without trauma as opportunities are recognised and pursued?

The answers to these six questions will be different for each firm that attempts to take action: they are highly dependent upon the industry, the individuals, and the resources available. But failure to address these questions leads almost inevitably to increased emphasis on the trusteeship role of management and to rapidly decreasing emphasis on the responsibility for identifying and pursuing opportunity.

If entrepreneurship is important, then organisations and society must find ways to encourage it. The data presented argue strongly that it is important, and it is, in fact, different from simply good business practice as previously defined. The individual entrepreneur is a person who perceives opportunity, finds the pursuit of opportunity desirable in the context of his or her life situation, and believes that success is possible and these elements distinguish the entrepreneur from the vast majority of people. In the individual, these three aspects have certain manifestations: the individual's ability to perceive opportunity is founded upon knowledge of products and markets; the entrepreneur has to have a 'better idea' and/ or a better way to deliver a product or service to a paying customer. The desire to pursue opportunity is based upon a complex balancing of risk and reward. Success often is the major impediment to continual pursuit of healthy change. We are fortunate that success is perceived as valuable, and failure is seen as only temporary or else few would try. Individual entrepreneurs believe success is possible and often, this belief is founded upon the example of the friends and associates with whom the start-up entrepreneur identifies. There must also be a belief and a commitment to the outcome; delusions are costly if they are reflected in misperception of markets, technologies or economics.

For the individual and for organisations, these same three factors

must be built into organisational life. The factors cannot be perpetuated
by cloning founders or by developing a mechanistic set of rules that
ensures extensions of the brilliant thoughts of the leader: they require
the building of an adaptive organisation and society.

Innovation and entrepreneurship are the keys to renewal. Every
company's initial success is dependent upon the identification and
pursuit of a sound opportunity. Every opportunity has a finite life.
Renewal is the key to survival and success, but renewal requires abandoning the old and pursuing the new. That is the essence of entrepreneurship.

Case Study: Atlas Lighting Company[2]

It was Friday, 16 March 1984, and James Ryan, Art Silver and Lois Price bid
each other goodbye as they headed home for the evening. Ordinarily, they
would have been looking forward to a relaxing weekend, but these three
principals of Atlas Lighting were planning to meet the following day to discuss
and plan for the future of their company. It was bound to be a lively discussion,
for they each sensed that the firm was at an important point in its evolution.

History

The early years

The Atlas Lighting Company was founded in 1930 by James Ryan's father,
Kenneth. In 1957, however, James elected to drop out of an MBA program and
return to Los Angeles to run Atlas:

> My father had a heart attack, and I felt it was my responsibility to head home
> and run the family business until my father regained his health. I was six
> months into the program; I had graduated from college in 1956 and then spent
> two years in the Air Force. My goal was to get my MBA and then head off to
> Wall Street – that's where the action was. Instead, I was in Los Angeles
> running a lamp business I knew very little about. I just wanted to keep it going
> until my father was well enough to come back.

At that time, the firm had sales of roughly $250 000 and employed six individ-
uals. Lamps were sold by manufacturers' representatives, mostly on the West
Coast. The product line consisted largely of lamps in the early American style.
Manufacturing the lamps involved assembling and wiring metal and glass parts
in a small, single-storey building on the outskirts of the city.

By the end of the following year, his father's health had improved enough to
allow James to return to school. But James felt that he had learned a great deal
in the year and a half he had been running Atlas, and could not picture being

back in the classroom after having managed his own business. He and a college class mate thought that Los Angeles was going to grow quickly in the coming years, and that there would be great opportunity for a personnel placement service.

This business had barely got off the ground when, in early 1960, James's father again became seriously ill. It was clear that James had to either close Atlas or take over the business:

I just couldn't imagine closing down a business my father had worked thirty years to build. True, it was no goldmine, but it stood for a lot of the same values my father stood for.

James went back to Atlas, this time with a long-term commitment to running the company. No longer in the 'caretaker' frame of mind, he saw several opportunities to improve Atlas's operations. He spent his first year or so really trying to learn the business; then he began implementing some changes. First, it had been his father's policy to maintain the minimum level of inventory, on the theory that heavy investment in styled merchandise was risky. James discussed the situation with the production foreman, Bud Lucas, and they concluded that they would be able to forecast sales with sufficient accuracy to justify manufacturing to inventory rather than orders. James also decided to move the company to Palisade, a suburb of Los Angeles. Rents were rising in the metropolitan area, and James decided that the company would need more space to implement its new manufacturing policy. Atlas moved from its 4000 sq ft building to 18 000 feet of space. Of this, about a third was initially partitioned off as rental space to be let. This new facility had a capacity of $3 million in sales.

In addition, James began implementing a number of personnel decisions:

I felt that people were our most important asset. My father suffered from an affliction common to many entrepreneurs – the desire to control every aspect of the business. Because of this, my father had staffed the business with people who would carry out his orders.

But I felt that we would not be able to grow rapidly with that kind of an attitude. I wanted people whom I could trust as loyal, devoted employees, but who would have some ideas of their own, and who weren't afraid to fight with me.

James fired the office manager/bookkeeper who had been employed by the company for six years; he hired a woman as bookkeeper and took over some of the other tasks himself. James also began looking for some talented people to staff the sales and marketing side of the business and finally, he streamlined Atlas's product line. In 1962, Atlas was producing close to seventy different styles: James and Bud pruned the product line back by almost half, focusing on the more profitable, better-selling items.

The success of these early moves was witnessed in 1962–63. Although sales climbed only moderately (see Table 5 CS.1(a), (b) and (c) for historical financial statements), James felt that he was building a solid base of people and a good reputation among his customers. While Atlas had always been known for the

Table 5.CS.1   Atlas Lighting Company: Historical financial statements

(a) Income Statements ($)

	1969	1963	1960
Net sales	1 138 404	293 967	278 675
Cost of goods	747 966	201 736	191 468
Gross profit	390 438	92 231	87 207
Expenses			
Shipping	33 923	8 018	8 832
Selling	125 141	34 275	34 238
Showroom	11 320	4 906	–
General	45 167	22 749	22 861
Taxes	18 980	4 149	2 923
Officers	117 000	14 500	15 000
Depreciation	3 740	3 140	752
Bad debts	3 815	41	366
Life insurance	7 765	–	–
Profit sharing	–	–	–
Total Expenses	366 851	91 778	84 972
Operating profit	23 587	450	2 235
Interest income	429	801	1 864
Profit	24 016	1 251	4 099
Less tax	5 291	448	985
Net profit	18 725	805	3 114

quality of its products, James's new policies made Atlas's delivery speed and customer service a new source of competitive strength. By this time, James had assumed the presidency (see the organisation chart in Figure 5. C.S. 1) and his father, as Chairman, had become less involved in the day-to-day operations of Atlas.

Bringing in a sales manager

James felt that the business was not reaching its potential and he accelerated his search for a sales manager.

First I turned to people I knew in the industry whom I thought I would get along well with. I was about to take on a partner from a competing lighting company. We had reached an agreement whereby he would receive a one-

(b) Balance Sheets ($)

	1969	1963	1960
Current Assets			
Cash	34 071	67 902	45 234
Accounts receivable	163 157	32 521	24 670
Inventory	139 079	37 829	11 385
Marketable securities	–	–	47 953
Total Current Assets	336 307	138 252	129 242
Fixed assets	31 643	9 256	3 737
Other assets	3 764	906	960
Total Assets	371 714	148 414	133 939
Current Liabilities			
Notes payable	60 000	–	–
Accounts payable	39 457	6 469	4 477
Accrued liabilities	37 182	8 895	6 124
Total Current Liabilities	186 639	15 364	10 601
Deferred Liabilities			
Mortgage	–	–	–
Total Liabilities	186 639	15 364	10 601
Capital			
Capital stock	94 750	100 000	100 000
Capital surplus	25 250	– –	–
Retained earnings	65 075	33 050	23 338
Net Worth	185 075	133 050	123 338
Total Liabilities and Capital	371 714	148 414	133 939

third equity in the business if we met certain financial milestones. I was just about to finalise the arrangements when I met Art Silver.

Art was working as the sales manager at one of Atlas's competitors. He was hard-working and aggressive – I knew Art was the man I was looking for.

Art talked about his decision to join Atlas:

I'd been on the road selling since I was eighteen. I had been making an excellent living in the lamp business, but I knew I was making even more for my boss. I decided to join Atlas for a piece of the equity – I'm in love with the American dream of making a fortune.

Table 5.CS.1

(b) Comparative statements of profit and loss ($) for the years ended December 31

	1983	1982	1981	1980	1979	1978
Net sales	$18,774,035	$16,408,675	$16,124,549	$13,213,970	$12,770,025	$9,711,750
Cost of goods sold						
Materials used	$ 9,188,279	$ 8,335,887	$ 7,686,977	$ 6,165,198	$ 6,358,607	$4,839,589
Labor	1,684,368	1,436,068	1,222,757	963,271	897,703	628,236
Factory Overheads	819,933	779,536	904,536	818,009	744,133	533,214
Cost of goods sold	$11,692,580	$10,551,491	$ 9,814,270	$ 7,946,478	$ 8,000,443	$6,001,039
Gross profit	$ 7,081,455	$ 5,857,184	$ 6,310,279	$ 5,267,492	$ 4,769,582	$3,710,711
	37.7%	35.7%	39.1%	39.9%	37.4%	38.2%
Expenses						
Shipping expenses	$ 531,791	$ 473,088	$ 476,216	$ 376,562	$ 361,649	$ 283,059
Selling expenses	1,546,300	1,293,605	1,257,942	995,813	856,431	635,229
Commissions	1,285,372	1,198,518	1,215,551	1,127,601	1,056,966	765,823
General and administrative expenses	1,024,790	1,054,120	1,016,864	656,440	664,345	591,864
Officers' salaries	531,493	430,041	424,890	369,079	360,600	298,243
Taxes	252,543	209,682	198,698	196,463	194,158	131,147
Depreciation	156,413	139,389	133,615	123,278	111,181	132,804
Bad debts	71,943	209,319	112,489	89,826	31,189	27,662
Profit sharing plan	359,187	329,298	325,150	298,529	270,944	180,322
Total expenses	$ 5,759,832	$ 5,368,060	$ 5,161,415	$ 4,233,591	$ 3,907,463	$3,046,153
Net operating profit	$ 1,321,623	$ 489,124	$ 1,148,864	$ 1,033,901	$ 862,119	$ 664,558
Sundry income	50,315	86,203	6,145	73,638	46,208	13,897
	$ 1,371,938	$ 575,327	$ 1 155,009	$ 1,107,539	$ 908,327	$ 678,455
Moving expenses	–	–	–	–	–	132,736
	$ 1,371,938	$ 575,327	$,155,009	$,107,539	$ 908,327	$ 545,719
Federal and State income taxes	629,888	256,565	504,437	493,528	329,248	221,339
Net profit for the year	$ 742,050	$ 318,762	$ 650,572	$ 614,011	$ 579,079	$ 324,380
Ratios (shown as %)						
Materials used to average inventory	3.7	2.9	3.1	4.7	5.3	4.5
Sales to average inventory	7.5	5.7	6.5	10.0	10.7	9.1
Working capital to sales	22.4	20.6	17.6	17.2	11.9	11.3
Year end accounts receivable to sales	21.7	21.1	20.8	20.1	17.8	18.7
Sales to average net worth	4.3	4.3	4.9	5.0	6.3	6.3
Year end inventory to sales	14.2	14.3	21.4	11.2	9.1	12.6
Net profit on beginning net worth	18.8	8.1	22.1	26.6	35.8	23.5

Table 5.CS.1

(b) Comparative statements of profit and loss ($) for the years ended December 31

1977	1976	1975	1974	1973	1972	1971	1970
$8,468,873	$7,350,678	$5,568,335	$5,274,153	$4,358,876	$3,061,423	$1,853,482	$1,502,164
$4,197,980	$3,637,370	$2,508,778	$2,497,755	$2,180,028	$1,614,439	$ 958,065	$ 776,409
548,302	464,874	365,830	360,435	355,161	262,462	200,341	172,159
427,806	400,644	330,132	285,086	271,250	129,382	108,704	87,460
$5,174,088	$4,502,888	$3,204,740	$3,143,276	$2,806,439	$2,006,283	$1,267,110	$1,036,028
$3,294,785	$2,847,790	$2,363,595	$2,130,877	$1,552,437	$1,055,140	$ 586,372	$ 466,136
38.9%	38.7%	42.5%	40.4%	35.6%	34.4%	31.6%	31.0%
$270,135	$ 245,083	$233,968	$ 225,453	$ 176,692	$ 95,973	$ 62,402	$ 53,882
570,261	457,107	374,782	318,272	167,036	85,213	94,323	78,531
741,244	677,256	484,407	446,237	349,110	265,269	123,322	95,438
491,052	345,881	238,559	241,590	170,558	101,666	85,449	68,902
280,000	249,600	261,800	263,900	242,800	245,500	132,400	111,000
101,358	78,593	63,741	60,479	64,697	37,138	29,245	22,521
123,923	83,936	77,759	73,626	40,150	11,400	12,938	9,048
9,762	60,608	12,788	48,011	13,693	3,002	4,599	3,523
124,665	63,020	61,593	56,446	–	–	–	–
$2,712,400	$2,261,084	$1,809,397	$1,734,014	$1,224,736	$ 845,161	$ 544,678	$ 442,845
$ 582,385	$ 586,706	$ 554,198	$ 396,863	$ 327,701	$ 209,979	$ 41,694	$ 23,291
7,889	16,309	8,646	4,340	–	315	270	–
$ 590,274	$ 603,015	$ 562,844	$ 401,203	$ 327,701	$ 210,294	$ 41,964	$ 23,291
–	–	–	–	–	–	–	–
$ 590,274	$ 603,015	$ 562,844	$ 401,203	$ 327,701	$ 210,294	$ 41,964	$ 23,291
301,885	303,159	289,699	203,377	159,209	105,762	17,414	8,082
$ 288,389	$ 299,856	$ 273,145	$ 197,826	$ 168,492	$ 104,532	$ 24,550	$ 15,209
4.6	4.9	4.7	5.2	6.6	7.6	5.1	5.2
9.2	10.0	10.5	10.9	13.1	14.4	9.9	10.1
11.7	12.5	12.4	7.7	5.1	8.8	10.3	10.1
15.3	16.4	14.6	13.9	15.4	15.9	15.8	14.9
6.9	7.2	6.7	8.8	10.5	7.5	8.7	7.8
10.7	12.6	9.9	9.6	10.5	6.8	11.7	10
26.6	31.0	39.3	39.7	51.2	46.5	12.3	8.2

Table 5.CS.1

(c) Comparative balance sheets as at December 31st

	1983	*1982*	*1981*	*1980*	*1979*	*1978*
Assets						
Current assets						
Cash in bank and on Hand	$ 104,089	$ 127,814	$ 138,457	$ 354,606	$ 158,711	$ 89,284
Accounts receivable	4,069,439	3,460,698	3,353,720	2,659,224	2,275,363	1,819,962
Inventories	2,659,912	2,342,731	3,448,798	1,475,730	1,160,710	1,222,380
Prepaid expenses	9,875	27,257	49,300	53,403	53,114	40,846
Miscellaneous receivables	2,164	9,937	7,933	62,195	983	30,033
Total current assets	$6,845,479	$5,966,437	$6,998,208	$ 4,605,158	$3,648,881	$3,202,505
Fixed Assets						
Furniture and fixtures Leasehold improvements, vehicles, computer, land and building	$3,625,985	$3,532,994	$3,536,956	$3,372,246	$3,376,528	$3,144,940
Less: accumulated depreciation	1,514,438	1,320,326	1,077,574	842,413	627,422	402,770
Total fixed assets	$2,111,547	$2,212,668	$2,459,382	$2,529,833	$2,749,106	$2,742,170
Other assets						
Security deposits	s$ 9,142	$ 3,067	$ 3,067	$ 3,067	$ 3,067	$ 3,067
Prepaid Mortgage Costs	19,191	21,228	23,266	25,304	27,342	29,380
Investments	16,224	17,803	47,177	–	–	–
Cash Surrender value officers Life Insurance	53,744	67,266	76,685	64,495	74,795	48,637
Total other assets	$ 98,301	$ 109,364	$ 150,195	$ 92,866	$ 105,204	$ 81,084
TOTAL ASSETS	$9,055,327	$8,290,469	$9,607,785	$7,227,857	$6,503,191	$6,025,759
Liabilities						
Current liabilities						
Notes payable – banks	$ 650,000	$ 500,000	$1,800,000	$ 100,000	$ 100,000	$ 650,000
Notes and mortgages payable – current	247,397	254,306	116,806	228,486	248,068	303,079
Accounts payable	948,523	1,068,338	1,224,031	1,147,665	1,071,324	851,542
Employees deductions	65,860	57,009	93,557	123,849	22,838	17,655
Accrued expenses and taxes	722,595	710,317	926,062	732,294	685,949	316,964
Total current liabilities	$2,634,375	$2,589,970	$4,160,456	$2,332,294	$2,128,179	$2,139,240

1977	1976	1975	1974	1973	1972	1971	1970
$ 281,242	$ 88,156	$ 144,410	$ 24,913	$ 21,541	$ 53,390	$ 59,045	$ 35,854
1,292,117	1,208,725	812,390	732,276	672,167	487,262	292,538	223,690
907,470	926,290	549,960	507,730	456,280	207,600	217,450	158,655
16,560	–	–	–	–	–	–	–
–	13,520	10,781	658	–	1,505	1,052	473
$2,497,389	$2,236,691	$1,517,541	$1,265,577	$1,149,988	$ 749,757	$ 570,085	$ $416,702
$1,108,592	$ 596,991	$ 523,244	$ 458,915	$ 337,896	$ 99,829	$ 83,747	$ 74,690
384,806	291,249	209,830	134,637	74,564	51,089	44,023	31,086
$ 723,786	$ 305,742	$ 313,414	$ 124,278	$ 263,332	$ 48,740	$ 39,724	$ 43,604
$ 69,269	$ 26,926	$ 14,664	$ 13,808	$ 13,000	$ 11,674	$ 4,829	$ 4,240
–	–	–	–	–	–	–	–
–	–	–	–	–	–	–	–
38,605	23,473	–	–	–	–	–	–
$ 107,874	$ 50,399	$ 14,664	$ 13,808	$ 13,000	$ 11,674	$ 4,829	$ 4,240
$3,329,049	$2,592,832	$1,845,619	$1,603,663	$1,426,320	$ 810,171	$ 614,638	$ 466,546
$ 300,000	$ 200,000	–$ 125,000	$ 225,000	–	$ 130,000	$ 125,000	
415,122	177,672	$ 25,000	23,550	–	–	–	–
659,745	769,991	547,883	397,827	443,345	203,383	164,079	68,276
46,215	2	3,641	3,135	966	1,889	2,554	2,248
335,303	173,325	250,843	306,650	259,149	275,531	93,170	70,738
$1,756,385	$1,320,990	$ 827,367	$ 856,162	$ 928,460	$ 480,803	$ 389,803	$ 266,262

Table 5.CS.1   (contd)

(c) Comparative balance sheets as at December 31st

Other liabilities						
Notes and mortgages payable – long term	$1,648,658	$1,752,255	$1,835,847	$1,952,653	$2,064,113	$2,172,699
Total liabilities	$4,283,033	$4,342,225	$5,996,303	$4,284,947	$4,192,292	$4,311,939
Capital						
Capital stock	$ 554	$ 532	$ 526	$ 520	$ 514	$ 508
Capital surplus	256,333	174,355	91,228	73,234	55,240	37,246
Retained earnings	4,515,407	3,773,357	3,519,728	2,869,156	2,255,145	1,676,066
Treasury stock	–	–	–	–	–	–
Net worth	$4,772,294	$3,948,244	$3,611,482	$2,942,910	$2,310,899	$1,713,820
TOTAL LIABILITIES AND CAPITAL	$9,055,327	$8,290,469	$9,607,785	$7,227,857	$6,503,191	$6,025,759
WORKING CAPITAL	$4,211,104	$3,378,467	$2,837,752	$2,272,864	$1,520,702	$1,063,265
CURRENT ASSETS TO CURRENT LIABILITIES	2.6	2.3	1.7	2.0	1.7	1.5
CURRENT LIABILITIES TO NET WORTH	.6	.7	1.2	.8	.9	1.2

James struck a deal with Art wherein Art put $20 000 into the business and, in return, received 50 per cent of the equity once certain financial targets were reached. Art took only a small salary ($150 per week). He joined Atlas as Vice President, Sales at the end of 1963, with full responsibility for sales and marketing.

James recalled his first year working with Art:

> He really injected new life into the company. I had been so busy managing the production and financial side of the business, that there was a lot of untapped potential. Remember, up until this time, our only sales force had been reps, who also sold other lighting lines. Art spent 90 per cent of his time on the road, calling on accounts. When he made it back to the office, it was usually to pack-up merchandise and load the truck for a customer who needed a rush delivery.
>
> It was not an easy time, and we had very little opportunity to talk to each other. We really developed a great deal of trust in one another.

$ 193,224	$ 85,791	$ 49,421	$ 49,815	–	–	–	–
$1,949,609	$1,506,781	$ 876,788	$ 907,977	$ 926,460	$ 480,803	$ 389,803	$ 266,262
$ 504	$ 504	$ 171,504	$ 171,504	$ 171,504	$ 94,750	$ 94,750	$ 94,750
27,250	25,250	25,250	25,250	25,250	25,250	25,250	
1,251,686	1,068,297	772,077	498,932	301,106	209,368	104,835	80,284
–	(8,000)	–	–	–	–	–	–
$1,379,440	$1,086,051	$ 968,831	$ 695,685	$ 497,860	$ 329,368	$ 224,835	$ 200,284
$3,329,049	$,592,832	$ 845,619	$1,603,663	$1,426,320	$ 810,171	$ 614,636	$ 466,546
$ 741,004	$ 915,701	$ 693,174	$ 407,415	$ 221,528	$ 268,954	$ 180,282	$ 152,440
1.4	1.7	1.8	1.5	1.2	1.6	1.5	1.60
1.3	1.4	.9	1.2	1.9	1.5	1.3	1.3

Developing the product line

By 1968, sales had hit the $1 million mark, and James and Art felt it was time to reassess their strategy. Up to that point, they had been focusing on building a sales network and a reputation for quality and service. Now, they felt it was time to focus on the product itself. Atlas's product line had expanded to a hundred or so lamps, mostly in the early American style. These lamps were designed by James and the production manager, who would mix and match readily available components to form designs they found aesthetically appealing.

In 1968, James also let Bud Lucas go. It was difficult, for Bud had been so helpful in the early years, but he clearly did not have the skills to manage a larger group of people, and Paul Ellis was hired to replace him.

Another management change was made in 1968. The bookkeeper whom James had originally hired was not well suited to handling other secretarial or administrative tasks. As the business expanded, James wanted to bring in a skilled office administrator and Lois Price was hired as office manager. She did the bookkeeping, and also managed two part-time secretaries. By this time, Atlas had also taken over the space it had previously leased, and was considering enlarging the original structure.

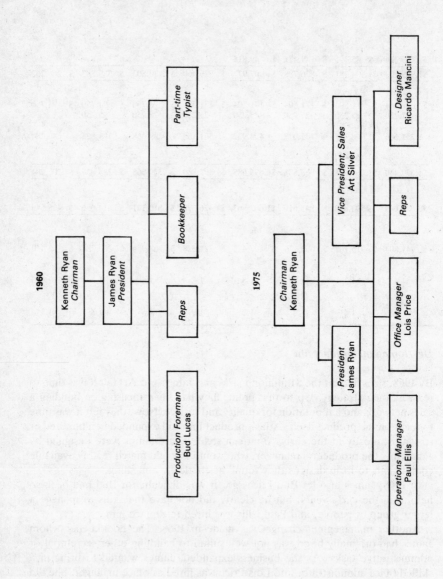

1960

Kenneth Ryan
Chairman

James Ryan
President

Production Foreman
Bud Lucas

Reps

Bookkeeper

Part-time
Typist

1975

Chairman
Kenneth Ryan

President
James Ryan

Vice President, Sales
Art Silver

Operations Manager
Paul Ellis

Office Manager
Lois Price

Reps

Designer
Ricardo Mancini

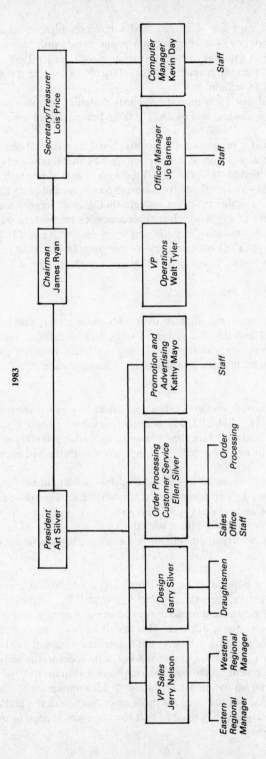

Figure 5.CS.1 Organisation charts, 1960–83

1983

James and Art now felt that they had sufficiently high volume to justify designing their own line of lamps. But they would need a professional designer. Art knew a designer who was with his former employer; and in 1969, Atlas hired Ricardo Mancini. Ricardo received a base salary plus a 1 per cent royalty on all sales in excess of $1 million.

Ricardo's initial work was directed towards designing custom components – bases, stems, glass shades, and so on. He talked about his efforts:

Atlas always had a reputation for quality, but I wanted to bring a sense of style and originality as well. Atlas' reputation was built on the early American style, and I decided to stick with this. I did a good deal of research to unearth authentic designs, and used quality materials like brass and hand-blown glass.

As a student of design, I always thought that artistic integrity was the most important aspect of my work. But the economics of my arrangement with Atlas give me the incentive to concentrate on designing popular lamps. If I ever feel as though I'm losing my creative integrity, I work it out on carpentry and painting at home. The reality is that I like making a good living.

Focusing on sales and marketing

By 1973, sales volume was slightly over $4.3 million. Art felt that he had developed a loyal and devoted group of sales representatives. He had spent most of his time working with reps and selling personally to major accounts. In mid-1973, though, he thought it was time for a major shift in Atlas's marketing policy:

I walked into our accountant's office and asked how much money we could afford to risk. He said $100 000 was the maximum. Then I walked into James's office, and told him that I wanted to spend $100 000 on a TV ad campaign. He turned a bit pale. No one in our industry had ever done TV advertising.

I felt that a well-executed merchandising *program* would help our product immensely. The ads themselves would stimulate consumer demand. At the same time, reps and retailers would be more likely to push our products if they knew that we supported them with this kind of *program*: They would feel that Atlas was really trying to help *them*. I convinced James that it was worth the risk.

Ricardo selected a popular group of lamps and co-ordinated a product line around them. Art developed three commercials with the help of a local producer. They purchased time through a local advertising agency, who also helped Atlas develop point-of-sale displays. The ads which were developed included space at the end for a 'trailer' which would feature the names of five or six Atlas retailers in the area. Reps were given video-cassette recorders to show retailers the ads before they went on the air. The campaign was quite successful, and by 1974, sales had shot up by almost $1 million to $5.3 million.

As James and Art saw the need for more co-ordination of the marketing and merchandising functions, they realised that someone was needed to manage the salesforce. Lance Taylor was a sales rep for one of Atlas's competitors and he was hired to manage the salesforce and assist Art in planning marketing programmes, but after a year, it was clear that Lance did not possess the required administrative skills, so he went back into the field as a rep, and Art hired a long-time friend, Jerry Nelson. Jerry had been managing the sales force at a local insurance firm. One of Jerry's first projects was to review the performance of Atlas's existing salesforce. Because reps were paid on a straight commission, their earnings had risen along with Atlas's sales. In 1974, for example, one rep had earned over $60 000.

In many companies, once a rep had become this successful, his territory would be divided up, or the commission rate cut. Yet, Art and Jerry felt that:

> There is no such thing as making too much money at Atlas. The more money they make from us, the more loyal and dependent on us they are.

Jerry and Art decided to run a sales contest. Reps were given sales quotas, and those who beat their quotas were eligible for cash bonuses. In addition, everyone who beat their quota won an expenses-paid holiday to Las Vegas. Sixteen reps exceeded their quotas, and Atlas opened up 200 new accounts; overall sales for the period increased by 50 per cent.

At this time Atlas estimated that it had 2500 accounts, distributed as follows:

	%
Gift shops	5
Department stores	20
Furniture stores	35
Lighting fixture stores	40

In 1975, a new operations manager, Walter Tyler, was hired to replace Paul Ellis. Ellis remained on as plant manager, reporting to Tyler. During this time, the production facility was expanded to 46 000 sq. ft. and no further expansion could be made at this site because of zoning regulations.

Developing new products

In 1976, Atlas began considering an expansion of its product line. Its traditional glass line was still Atlas's only product line, and the company had become the leader in this area; the company now had 400 or so different lamp styles. Ricardo had done a modern line for his previous employer, and was anxious to design such a line for Atlas. In addition, James and Art were also considering an expansion into traditional brass lamps, and a lower-priced line for sale to mass merchants and discount department stores, so James and Art decided to enter both the contemporary and brass markets. James recalled this decision:

> Ricardo had been so succesful with the early American line, and was so anxious to go ahead with the contemporary line, that we gave him free reign. He tried to be extremely innovative – we didn't do any market research or testing. We used our traditional approach, purchasing from suppliers and assembling in-house. In spring of 1977, we came out with this new line of

about forty lamps. At the time, I think we felt that we had become so important to our customers that they would try anything we produced. They did order the line, but it didn't sell, and we took back a lot of product from them. This project cost us about half a million dollars.

At roughly the same time, Atlas also introduced two other new lines:

A line of decorative wall sculptures. On a trip to Italy, Art had been struck by some unusual glass and mirrored wall sculptures. Ricardo designed several pieces in this style, but they were poorly engineered: customers didn't feel the high price was justified, and the line did not sell.
   A line of brass lamps. Here again, Atlas had brass pieces manufactured to its specifications, and then assembled and wired the lamps. This line sold moderately well, although the Atlas product was perceived as inferior in quality to the main competitor in this business, who continued to maintain the dominant share.

Changing management structure

In 1976, James's father died. Up to that time, James, the President, his father the Chairman, and Art, Vice President, Sales, had each held a one-third interest in Atlas, although Art and James split the voting control 50:50. Art had been hired, however, with the understanding that he and James would each ultimately own 50 per cent of the equity.
   Following the Chairman's death, James and Art took the opportunity of restructuring the equity to reward Lois Price. James recalled their decision:

Lois had always worked like it was *her* business. She came in weekends, worked nights. Even her husband, Bob, had gotten very involved in the business, helping us choose our computer system and advising us on a number of other important decisions. It was this kind of attitude which had made Atlas grow and prosper. Art and I each gave Lois 5 per cent of our stock, to give her a 10 per cent ownership position.

In addition, James assumed the title of Chairman and Art moved to the position of President; Lois Price was named Secretary/Treasurer.

Adding new facilities

By 1977, it was clear that a new facility would be needed. The Palisade plant had a capacity of about £7 million in sales. Rather than build another, separate plant, Atlas decided to consolidate its operations into one, larger facility and purchased a plot of land in Ellentown, about 20 miles from its existing facility. Plans were drawn up and the process of looking for a contractor began, then, in late 1977, Atlas discovered an old aircraft plant which was available in the area; it was cheap, and would need only minor improvements, so the plans were scrapped, the land sold, and five months later, Atlas was in its new 110 000 sq ft plant.

At about the same time, Atlas dramatically upgraded its computer system. The company had purchased its first system in 1973, and added another computer in 1976. In 1977, this entire system was sold and a new IBM system put on line.

Reorganising the sales force

In 1977, another important change occurred. Atlas reorganised its sales force, and asked all its reps to become full-time, commissioned employees of Atlas. Virtually all of them dropped their other lines and began working exclusively for Atlas. Art recalled this period:

> We had developed a group of loyal and talented reps, but we just didn't have the kind of control over them that we wanted. We knew that they were making a lot of money with our line, and thought that, if they would agree to become our exclusive agents, we could start doing a lot more with them. We dropped the commission rate from 10 per cent to 9 per cent but started giving them benefits and profit sharing.
>
> At this point, we were really in a position to start implementing some good marketing programs. Jerry Nelson and I worked on a number of fronts. First, we started doing a lot of training. We had sales meetings, and really educated our people on our products and on selling techniques. Jerry was also very creative, and very good about staying in touch with the sales force and getting ideas from them.
>
> We also put some excellent merchandising programmes together. A lot of our customers were lighting fixture stores – they had lots of stuff hanging from the ceiling and walls, but nothing else – no table lamps. We came up with the display concept. If a customer ordered a certain merchandise package, he got a wooden display rack. Our salesmen policed it to be sure that no competitors' merchandise was ending up on our displays.
>
> One of Atlas's keys to success was selling the entire merchandising concept, not just the product. The idea was to get the product into the home, not just into the store. We would help our customer build his business. We had a whole package – the display, TV advertising, promotion money for the store. By 1979, we had customers who were buying entire packages of merchandise without even seeing the product, they trusted us that much.
>
> Salesmen would conduct seminars for the stores on how to sell the product. We had in-store contests for our customers' salespeople.

During this time, Atlas was still using a good deal of TV advertising.

Design

In 1978, Ricardo left Atlas. James and Art felt that there were several reasons for this:

> First, Ricardo was upset because we had given Lois, and not him a piece of equity. Our feeling was that, while she always worked like it was her business,

Ricardo was more of a 9-to-5 type. Second, he was very shaken by the failure of his contemporary line. Finally, he really was a temperamental artist. The pressure and growth of the organisation were beginning to get to him.

Ricardo's departure did not hurt Atlas; he had left enough work 'in the pipeline' to carry the company for a year or so. Finally, Ricardo had become quite expensive: because of his compensation agreement – he received 1 per cent on all sales over $1 million – Ricardo was making more money than Atlas's principals. He had also been quite conservative, and after his failure with the contemporary line, was reluctant to try anything too new. James, Art and Lois were anxious to get into the fan business, but Ricardo had been opposed to this. (Ceiling fans were beginning to become a popular home accessory.)

More changes

In 1979, Jerry Nelson was also made a principal of Atlas. James and Art each gave up 2 1/2 per cent of their stock so that Jerry could have a 5 per cent ownership share. Also in 1979, Art's son, Barry, joined Atlas as its new designer. Barry had been an artist and a glassblower, and had owned a shop where he blew and sold unique glass objects. Later that year, Atlas opened up a large showroom in Dallas, Texas. This area had become an important growth market for Atlas, and they felt that this facility would expand their presence in the Dallas area.

In 1980, Lois Price transferred many of her formal responsibilities as an office manager to a new office manager who was promoted from within the staff. A computer manager was also hired. In addition to managing these two individuals, Lois also became more involved in the human resources area. She became more active in the marketing area as well, working in the field, and getting involved with sales promotions.

More new products

In 1979, Atlas brought in a designer to focus on 'Tiffany lamps'. There was a revival of sorts going on at the time, and Atlas allocated a portion of their plant and production workers to the lamps. Art recalled the experience:

It was a very labour-intensive operation; workers cutting and soldering small pieces of colored glass into lamp shades. We had such high overheads that our product was priced too high; we couldn't compete.

Then, in 1980, Atlas did finally get into the fan business. The company joined forces with a fan company, and formed a joint venture, of which Atlas owned 75 per cent. The new company imported fans from Hong Kong, and Atlas sold them to its existing customer base. Art recalled this experience:

We got a lot of fans out there, into the stores, based on our relationship with our customers. But the damn things didn't work. They were priced at about the average of competitor's products, and at this time there was a flood of product from Hong Kong. The quality of our product was about average, too. But our customers wouldn't accept average quality from *us*. I went over to Hong Kong and talked to the manufacturer. I made about a hundred suggestions on how to improve the product, and they wrote them all down and said yes to every one. But nothing changed. We ended up taking back a lot of product, and dissolved that partnership.

During this time, Barry had been working on a custom fan for Atlas. This fan incorporated the typical rotating blades, but the stationary housing contained a lighting fixture. At the start of 1981, Atlas introduced this fan, which quickly became a $3 or $4 million business.

Recent marketing efforts

In 1980, Atlas began the 'Atlas Ace Club'. Customers who purchased over a certain dollar amount of merchandise in a given year were taken on holiday with their wives. Between 1980 and 1983, Atlas took many of its best customers on trips to London, Israel and Palm Springs.

In 1982, in response to a downturn in the economy, Atlas begao a special newspaper tabloid insert. It realised that many of its customers were having a vesy difficult time surviving, so the company pulled together a special group of lamps which would be sold at a discount price. The tabloid was very successful, generating sales for both Atlas and its customers. The company tried the 'tab' again in 1983, but this time, merchandise did not sell well. Atlas's customers purchased in large quantities, but the consumer didn't buy. Art speculated that, because the 'tab' was in the spring, customers were more concerned with the 'outside' of their houses than with the inside.

In late 1983, Atlas suffered a serious blow: Jerry Nelson was killed in a car accident:

> We all miss Jerry a great deal. He was a very creative guy, and a constant source of new ideas. He was always talking to our salesmen, and they were continually giving him feedback and ideas.

A personal perspective

Each of Atlas's managers talked about the changes they had witnessed during their years at Atlas, and how they viewed their role in the company.

James Ryan

> It is incredible to me how Atlas has changed. [See page 134.] In the early years, before Art came, it wasn't at all unusual for me to put on a smock, wire some lamps together, pack them up and ship them off.
>
> Bud Lucas and I would 'design' a few lamps and take these models to a regional show. Based on these show orders, we would order parts, and put the lamps together when the parts came in.
>
> Even after Art joined, there was still a lot of hands-on work to do. Up until

1980, I did all the hiring and firing. Now, I do let Walt run the factory pretty much on his own. I don't get involved in many of the decisions. My attitude is, if things are working well, to push responsibility and authority down. Now, relations with the bankers take up more of my time. I spend more time thinking about marketing and sales issues. Finally, I don't put in the hours I used to; I enjoy spending more time with my family and friends, and on a number of civic activities and charities.

Art Silver

When I joined Atlas in 1964, I was on the road 90 per cent of the time; we had about nine reps. I sold and delivered products. Even as sales manager, I was still the salesman for the metropolitan area. I worked closely on collections with Lois. Weekends I would be in one of my accounts selling, or helping them with inventory. I did all the advertising, promotions. I travelled with the reps, and trained them, I brought design ideas back to Ricardo. Once Jerry Nelson joined, I still travelled a lot, but he took over more and more of the advertising, merchandising and promotion. I gave up the metropolitan area, but still spent a lot of time on the road.

Lately, I've been less involved with the sales force, which now numbers 26. I still work on developing merchandising concepts, and travel to bring ideas back to Barry. I'm heavily involved in a local charity, and in building a local youth tennis program.

Lois Price

When I joined Atlas in 1968, I did practically everything. It took a lot of weekends and nights, but I really felt like I was accomplishing something. I remember being surprised when, after *one* week, James gave me a key to the building.

When an order came in, I would do the credit check, enter it on the books and it would go to the factory. Pedro would manually write out *all* of the parts – from memory – which those items required. He would know what was in stock and what wasn't. When it was shipped, they would send the invoice back, and we'd send it out. We sent our records out once a week, and got them back two weeks later – this was how long it took to get inventory data. I would call up customers who hadn't paid, and keep on top of the accounts receivable.

Now the system is incredibly complex. We have 25 office workers, up from 15 in 1980 and 4 in 1972. When an order comes in, one person checks it to be sure the numbers are right. Then it goes to the order processing department. The name and address of the customer are accessed in the computer. The order is typed in, and invoice is created. All inventory records for every part required for every lamp ordered are checked, and an order record is created. A work order is created, with four copies – one for the salesman, one for parts picking, one for shipping and one to be used as the packing slip.

The optimal shipping method and charges are automatically computed. Back orders are automatically created and stored. Every night, we can create an inventory record, and a record of sales by customer, salesman and lamp style. We send salesmen a monthly record of their sales by customer and style. We can call up a customer's entire credit and sales history on the CRT.

Over time, my own job has become more removed from the day-to-day. I spend time on human resource issues, employee benefits, and talking to customers when a problem comes up.

My management style is different from either James's or Art's. James has turned over complete control of the factory to Walt. Art, on the other hand, is very authoritative. He gets involved in every decision. I like to know most of what's going on, but I don't get too actively involved unless someone drops the ball.

Walt Tyler

When I joined Atlas in 1975, we had about forty employees in the factory. The same person would do receiving, warehousing, stocking and inspection. Now, several different people, and even several departments are responsible. When I first joined, I had to fight with James and Art for weeks to get them to spend $12 000 on a fork lift. Last year, I spent $50 000 for two fork lifts, and this year I have a $300 000 budget for mechanical equipment.

Our sales growth has forced me to organise the factory in a more structured way. We have about 1000 different lamp styles now. [See Figure 5. CS. 2 and 5, CS. 3]. First, you can't manage unless you can measure, and in order to hold people accountable, you need to define their jobs in fairly specific terms. Also, I can't afford to be dependent on any one person. In 1975, we didn't have any inventory system; Betty *knew* where every one of 2000 parts was. But Betty left!

It took a year to train someone to replace Betty. Now, we have an organised, computerised system; I can get someone up to speed in two weeks.

Current situation

As 1984 began, Atlas's principals saw the firm confronting a number of issues.

Jerry's absence

Following Jerry's death, Art moved the two regional sales managers into a joint position as Regional/National Sales Manager. The two would share the duties which were previously Jerry's, as well as continue their responsibility of managing the sales force.

It was a condition of all of the principals' equity positions that Atlas would purchase the individuals' stock at its 'appraised value'; and the most recent appraisal of the company placed its value at roughly £10 million.

New product lines

James and Art felt that Atlas should get into some new product areas. Art and his son, Barry, went on a buying trip to Spain and Portugal, and brought back a

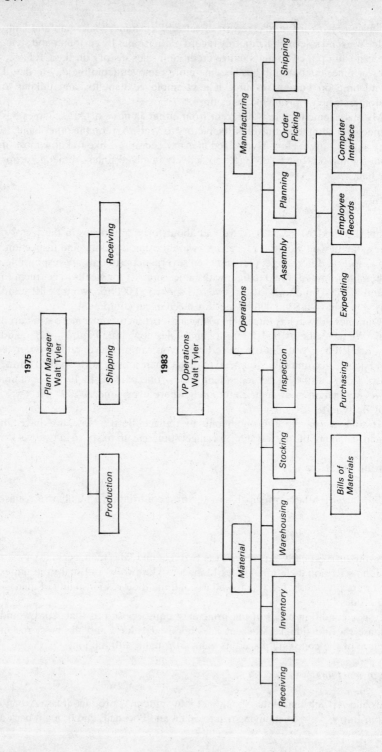

Figure 5. CS.2 Plant organisation charts, 1975 and 1983

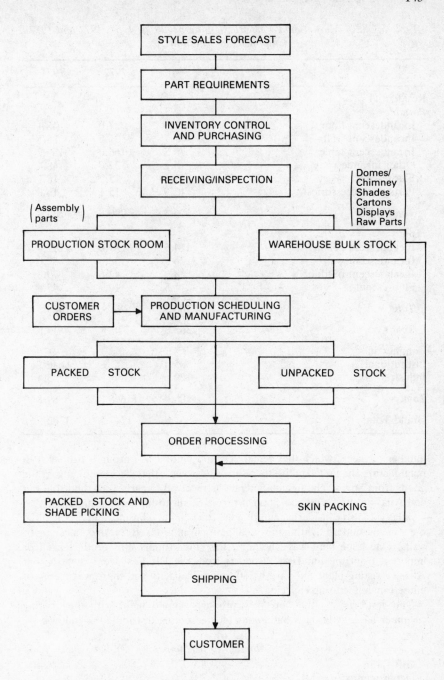

Figure 5.CS.3   Organisation flow chart

Table 5.CS.2   Market data – electric lighting products; 1967, 1972 and 1977
(shipments in $ millions)

	1967	1972	1977
Residential			
Portable			
Incandescent floor	41.6	27.0	48.1
Incandescent wall	11.7	35.5	25.5
Incandescent table	78.3	166.0	189.2
Other incandescent	18.2	32.0	48.4
Fluorescent	13.6	15.2	16.7
Parts and accessories	12.9	15.1	16.0
Total	176.3	290.8	343.9
Fixed			
Incandescent ceiling	114.5	185.0	292.4
Incandescent wall	26.5	38.6	52.0
Incandescent outdoor	28.0	44.6	79.3
Fluorescent	11.5	19.7	45.4
Total	180.5	287.9	469.1
Totals	365.8	578.7	813.0
Commercial			
Institutional	385.4	502.1	646.1
Industrial	120.6	166.7	243.4
Total	506.0	668.8	889.5
Grand Total	862.8	1247.5	1702.5

number of pieces which they felt they could build a line around. Rather than manufacture the merchandise themselves, however, they decided to import the goods from Spain. The first shipment was received in early 1984, and sold out and Atlas awaited a second shipment from Spain to fill outstanding orders.

Atlas was also considering entering the track lighting business. (Track lighting is a style of modern lighting in which lamps sit in grooved tracks on a ceiling or wall.) One issue here was whether Atlas should make this product itself or import it from the Far East. Products from the Far East were cheaper, but Atlas's existing plant did have a £30 million capacity and there was plenty of unused manufacturing capacity.

One concern was that any new products should fit in with the existing customer base. Atlas now had about 1400 accounts, distributed as follows:

	Number of accounts (%)	*Dollar volume (%)*
Gift shops	8.9	3.7
Department stores	2.0	2.0
Furniture stores	30.1	9.8
Lighting outlets*	59.0	84.5

*Includes stores selling fans

Acquisitions

Atlas's management was also considering the possibility of making a series of acquisitions to get into new product areas. They wanted to bring more volume into their existing facility, which they estimated had a capacity of roughly $30 million in annual volume.

Atlas's future

One issue which had only recently begun to concern Atlas's principals was the future management of the company. James was 52, Art 57 and Lois 56. Lois had mentioned her desire to retire during the next five years; and James and Art were spending less time on the business and more time with their families and on personal activities.

In this regard, one related issue was that of Art's children working for the business. Currently, two of his children were working for the company; while James and Lois felt comfortable with the existing situation, they were uneasy with the notion of extending family involvement in Atlas. They thought that having family of the principals working for Atlas had two negative effects. First, if other employees thought that responsibility and financial reward were more a function of family ties than effort, they would be less likely to put forth their maximum effort, and employees might feel uncomfortable or 'spied upon' if they were working with one of the principals' relatives.

Art, however, saw several benefits to having family and relatives working for Atlas:

> They are people you can trust. In a small, growing business you don't have time to keep a close watch on everyone. I *know* that these people are working for *Atlas's* best interests. In addition, these people are our 'eyes and ears' in the rest of the company. If something is going on that I should know about, they will tell me.

Going public

In the past few months, Atlas had been considering the possibility of going public. Another lighting company of a similar size had recently gone public at a price/earnings ratio of 15, and the hot new issues market had brought several proposals from investment bankers.

James thought that, no matter which strategy Atlas pursued, it would need more financing; whether it was to acquire other companies, finance inventory of imported merchandise, or internally develop new product lines. In addition, the principals had some personal reasons for thinking that a public offering might be attractive. They felt that it would establish a value for the company and their stock, and provide them with liquidity in the future. It would also provide a vehicle for getting some funds at the time of the offering. They realised, however, that being a public company would have an impact on the company. The firm's salary and expenses structure would change as maximising earnings became more important. In addition, dealing with financial community would place more demands on James's and Art's time.

The consultant's report

In an effort to produce a business plan which Atlas could use in some preliminary discussions with underwriters, Lois called in a small-business consultant who had some experience in helping companies draft business plans, and who was a personal acquaintance of hers. The principals were surprised to receive a memo (see Appendix A on page 149 for excerpts from the consultant's notes and the final memo) which was not a business plan but a series of recommendations about the business.

Where do we go from here?

James, Art and Lois each had their own perspectives on where the company should be headed.

James

> There is no doubt about the fact that we do need more discipline in our approach to decisions; we need a strategy for growth. We still have a 'seat of the pants' approach to decision-making. This has hurt us in the area of new product introductions which were not as carefully thought out as they should have been. Yet our underlying strength is our ability to react quickly and serve our customers. We've already added a lot of systems and controls. I don't want to lose the 'entrepreneurial spirit' that has made this company what it is.

Art

> We don't need any more layers of management than we already have. We have plenty of good ideas and the people to implement them. Sure, we've made some mistakes but we've had some great successes too. In a business like this, you *have* to be willing to take risks – and we do. With a lot of ideas, you just don't know which ones are going to be successful until you try them out.
>
> Our existing product line can easily support 15 per cent growth. We have excellent sales and marketing systems in place, and once we find the right product, we should have no problem selling it.

Lois

> As we have grown, we've gotten further away from our customer. It disappoints me to look at our income statement and not see the kind of percentage gains we saw in the early and mid-1970s. James and Art have built an incredible business over the course of twenty years; I've contributed a lot during my fifteen years here. But the next twenty years can't be like the last twenty.

We need to put some systems and structures in place so that we can be more deliberate and analytical about the important decisions. We also need to be training a new generation of management.

And it was in response to the consultant's report and their own sense that there were some important decisions to be made, that the principals decided to meet to discuss their company's future.

Appendix A: Consultant's report – excerpts from interview notes

James Ryan

We need to develop a strategy to grow. We have a lot of unused capacity in this facility, and very high overhead. Acquisitions offer some potential in this area . . . Financially we are quite sound. Our maximum seasonal borrowing needs don't come close to exhausting our credit line. However, as we begin to import more product, this will undoubtedly tie up capital . . . I think we could get into lower-priced, higher-volume lines, but this seems to imply lower quality. We have worked hard to build our reputation as a quality supplier, and taught our people how to make a quality product. I don't want to risk this.

Barry Silver

There are many potentially profitable opportunities for us to exploit. Up until now, we have concentrated on selling custom and 'exclusive' designs. There is a whole world of opportunity out there. We are selling more than a product . . . There is plenty of good quality product overseas in Spain, Italy and Taiwan. This material is far cheaper than the material that we are currently buying in the US. We should be buying more of this.

Lois Price

We have excellent systems and controls in place. Our bad debts are very low . . . One thing that we don't have is a controller or any sort of financial planning.

Art Silver

We are the leader in the traditional/glass segment of the business with a 60 per cent market share. We have really created consumer demand for our product through advertising and merchandising. We should be able to grow this business at 15 per cent to 20 per cent per year . . . We will soon be coming out with a line of track lighting and a line of less expensive merchandise targeted towards the mass merchant . . . We have a great many competitive strengths: we are one of the few firms with a full-time design staff; we are the most aggresssive merchandisers of product; and we have excellent quality, superb delivery and service . . . We would prefer to maintain our existing customer base. Department stores are more trouble to sell than they are worth. They want a better deal, don't pay freight, need more advertising dollars, and generally are a pain in the neck.

Consultant's Memo

TO   :   Atlas Management

FROM :   Steven Evans

DATE :   March 11, 1984

As part of its effort to prepare the company for a possible initial public offering, the management of Atlas requested that I assist in the preparation of a business plan. At the time, it was envisioned that this plan would:

- lay out the history of Atlas;
- detail its current operations;
- present Atlas's objectives, and its strategy for achieving them;
- identify the resources which would be required to carry out these plans; and
- project the financial results which might result.

Based on my discussions with the management of Atlas, I would make the following observations and recommendations:

1. Rather than attempt to document its objectives and strategies as outlined earlier, Atlas should *first* undertake a serious effort to formulate precisely its objectives and strategies.
2. This strategy formulation should be based on:

   - a well-thought-out and detailed statement of what Atlas management's financial and non-financial goals are;
   - a thorough analysis of Atlas's existing business to determine what the company's competitive strengths and weaknesses are;
   - a thorough analysis of the attractiveness of each of the product/market segments which Atlas could potentially serve to determine where opportunities lie; and finally,
   - an evaluation to determine which of these potential opportunities are attractive and represent the best fit with Atlas's own strengths and capabilities.

3. Following this strategy formulation phase Atlas should map out a detailed plan for implementing this strategy including, but not limited to, the securing of:

   - financial resources
   - physical plant and equipment
   - design and creative staff
   - marketing and sales management
   - financial management

- general management
- sources of material supply.

Only after each of these steps has occurred will management truly and realistically be able to document its 'business plan'. These steps will provide the data and analysis necessary for good decision-making. In addition, this process will provide a vehicle for the discussion of important issues and the building of consensus among management which is so critical if the resultant decisions are to be successfully implemented.

I will discuss, in more detail:

- The specific issues which Atlas's management must resolve at each one of these steps; and
- My conclusions as to the course of action Atlas should pursue.

ISSUES

Atlas's management should address the following issues in order to accurately assess its current position and plan its future accordingly:

Objectives

Clearly, any attempt to formulate and implement a strategy must be based on a conception of what Atlas's goals and objectives are. During the course of my discussions with management, I heard a number of goals mentioned or alluded to:

- Achieve 25 per cent to 30 per cent growth in sales for the next 3 to 5 years;
- Maintain quality image: high product quality, excellent service and rapid turnaround on order delivery;
- Maintain focus on 'exclusive' designs.

While any *one* of these objectives is probably attainable, they may not *all* be achievable simultaneously.

It is my sense that the first step in the goal-setting process should be a realistic assessment of what each of the principals of Atlas wants for him/herself. These goals should be laid out in both financial and non-financial, qualitative terms.

From this set of more personal goals can arise a set of objectives for the business. Yet, the range of possible options can only be evaluated once the principals' own desires are known. Rapid growth, for example, probably implies the injection of some additional management. The objective of becoming a public company implies a commitment to growth.

I believe that Atlas has the base of management and financial resources which make continued rapid growth a realistic and attainable goal.

Existing business

Atlas should undertake an examination of its existing operation to determine its own competitive strengths and weaknesses. Such an examination might include:

- A financial analysis to assess sales and profit by product, over time;
- A qualitative assessment of each of the elements of Atlas's business system:
    Design
    Manufacturing
    Marketing
    Sales
    Distribution
    Service;
- A market survey to determine how Atlas is perceived by customers (existing and potential) *vis-à-vis* its competitors on each of the fundamental dimensions of competition:
    Design
    Product Quality
    Service
    Support
    Price
    ???

Such an analysis should unearth the nature of Atlas's competitive strengths, and it is upon these strengths that its strategy should focus.

Potential opportunities

Undoubtedly, rapid growth will require a well-thought-out and carefully executed strategy. Growth will require:

- serving existing customers with new products;
- serving new customers with existing products; and
- some combination of these, for example serving new customers with new products.

This statement is predicated on the assumption that Atlas has virtually saturated its 'existing' product market. That is, Atlas has a dominant share of the product market defined by:

- Colonial/early American style;
- predominantly glass;
- sold through lighting outlets.

Further, it assumes that this *particular* market segment is not growing rapidly to generate the desired level of corporate growth. Both of these assumptions are certainly open to question, and could be resolved through analysis.

If analysis does bear out this assumption, Atlas's growth will have to come from developing new product lines or serving new customers, or both.

Product line opportunities In order to develop an array of potential product line opportunities, one must:

– define the market in general;
– list each of the dimensions which create segments in this market; and
– list each of the ways in which these segments can vary.

For example, if we define the market, in general, as 'decorative home lighting' we can envision the following 'dimensions':

– room of house;
– style of lamp;
– material of lamp;
– kind of lamp (table, floor, fixture, etc.); and
– price/quality.

For each of these dimensions, we can envision a number of different variables:

Room of house
  living room
  dining room
  bedroom
  bathroom
  hall
  kitchen
  outdoors
Style
  Colonial
  traditional
  contemporary
    track
    strip
    other modern
  oriental
Material
  glass
  brass
  white metal
  ceramic
Kind of lamp
  fixture
  wall
  table
  floor
Price/quality
  high
  medium
  low.

This approach creates a huge number of potential product market opportunities. This range of opportunities is expanded even further by looking at the channel of distribution.

Distribution channel opportunities   Conversely, Atlas could attempt to sell its existing product line through a broader range of distribution channels. The range of channels would appear to include:

- lighting/electrical outlets;
- contract sales;
- department stores;
- catalogue houses;
- speciality stores; and
- furniture stores

Conceivably, such an array could create a description of over 3500 potential *different* market subsegments.

Evaluation

Once these opportunities have been arrayed, they must be *evaluated*. That is, each 'cell' that is, high-price/quality ceramic, oriental, table lamps for the living room sold through department stores, for example, must be assessed. The characteristics which will determine the attractiveness of the opportunity are two-fold in nature:

Absolute, i.e.:
  size
  growth
  profitability
  competitors' profile;
Fit with Atlas, i.e.:
  What are the key factors for success (KFS) in market:
    price
    quality
    distribution
    advertising
    service
    design exclusivity;
How do KFS fit with Atlas's skills and resources?

CONCLUSIONS

Based on my discussions with management, I will offer my conclusions on some of the issues I have highlighted in the previous section.

Objectives

I believe that rapid and sustained growth in the order of 20–25 per cent per annum is a realistic and obtainable goal for Atlas:

- The company has the physical plant, and base of financial and management resources necessary to fuel this growth;
- There are attractive opportunities in the market-place which are well-
suited to Atlas's strengths; and
- Management's own desires to enjoy both the challenges and rewards,
financial and otherwise, which are increased by a growth strategy.

I believe that, in order to create a solid base which will carry the company for
many years to come, Atlas's management should focus on building the structure, systems and management staff which are required in a *major* business firm:

- Top management already seems to be stretched. This is not to say that
there is not enough management talent to sustain several years of rapid
growth. Rather, plans must be made *now* to identify potential weaknesses, and develop the people capable of filling important roles in years to
come.
- The pressures on management will only become greater as:
growth continues;
the company expands into other product lines;
the company (perhaps) becomes a public concern.

Existing business

It is easy to identify Atlas's strengths:

- A high quality product;
- Aggressive and innovative merchandising, including advertising and
promotion;
- Customer services, including rapid delivery and the extensive knowledge
of the sales force; and
- Integrity, dependability and trust on the part of the customer.

The company's weaknesses are more difficult to define. I would suspect that one
would be cost; Atlas is not a low-cost manufacturer. Its policies are far more
orientated towards service and quality than to low cost. Therefore, it would
seem unadvisable for Atlas to compete in any market segments where price is a
major dimension of competition.

A final, but potentially more serious, weakness has been alluded to earlier. It
seems that Atlas's management structure and systems have several weak points
now, and that this situation could be exacerbated by growth.

The current problems appear to be primarily in the area of 'product management'. While each of the individual areas (design, sales) appears to function
well, there is a problem in co-ordinating the various information flows and tasks
required to introduce new products.

Another problem may be in the area of financial management. It is unclear
whether the 'controller' function is adequately constituted.

These problems, to the extent they exist, will grow as the company expands
and its products proliferate.

Potential opportunities

Potential opportunities exist in a number of areas:

- Within the home decorative lighting area, the following were mentioned:
  Track lighting
  Porcelain lamps
  Brass
  Bathroom lighting
  Strip lighting
  Lower-priced merchandise
  Import goods
- Higher-priced decorator merchandise
  Quartz halogen-based lighting;
- In addition, certain channels were mentioned as offering potential for lighting products:
  Contract sales
  Catalogue houses
  Mass merchants
  Department stores
  Furniture stores;
- Finally, there exists the possibility of selling products which fall outside the domain of lighting:
  Mirrors
  Decorative arts
  ???

Perhaps, at this point, it is appropriate to comment on the topic of acquisitions. In general, acquisitions do not appear to offer attractive opportunities to Atlas:

- The firm does not need to acquire any physical plant. In fact, having the plant away from the main facility would probably hinder management's ability to control the design, manufacturing and distribution process to the extent desirable;
- To the extent that acquisitions are attractive because they represent a collection of design marketing, etc., talent, there would seem to be less expensive means of acquiring this talent than purchasing the entire firm.

Evaluation

Once potential opportunities have been identified, they need to be evaluated. In discussing potential product lines, several important dimensions were discussed.

First, all of the potential distribution channels were found to be attractive by some individuals. There was controversy over the appropriateness of contract sales ('pay-offs required') and department store sales (too tough to deal with). Of course, these impressions are based on Atlas's existing product line. For new product lines, certain distribution channels may be more or less attractive.

There are also some conclusions which can be drawn about potential new product lines:

- Brass: one competitor is already competing with a high-quality/premium price strategy and doing very well. Atlas would seem well-advised to focus its resources on a market where there is not a dominant firm using the same high-quality/premium price strategy as Atlas;
- Track lighting: attractive, large and growing market – Also appears to be poorly served by existing competitors;
- Lower priced merchandise: undoubtedly a large market, but unclear as to strategy required to succeed. Some question about the advisability of introducing lower-quality merchandise into a plant which is orientated towards high quality.

Throughout there was an important consideration given to the issue of whether a particular product line would 'get us into new, desirable customers'. Yet it was unclear precisely who those customers were and what products would be successful wedges for Atlas.

Again, the most important influence upon the choice of a product market opportunity should be its ability to own Atlas's existing resources and strengths, as opposed to requiring a new set of skills and abilities.

ACTION STEPS

I recommend that:

- Atlas hire an individual into the Sales Manager position left vacant by Jerry Nelson's death;
- Atlas hire a Controller/Vice President, Finance, responsible for:
    financial and strategic planning;
    capital budgeting;
    financial controls; and that
- This individual, in conjunction with a cost-accounting staff, should also establish a product-specific cost accounting and profitability system to permit Atlas to weed out those products which are not profitable; and that
- Atlas hire two Product Managers to co-ordinate the design, merchandising and support of its product lines:
    one of these managers to be responsible for the existing early American line; and the other, for developing a new product line.

CHAPTER 6

Employment Relations in the Small Firm

John Stanworth and
James Curran

1. Small firm stereotypes

There can be few areas of small business activity less well researched and understood than that of employment relations. This observation is perhaps surprising, on two grounds. First, the job creation potential of the small firm sector often features at the centre of the debate on the role of the small firm in today's economy. Second, the majority of people involved in small business occupy roles as *employees* (including those who hold managerial and/or professional titles) rather than as small businessmen. Yet they are seldom mentioned in any direct sense. Rather, a small business is equated all too often with a single individual – the owner-manager.

  Two stereotypes have dominated views on employment relations in the small firm and these are worth examining initially before passing on to look at the more complex, though more plausible, everyday reality of working relationships in the real world of the small firm. First comes the view of the small firm as a 'sweatshop' which involves an exploiting employer offering poor conditions in return for low wages and long hours of work, and replacing any worker who either objects to the wages and conditions or cannot meet the output targets set. This stereotype has been particularly associated with certain industries such as clothes manufacture (the 'rag trade') and usually marks the presence of fierce competition amongst firms resulting in intense pressure on wages and working conditions. Of course, there *are* sweatshop firms but they appear to be in the minority and the limitations of the managerial strategies they embody are obvious. Employee goodwill, commitment and ingenuity are valuable assets to any enterprise and are less likely to prevail under sweatshop conditions. Further, sweatshop firms are likely to acquire an unsavoury reputation which is unlikely to enhance the personal status of those who own and manage them.

By way of contrast, the second stereotype posits the small firm as the centre of an almost Utopian social setting involving highly satisfying and conflict-free relationships. Everyone in the firm relates to everyone else in a friendly manner; the owner-manager knows all employees person-ally and takes a close personal interest in their welfare. The Bolton Report adopted this view:

> In many respects the small firm provides a better environment for the employee than is possible in most large firms. Although working conditions may sometimes be inferior, most people prefer to work in a small group . . . The fact that small firms offer lower earnings than larger firms suggests that . . . generally the non-material satisfactions of working in them, more than outweigh any financial sacrifice . . . In a small firm an employee nor-mally may, if he wishes, speak to the owner himself. In a large firm problems of communication arise and some kind of organisation to represent employ-ees' interests is necessary.[1]

Perhaps the best-known formulation of such ideas was that of Schumacher[2] whose somewhat romantic view of social relations in the small firm is summed up in the catch-phrase 'small is beautiful'. How-ever, industrial relations experts themselves have usually been sceptical of this simplistic stereotype and, in a much quoted article, Henderson and Johnson argue:

> The belief that all is well in small firms' industrial relations seems to be based on the simple, but fallacious, reasoning that because large size and complexity of organisation can create problems, smallness and simplicity automatically eliminate them . . . because of the enormous diversity of small firms any generalisations about their industrial relations are likely to be either plain wrong or so broad as to be pointless.[3]

However, this is not to deny that many small firms will have common features by virtue of being small, albeit intermeshed with industrial-subculture influences as well as a range of other factors reaching from entrepreneurial management styles to historical and market factors. Research conducted in the post-Bolton era has resulted in a rather more complex view of social relations in the small firm which attempts to take into account this range of factors and combines both the 'top down' view adopted by the Bolton Committee with the 'bottom up' perspective of the employee.

2. The entrepreneurial quest for independence

Given that, in the small firm, there are usually very few managers and that ownership and control is often concentrated very closely in the hands of a single person – the owner-manager – it should not be surprising that the psychological make-up, attitudes and values of that one person can have an enormous impact on the enterprise's organisational framework, policies and social relations. The psychological profile of the owner-manager offered by the Bolton Committee has been broadly supported by a considerable amount of other research and offers a picture which needs to be kept in mind later when the nature of social relationships is dealt with more specifically. They described the underlying motivation in terms of the need to 'attain and preserve independence':

> This need for 'independence' sums up a wide range of highly personal gratifications provided by working for oneself and not for anybody else. It embraced many important satisfactions which running a small business provides – the personal supervision and control of staff, direct contact with customers, the opportunity to develop one's own ideas, a strong feeling of personal challenge and an almost egotistical sense of personal achievement and pride – psychological satisfactions which appeared to be much more powerful motivators than money or the possibility of large financial gains.[4]

In turn, these dominant psychological characteristics of entrepreneurs and small-firm owner-managers have been repeatedly reported as manifesting themselves in a distinct managerial style. Kets de Vries, in a summary of much of the available literature, argues that this managerial style is autocratic, impulsive, egocentric and essentially unpredictable. Forward planning is limited to the short term and relations with employees are highly particularistic:

> What we frequently encounter in an entrepreneurial organization is an organizational structure and work environment completely dependent and totally dominated by the entrepreneur . . . We are also faced with an individual who refuses to delegate, is impulsive, lacks any interest in conscious, analytical forms of planning, and engages regularly in bold, proactive moves . . . [which] . . . make for the initial successes and may contribute to the continued success of the enterprise, but due to the absence of a conscious planning effort also carry a high risk component . . . Within the organization power depends on the proximity to the entrepreneur, is constantly changing and creates a highly uncertain organizational environment. This state of affairs contributes to a highly politically charged atmosphere where changing coalitions and collusions are the order of the day.[5]

Kets de Vries goes on to argue that job descriptions and job definitions are poorly defined, contributing to a high incidence of role ambiguity and role conflict. This, finally, leads to low levels of job satisfaction, and 'withdrawal or avoidance' behaviour among employees becomes symptomatic. Of course, we must beware of over-generalisation here. There is no single entrepreneurial or owner-manager type and, in practice, behaviour will usually result from a subtle interaction between entrepreneurial personality, type of economic activity, age of the enterprise, level of success and whether the small firm executives are first generation entrepreneurs or those who have inherited ownership. None the less, the above picture has emerged from repeated studies of the small business and must now be regarded as approximating to the most 'typical' pattern. This is perhaps not surprising considering the owner-managers' motivational and personality patterns discussed above. In addition, they are not usually very well educated or trained in managerial skills. For example, the Bolton Report showed that, amongst their sample of manufacturing small firm chief executives, 71 per cent had no higher education and only 1 per cent had any form of management qualification.

In addition to the impact which the small businessman himself can have on employer–employee relations in the small firm, there are influences stemming from the operation of the labour market. Economists and others[6] developed theories in the 1970s based on the notions of 'dual' labour markets, or labour market segmentation. Basically, such theories suggested that large firms had particular preferences for certain types of employees – well-qualified, experienced, married rather than single, with stable work histories and, where appropriate, members of relevant trade unions or professional associations. For such employees, large firms were prepared not only to pay well but also to offer a wide range of fringe benefits and opportunities for career advancement within the enterprise.

Small enterprise, on the other hand, could not match the reward packages of the larger companies and were unlikely to be able to offer many internal career opportunities. As a result, small firms were inclined to recruit from a 'secondary' labour market rather than compete with large firms in the 'primary' market. Small firms generally tend to recruit younger, less well-qualified and less experienced employees often with unstable work histories. In some ways, owner-managers tend to adjust to this situation since their recruitment policies are more personalised or particularistic. Whereas large firms use bureaucratic recruitment procedures emphasising credentials and hard evidence of previous achievement, small-business owners are typically more willing to back their personal judgement of a job applicant and to attach less importance to paper qualifications or previous work record. Owner-managers tend to look for people who will 'fit in', and trade union members, for example, are often rejected because of the owner-manager's dislike of unions which, he feels, may reduce his much valued independence.

Obviously, the divide between large and small firms into primary and secondary labour markets has never been absolute and may become increasingly complex as a result of the current recession and economic restructuring. For example, high-technology small firms, growing rapidly and requiring the cream of scarce specialised skills, have often needed to enter the primary labour market and adopt primary labour market strategies. On the other hand, large firms seeking low level labour skills in areas of surplus, have traditionally encountered reduced pressures to adopt primary labour market strategies.

3.   Job satisfaction and social relations in the small firm

There appears to be a widespread popular acceptance of an inverse relationship between size of firm and job satisfaction among employees at all levels. The small firm is seen as offering a higher level of job satisfaction compared to the large firm and as being especially superior in relation to intrinsic aspects such as satisfying social relations (both with fellow workers and superiors), more varied and interesting work roles, and opportunities for identifying with the enterprise as a whole.

Academic literature reviews of this topic have been inclined to follow the above view, albeit not without qualification. An examination of the studies cited to support the above view[7] identifies a comparatively small number of studies that are repeatedly mentioned. Most of these were published more than a generation ago and adopt methodological strategies and associated levels of conceptual sophistication which are poor by modern standards.

One of the most sophisticated theoretical approaches to the question of worker involvement in the small firm is that of Ingham.[8] He argued that, as work experience lengthens, workers develop a distinct set of orientations which, other things being equal, results in self-selection into work environments congruent with those orientations. In job satisfaction terms, Ingham argued that the typical small-firm worker placed great emphasis on intrinsic aspects of the work task and social relations within the firm. Equally, he argued, the small firm offers job rewards of a positively intrinsic character involving opportunities for greater job involvement and socially and psychologically satisfying relations with others. Conversely, the rewards profile of the large firm which offered relatively high extrinsic rewards (monetary and material rewards) but low levels of intrinsic rewards, would not be attractive to these workers but, rather, would attract workers who defined work in a highly instrumental fashion and sought to satisfy their intrinsic goals mainly outside their work.

Overall levels of job satisfaction amongst small and large firm workers were very similar, according to Ingham. On extrinsic aspects, as measured by monetary rewards, small-firm workers were paid less but their expectations were also lower, so that the experienced level of job satisfaction was similar to those reported by large firm workers. On intrinsic aspects, as measured by perceived opportunities for using abilities to the full, results were rather more mixed. Small-firm *semi-skilled* workers were much less satisfied than their large firm counterparts; they had very high expectations on this aspect which the small firm clearly failed to meet. Small-firm *skilled workers*, on the other hand, were more frequently satisfied on this aspect than their large firm equivalents.

Despite the plausibility of Ingham's thesis, subsequent researchers have been very critical since it conflicts with the overwhelming bulk of the literature on occupational placement for the groups concerned. It overstresses the extent to which such workers are likely to develop a single and well-defined orientation to work lasting through time and, finally, it exaggerates the element of choice in job-finding. Other researchers[9] argue that, for most workers, finding a job is less a matter of choice or rational decision-making than the result of a host of influences over which the employee has little control. In a recession, the force of such influences is likely to weigh ever more heavily in the job placement process.

The largest and one of the most recent studies in this area[10] interviewed a large sample of workers and managers from small and large firms in the printing and electronics industries. When asked to identify what they saw as the most important aspect of a job, small-firm workers did indeed come out as more intrinsically-minded than their large-firm counterparts. However, it was found that the small firms in the sample tended to employ younger workers (consistent with a 'dual' labour market strategy) and this emerged as the principal reason for the differences. Single workers in both small and large firms were the most intrinsically-minded. Married workers, given their family responsibilities, were more likely than unmarried workers to stress extrinsic factors. When age was controlled for, the differences between small-firm and large-firm workers disappeared. In fact, once controls were operationalised for age, marital status, and the presence of contract workers, it was the electronics workers (small firms and large) that showed the greater preference for intrinsic job aspects. Hence, discussing small-firm workers without reference to the industry in which they work can lead to misleading over-generalisations.

The research supported the view that peer relations were perceived as somewhat friendlier by small-firm workers than by workers in the large firms. However, when shop-floor workers were asked whether they regarded any of their workmates as *close* friends, a slightly higher proportion of large firm workers claimed to regard a fellow worker as a close friend, though small firm workers were more likely to see close friends outside work as opposed to merely *at* work. The differences here were much reduced when marital status was controlled for since the younger small-firm workers were the most likely to see workmates outside.

Although it may be argued that people are thrown more closely together in small firms and are thus more likely to get to know one another, this can highlight disagreements as well as cement good relations. Since the small firm contains, by definition, fewer people, it will also contain fewer people of similar age, outlook, tastes and interests and, therefore, may actually be a less likely source of friends than a larger firm. Lower labour stability rates amongst small firm workers may also be unfavourable to the formation of close personal relations.

On the question of *vertical* social relations, there were no apparent relationships between size of firm and workers' perceptions of their relations with first-line supervisors. While the small electronics firm workers appeared most enthusiastic about such relations, the small printing firm workers were the least enthusiastic. The differences are probably explained by industry subcultures. In printing, the shopfloor worker is, ideally, a 'journeyman' or craftsman, a status gained after a long period of training. In the industrial subculture, the journeyman is autonomous and self-directing and relations with the supervisor minimal. The large-firm printing department approximates most closely to this since the supervisor has less opportunity to violate this ideal. The department tends to be specially bigger and workers more highly skilled, thus requiring less supervision than in the small firm.

In the electronics industry, on the other hand, organic organisational structures are more typical[11] and there is a relative absence of sharp distinctions between shop floor and management. Supervisors are frequently used in a consultative capacity as a technical resource by workers and the nature of interaction is more relaxed and less authoritarian than is typical of much of manufacturing industry. The ideal 'consultative' relationship is, however, more likely to be realised in the small firm since the larger size of department and span of control in the large firm makes it more difficult for workers and supervisors to achieve this consultative relationship fully.

On the question of relations with owner-managers, rather less than one in three shop-floor respondents felt they knew their owner-manager 'very well' or 'fairly well'. The figure was well *below* this for the electronics workers since, in a market-orientated industry of rapid technological change, owner-managers are heavily constrained to adopt an 'external' orientation, leaving less time for interaction with the shop-floor.

Whilst the above findings suggest that the closeness of social relations between workers and owner-managers in the small firm is easily exaggerated, there may well be a tendency to exaggerate the impersonality of worker–management relations in the large firm. The fact that large-firm workers often identify with the department in which they work rather than the firm as a whole strengthened relations between workers and their immediate managers in the large-firm sample.

A further indication on the social relations issue was a question on whether respondents viewed industry in 'teamwork' or 'conflict' terms. Like Batstone[12] before them, the investigators found little difference between the samples on this point. Unexpectedly, perhaps, the large-printing-firm workers, the most unionised subsample, were also the most likely to opt for a teamwork view while the large-electronics-firm workers, of whom less than half were union members, offered the lowest level of support. It appeared that 'teamwork' here was defined, by respondents, not so much in terms of consensus as in terms of participation via collective bargaining strength.

4. Managerial and professional employees

It has also been suggested that certain kinds of employees, for example highly qualified and professional people, will be reluctant to work for small firms as small firms are often unable to offer the rewards and career progression opportunities available in the larger firm. Also, such staff may feel that experience gained with a household name company in industry or commerce will carry more weight when they subsequently offer themselves to other employers.

Unfortunately, there is relatively little evidence to indicate the strength of these points but that which is available does support them broadly.[13] One study[14], reported that almost half of the small and medium-sized enterprises in the research sample employed no professionally qualified staff at all. Some respondents also indicated that they were reluctant to encourage managerial staff to develop their skills for fear they would leave and start up their own businesses as competitors.

Owner-managers hiring professional or highly qualified staff for the first time are often reluctant to delegate full authority and responsibility to the newcomer(s): having previously been responsible for tasks themselves, they find it difficult to abandon them to others. Equally, new entrants often felt they must demonstrate their expertise by reorganising the area of the organisation for which they have assumed authority. The owner-manager may well take this as implicit criticism of his previous efforts, leading to friction with the new employee.[15] In addition, functional experts are often 'cosmopolitans'[16], whose commitment to their specialist skills may override their commitment to any particular firm. In the extreme case, their current employer is regarded merely as a stepping-stone in their career, to be rejected when further possibilities for career advancement occur elsewhere. Unless the owner-manager can master this new situation by delegating authority to specialists (thus relinquishing an element of personal independence), integrating his longer-standing managers with his new specialists, and coping with the occasional loss of specialists, a quest for growth may be transformed into a battle for survival.

5.   Size and unionisation

An interesting debate has ensued for some time concerning correlations between size of firm, likelihood of unionisation and levels of conflict as evidenced by levels of strike activity. Some observers have heralded the statistics here as firm evidence of the superior industrial relations in small firms as compared with big. It is interesting, though, that the people most convinced by the figures in question are almost inevitably non-industrial relations specialists. Expert opinion, from the Commission on Industrial Relations onwards, has tended towards an alternative explanation of the data.[17] For example, Rainnie and Scott take the view that:

> Low rates of unionisation are . . . taken as a proxy measure of harmony. One should of course be most careful not to confuse correlation with causality. (There is a statistical correlation between the number of fire engines attending a fire, and the amount of damage caused by that fire. No one would make the mistake in saying that fire engines *cause* fires; yet the correlation between size of firm and strike proneness and unionisation rates, *is* all taken as causal.) More significantly, other statistics, which would equally act as proxy measures, are often neglected as evidence for potential conflict and these include figures for rates of pay, incidents of accidents, labour turnover and references to industrial tribunals for unfair dismissal.[18]

There are several reasons why one should not expect any segment of industrial or commercial life to be a bed of roses and one such feature is economic vulnerability, as Henderson and Johnson point out:

> For a variety of reasons, including the competitive nature of the industries which attract new small firms by their ease of entry, and their generally low cash reserves, many small firms are likely to be under pressure economically

with obvious implications for their employee relations . . . [also] . . . they are often overloaded with everyday matters and thus have little time or inclination for a planned approach to their role as employers.[19]

In any case, there is now a substantial body of research and theory which points towards a rather different picture of small-firm industrial relations than is suggested by either of the earlier stereotypes. First of all, the use of statistics relating to strikes or other overt forms of industrial conflict expressed as a measure of overall levels of conflict in the enterprise suffers from several drawbacks. Strikes or other collective expressions of employee protest represent only some of the forms such conflict may take and, indeed, may be relatively infrequent overall compared with individual expressions of disagreement. For example, labour turnover is probably a much more common expression of conflict, particularly in industries or firms with low levels of unionisation.

Where an employee finds himself or herself seriously at odds with his or her employer, staying on may be rather difficult. The employee may leave or the results may be dismissal. In a unionised firm, the employee may turn to a shop steward or other union official to negotiate on his or her behalf or to provide support in a dispute with management but where there is no union, this option is not open – nor is a one-person strike likely to be very effective. A recent detailed study of labour turnover bears out the above and provides evidence that, amongst firms in the same industries, labour turnover is substantially higher in small firms[20], as are dismissal rates. [21,22]

Small firms are environments in which people are likely to interact closely on a face-to-face basis, creating opportunities for friendly relations and strong personal links but, equally, the same conditions offer greater opportunities for interpersonal conflict. In large organisations, those who 'don't hit it off' can more easily avoid each other since departments or sections are that much larger. Alternatively, there may be opportunities for internal transfer so that contact is reduced. In a small firm, these solutions are less readily available, often leaving only one alternative, to leave, for either or both of those involved.

Evidence on the process of unionisation lends itself to an alternative explanation, which suggests that unionisation is a natural development of the growth process of the firm itself and seems to be mainly the outcome of two interrelated processes:

1. The development of group consciousness on the part of workers who share similar work situations. As the firm grows, it produces groups of workers who do similar jobs and who come to see advantages in acting collectively.
2. The standardisation of conditions of employment by management as

a strategy to ensure orderly management–worker relations and avoid charges of favouritism and victimisation, and so on.

Other factors such as the extent of unionisation in the particular area of the economy, prevalent government attitudes, attitudes towards union participation in the local economy, as well as the state of the economy, may all play a part, but are secondary to the two above processes.

Though owner-managers often feel inclined to resist strongly the onset of unionisation in their firms, some industrial relations experts claim certain advantages associated with the more formalised or bureaucratic conduct of industrial relations issues which that implies.[23] For example, it is claimed that the more formalised set-up provides a more efficient means for the resolution of employment problems as a result of employee grievances being more openly expressed. Without such channels, dissatisfactions may fester and lead either to a deterioration in morale or the loss of valued staff. Also, union representation allows employees to raise issues in an impersonal way and without fear of subsequent discrimination – the focus rests more on issues than on personalities. Otherwise, as Henderson and Johnson point out, the individual has no support in raising issues directly with his employer. The employer can be so subjectively involved in the business that he is unable to conceive that anything may perhaps be wrong. Alternatively, he may simply resent what he regards as interference in the running of the firm which he sees as his personal possession: 'Such an employer may have the interests of his employees at heart, but is not necessarily the best judge of them'.[24]

One reason why trade unions may be reluctant to invest heavily in attempting to organise workers in small firms is that small-firm employers are often very unwilling to concede union recognition and will often go to considerable lengths to resist it. Spectacular examples of employer resistance to trade unions in recent years are the Grunwick dispute in 1976 and, more recently, the disputes between Mr Eddie Shah and the National Graphical Association. Changes in trade union legislation in the 1980s have reinforced employer resistance by making it more difficult to insist on recognition. So, faced with the likelihood of stiff employer opposition, trade unions have a further reason for not embarking on a small-firm recruitment campaign. In addition to this, of course, any successful campaign to unionise a small firm is going to lead to only a minute net gain in membership.

Small-firm employees themselves do not appear to be anti-trade union despite their lower propensity to be union members. Research indicates that, like most British workers, small-firm employees are not especially 'ideological' about trade unions, one way or the other. For example, the largest study of its kind in this area found that, although the majority of non-union members did not think it would be a good idea if their present firm became unionised, many indicated that they would join if it did. In fact, only a minority – just over 15 per cent – disapproved of unions as such.[25] Thus, it appears that many small-firm workers, whilst not wishing to become directly involved in the difficulties associated with initially establishing a union presence in an owner-managed small firm, would not be averse to joining one if a formal presence were established. It was noticeable in the study in question that some employee respondents had previously been members of trade unions but had let their membership lapse whilst working in a non-union firm on the essentially instrumental basis that they would otherwise have been paying for benefits they were not going to receive. This, once again, indicates the non-ideological attitude towards trade unions which most workers in Britain adopt.

In some industries such as printing, furniture and footwear, unions are strongly present even in small firms and, against that, managements tend to be highly organised in terms of membership of employers' organisations. Just as unionisation increases with size of organisation, on the other side of the fence, so does managements' involvement in employers' organisations. Bolton found that membership of an employers' association was very positively correlated with size increasing from 31 per cent in those with 1 to 24 employees, to 63 per cent in those with 25 to 99 employees and, finally, to 77 per cent in those employing 100 to 199. A Commission on Industrial Relations study on employers' organisation claimed:

> Many very small firms do not join [employers'] associations because they do not want to be bound by agreements which may set unacceptable obligations, or because trade union organization in their company is low and likely to remain so, or because they do not require the services provided by the associations, or sometimes because they simply cannot afford membership subscriptions.[26]

Employers' associations, like their trade union counterparts, do not make strenuous efforts to recruit these firms and in many industries characterised by a large number of small firms, for example, clothing and road haulage, membership density is low.

6.   Employment legislation

A notable feature of the debate on the job creation potential of the small firm in recent years has been the effects of employment legislation. Central to the discussion has been the claim that this legislation was inhibiting the expansion of employment in the small business sector. For example, an all-party Parliamentary Select Committee postulated in 1978 that if 'each small business could take one more employee, the unemployment problem would be solved'[27] and called for continuing research into the extent that the Employment Protection Act (EPA) was a deterrent to 'small businessmen taking on additional personnel'.

Although a number of bodies undertook research, the findings appeared to be conflicting. For example, surveys conducted by business pressure groups appeared at odds with those carried out by independent research organisations and funded by the government. A sensitive analysis by Westrip[28] of two independent surveys and four conducted by employer interest groups threw up some interesting observations. For example, her analysis indicated that methodological differences held the key to the contrary claims made for research into the same area.

It is worthwhile at this point briefly outlining the development of the salient piece of legislation – that relating to statutory protection from unfair dismissal introduced in 1971. The background to this development had been the Donovan Report of 1968, which regarded the then existing situation as unsatisfactory. The prevailing legal view of employer–employee relations had seen both as free and equal parties to the employment contract whereby an employer was entitled to dismiss an employee whenever he wished, provided only that he gave due notice. Reasons did not have to be given, let alone justified. The Donovan Commission argued that this situation was unsatisfactory since, in practice, there is usually:

> No comparison between the consequences for an employer if an employee terminates his contract of employment and those which will ensue for an employee if he is dismissed. In reality people build much of their lives around their jobs. Their incomes and prospects for the future are inevitably founded in expectation that their jobs will continue. For workers in many situations, dismissal is a disaster.[29]

The majority of individual rights provisions of the subsequent EPA came into force in 1976, and less than one year later the Policy Studies Institute (PSI)[30] was commissioned by the Department of Employment and the Manpower Services Commission to examine some of the consequences of the legislation on firms employing between 50 and 5000 personnel. Before the results were published, the Department of Employment commissioned the Opinion Research Centre (ORC)[31] to undertake a complementary study of firms with less than 50 employees.

The PSI found 'very little sign . . . that employment protection legislation was inhibiting industrial recovery or contributing to the high level of unemployment by discouraging employers from taking on new people'. Where firms with increasing demand were not recruiting, respondents rarely cited employment legislation as the reason. Increased productivity or spare capacity were by far the major reasons given. Further, whilst 17 per cent of respondents considered that unfair dismissal legislation had had 'a good deal of effect' on their manpower policies, the effects were often very positive, such as improved procedures relating to disciplinary action, selection, recruitment and training.

The researchers also found that, whilst dismissal rates were higher in the smaller establishments, formal complaints of unfair dismissal showed an opposite trend. Then researchers felt that the legislation had had, in fact, more influence on the practice of large firms than on their small firm counterparts, but that it was more *unpopular* in small firms. They 'unequivocally' rejected 'the crude form of criticism' levelled principally by employer-interest groups.

Before the findings of the PSI study were published, the ORC began research on a sample of firms employing less than 50 people, with two-thirds employing 10 or less. Respondents attributed little effect to employment law when asked to list their main difficulties experienced in running their business – only 6 per cent mentioned any aspect of legislation. Issues of much greater concern included financial problems (44 per cent), staff shortages and related problems (35 per cent) and VAT (16 per cent). In a general question on the effect of employment legislation, 7 per cent indicated some reluctance to take on more staff, without prompting. However, when asked *directly*, 24 per cent (71 respondents) said they would have taken on more employees but for the legislation. Yet 56 of these had earlier claimed that they did not find any particular piece of legislation troublesome when confronted with a specific list. Hence, it seems that the form of the question suggested to respondents an effect that they would *not* have raised spontaneously. The researchers cautioned against viewing this prompted response in isolation, yet it is precisely this type of question that is generally used in surveys conducted by employer interest groups, as Westrip shows in some detail in her analysis.

Another key finding from the ORC study was the low level of understanding of the details of the legislation. In fact, no single respondent could correctly answer six straightforward questions, and only 24 per cent were able even to answer correctly a question on the statutory unfair dismissal qualification period.

The researchers concluded that their results countered the suggestion that the legislation was having massive and widespread effects on small firms. It was somewhat surprising, therefore, that one year after the preliminary results were made available to the Department of Employment, the Under-Secretary of State for Employment was able to proclaim 'overwhelming evidence that the present provisions frustrate and unreasonably curtail the creation of jobs'. Further, it was claimed that surveys 'undertaken by employers' organisations' showed convincingly the deterrent effect on employment. The fact that these surveys used leading questions, seemingly to indicate the type of replies required, and that they were based on low response rates from their own membership groups (hence being doubly self-selecting), appeared not to interest key political decision-makers in debates leading to legislative changes reducing the prevailing levels of employee protection.

Westrip, in a concluding remark to her analysis, said that 'many owner-managers appear to regard the legislation as a challenge to management prerogatives'. Given that this alone was the main basis for owner-managers' objections, Westrip concluded that changes in the law were unlikely to have any significant impact on levels of employment.

Legislative changes, stemming from the debate to which the above research contributed, did come about, however, and resulted in workers in small firms employing fewer than 21 staff receiving less protection from unfair dismissal than their counterparts in larger firms. This, it might be argued, reinforced the position of the small firm as a secondary labour market employer, putting it at more of a disadvantage *vis-à-vis* the large firm than previously. Added to this is another possible source of disadvantage for the small firm in the labour market. Small-firm employers have successfully ridden out the pressures imposed upon them in the last decade to adopt 'modern' industrial relations techniques and procedures. The rest of the economy, meanwhile, has shifted from the industrial relations of high unemployment and returned to an approximation of a *laissez-faire* economy. Given that it was previously large firms which were obliged, as a result of their high visibility and informed trade union presence, to obey the laws on employment, it could be argued that it will be essentially large, rather than the small, firms which will benefit from relaxations in the law and enjoy the greater flexibility in the use of labour which has traditionally been more pronounced in the smaller firm.

What this chapter has shown is that 'common-sense' views of employment relations in the small enterprise should be treated with caution. A research-based approach, in contrast, reveals that, as with most human relations, there are pluses and minuses for those involved. Some result from the different positions in the organisation that the various participants occupy: owner-managers have often invested not only their savings but a large part of their emotional and physical resources in the firm and may be expected to have a different level of involvement from the employee who may only stay a few months. Other influences on employment relations come from outside the firm and are beyond the control of either employer or employees. In short, analysis of these relations needs to go beyond the obvious if any level of real understanding of the reality of the small enterprise is to be achieved.

Case Study: Premier Printing Limited

The case study setting

Premier Printing is a growing family firm in the South East of England which currently employs nearly sixty people. Its activities range from the production of jobbing printing products and accounting stationery to short-run periodicals and specialist industrial photographic services.

The firm has reached a point where traditional patterns of informal and highly personalised management need to give way to more professional forms of management and more formalised organisational procedures. Attempts by the owner-manager and Managing Director, Julian Holt, to bring this about are proving disconcerting for all concerned, including Holt himself.

Background to the problem

Julian Holt joined his parents' family firm in 1960 after leaving grammar school at the age of eighteen. Not without certain regrets later, he turned down the option to read Biology at university and undertook general administrative duties in the firm 'whilst deciding what to do for a career'. In the event, he got 'sucked into the business', at least partly as a result of pressure from his parents when it became plain that his elder brother, who also worked in the business, was not interested in management and wished only to develop his specialist interest in industrial photography.

Holt found his parents' attitudes towards business to be very cautious and conservative. Much of this he put down to the failure in the 1930s of a small manufacturing firm they had owned. Holt eventually succeeded his father as Managing Director of the business in 1973 at the age of thirty-one. He immediately borrowed money from the local clearing bank to help expand and re-equip the firm and began to increase the size of the firm's workforce, which was around 20 at that time.

Shortly after this, Holt recruited an old school friend, Tony Allott, as a print machine operative – a task he had previously undertaken for another small printing firm. As the firm grew, Holt felt the need for more help with administrative and managerial tasks and he made Allott Production Manager. Though he had never received any professional training for this role, Allott proved very hard-working and was a great help to Holt.

Employment relations within the firm were very informal. Holt was always addressed by employees as 'Mister' Holt, in accordance with the custom originated by his father. Allott, on the other hand, was almost always addressed by his forename, though he personally considered that this was as much due to 'lack of respect' as 'family atmosphere'. Holt prided himself on the informal atmosphere within the firm and the fact that he knew practically all the employees' first names. When time permitted, he often indulged in informal discussions with employees concerning anything from their domestic circumstances to general issues such as what was currently in the newspaper headlines.

He felt that his efforts in this direction were highly valued by employees and contributed towards the maintenance of employee morale.

Against this, the firm experienced both high labour turnover and high rates of absenteeism. Turnover was so high that they were usually understaffed and could seldom afford to turn away anyone who wished to work for the firm. On the question of absenteeism, Holt, on particularly bad days, would look on the black side and say that management should 'count the number of employees present rather than the number absent'.

Premier Printers was a non-union firm and paid substantially below trade union agreed rates and as such, it was seldom able to attract fully trained and experienced printers. This did not worry Holt to the extent that such workers were almost invariably union cardholders and he always avoided knowingly employing union members since he wished to avoid a formal union presence in his firm. In his own words, he didn't want to 'have to negotiate with organised pressure groups' in an organisation which he personally owned. In short, he didn't see why he should share control.

The firm tended to employ relatively young and unskilled workers and to train them in just the specific areas of skill needed to meet the firm's immediate requirements. Many of the people that the firm recruited had a history of frequent job-changing and, in accordance with this, they did not stay very long with Premier Print Limited either – in fact, annual labour turnover ran at 50–70 per cent per annum. There was a hard core of employees who appeared to stay whatever happened but, none the less, the task of constantly recruiting and replacing staff was quite an arduous one. High rates of turnover, combined with the firm's growth, made it difficult to operate the administration of the firm's payments system. There was no formal system of employee grades and payment scales – Holt merely paid people 'what they were worth'. This situation stemmed from the early days of the firm's existence when the workforce was very small and everyone did a different job. Even though this was no longer the case, Holt saw the operation of a highly personalised payments system as justified on the grounds that employees varied greatly in terms of age, competence, experience and domestic obligations.

Increasing pressure

By 1980, the firm employed around 50 staff but still continued to operate in a highly informal manner and the family element was as strong as ever. In addition to Holt and his brother, two of Holt's cousins now worked on the shopfloor and his mother continued to assist with putting up the wages each week. Holt and Allott had found the length of their working week increasing with the firm's expansion; in fact, both often worked a twelve-hour day and Saturday morning working had become almost an institution. Both frequently felt exhausted and their long working hours were a source of recurring domestic pressure. Holt felt that the need for additional management talent was now urgent. Late in 1980, an opportunity arose when Sherwyn Simmons joined them as Sales Manager, taking over much of the quoting and estimating work from Holt who had done it previously.

Simmons was fifty years old and was an ex-Army major who had worked for several years in the reading room at *The Times* before holding a series of managerial posts in small print firms. In 1978, he had set up his own small printing firm to produce accounting stationery. He had some excellent contacts in large company purchasing departments and soon found that he was inundated with work. However, despite this, he lost money and the stress proved detrimental to his health. It was subsequently agreed that Simmons' firm would be absorbed into Premier Printing, at no direct cost to the latter, in exchange for Simmons being offered employment as Sales Manager and being paid a special commission on work from established large customers he brought with him.

By 1982, however, the pressure was worse than ever and Holt resolved to act. Firstly, he set up formal bi-weekly management meetings involving himself, Allott and Simmons. Holt himself appeared quite satisfied with the progress of these but not so Allott and Simmons. They claimed that all important decisions were still made by Holt who 'usually just dropped them in casual conversation'. When Allott and Simmons complained at their lack of personal impact and involvement in key decisions, Holt claimed that he was 'very receptive to good ideas', so Allott and Simmons felt that, by definition, 'good ideas were Holt's ideas'. They also felt that Holt used formal management meetings to quiz them about their own activities and often used this information to check up on them later. In many ways, then, they felt they had lost some of their authority, rather than extending it, as a result of these meetings.

Using consultants

In 1982, Holt said the firm would have to become better organised and more professional if it were to continue to be successful and if the pressures on existing management were to be reduced. To this end, he resolved to explore the use of management consultants. Via contacts he had made through a printing industry employers' organisation, he commissioned a two-day initial consultancy survey and was very pleased with the results, since they spelled out, in general terms, the need for increased attention to issues such as organisation structure, planning and administrative procedures. On the basis of this, he went ahead and commissioned a full-scale consultancy survey. However, he exploded when he read the final detailed report and refused to pay the bill. He claimed that the detailed recommendations for greater professionalism were inappropriate to Premier Printing and were 'just the sort of standardised recommendations for "systems" that consultants hand out regardless of the nature of the client'. Allott and Simmons, however, felt that the reasons for Holt's reactions were far more personal and emotional – that Holt saw the report as a pointed criticism of the way in which he ran the firm.

The firm struggled on though the pressures got worse, if anything. Overall financial performance was quite reasonable and the firm borrowed £50 000 from a venture capital organisation (in a deal which involved the latter in an option for 10 per cent of the firm's shares) and moved to larger, purpose-built premises some three miles away. The move from rented to company-owned premises gave Holt a feeling of considerable security since he felt that, if necessary, he could always live off the rent which such a building could attract.

In January 1986, Holt met a professionally-trained Production Manager from a larger printing company – Nigel Salmon – and was very impressed by his knowledge, experience and obvious enthusiasm. He offered him a job and Salmon accepted. Six weeks later, Salmon joined the firm but amid much consternation, for, whilst Holt felt that the firm had 'outgrown' Allott's abilities, he still felt some loyalty towards him and kept him on. What is more, Allott retained his old title and his old office whilst the new man, Salmon, had the same title but far more modest office facilities – a desk in a small general office. Salmon was formally given responsibility for the production function and told 'to make things happen', though all other aspects of the firm's structure and activities remained completely unchanged, and it was still Allott, not Salmon, who attended the bi-weekly management meetings. Although Allott felt very hurt at what had happened, he found his workload much reduced and, in fact, kept himself occupied with 'various little jobs that would otherwise have remained undone'.

Salmon began trying to make changes but found that the autonomy he had experienced in his previous job was lacking. Whenever he initiated changes, he was overwhelmed with questions from Holt to justify them. Salmon felt that Holt saw any attempts at change as an implied personal criticism of the firm's former systems and procedures. For a while, Salmon subdued his attempts at change only to be criticised by Holt for 'lack of progress'.

Salmon then resolved to resume his attempts at change but to reduce Holt's level of resistance by 'keeping him fully in the dark' and 'just getting on with the job'. This appeared to work for a while, until Holt realised what was happening and countered; whenever he realised that Salmon was in the process of making changes, he would insist that the plans for change were put to him 'for consideration'. 'Leave it with me' was typically the instruction he would issue, followed by an indefinite silence. In these situations, Salmon had usually already embarked upon a process of change and was often past the point of no return. To have stopped what he was doing would have had serious consequences, and yet to proceed appeared to be overstepping his immediate authority since the authority he had been formally given when he joined the firm appeared to have been informally taken away. By use of his quite considerable political skills, Salmon usually managed to survive the tough situations he sometimes found himself in, but he was certainly not enjoying his work at Premier Printing anywhere near as much as he had anticipated.

Personnel procedures

At Salmon's previous firm, up-to-date personnel procedures had been implemented and, four months after joining Premier Printing, Salmon told Holt that the lack of such procedures at Premier Printing was a major cause of concern. He claimed that the firm was at a size where it had to develop a proper job grading scheme with a workable and rationalised payments system. Also, Salmon claimed, it was time to set up a proper grievance procedure. His general view was that Premier Printing operated in an exceptionally amateurish manner and that the kind of employees Holt was used to hiring might not be expensive but nor were they very effective. In addition, the labour turnover rate was twice as high as it should be. Holt, however, was far from enthusiastic and, at this point, a furious debate ensued. 'Why do was need a grievance procedure?' enquired Holt, 'we don't have disputes, do we?' Salmon explained that some of the sackings that occurred in the firm might be eliminated if things were sorted out at an earlier stage by a system of staged warnings and that some of the employees who now left of their own will might not do so if there were channels for them to express and discuss their problems. Holt raised the question of what he saw as the possible threat of unionisation as a consequence of the firm's growth and how this might be countered. Salmon said that he had been used to dealing with unions and that good management usually had little to fear from them. On the contrary, he claimed, at a certain size, it could even be an advantage to management to be unionised and that, in any case: 'You usually get the industrial relations you deserve'.

'Why did you come to Premier Printing in the first place if you thought there was so much wrong with it?' an enraged Holt asked Salmon. 'Because I could see potential for growth and improvement,' claimed Salmon. Holt then played his usual trump card – 'leave it with me' – and both men withdrew to consider their positions, the crisis unresolved.

Case study issues

1. Review the reasons why Julian Holt seeks out change which he feels is necessary and yet resists it at the point of implementation.
2. What options are really open to Holt at the current stage in his firm's development and what would be the likely consequences of each of these?
3. What, if anything, can Salmon do to (a) improve his relationship with Holt and (b) extend his authority and influence to enable him to make the changes he feels are necessary within the firm?
4. Is there any room for Allott in the firm at its current stage of development? If you feel that the answer to this question is 'no', does this mean that the hard work and loyalty of people like Allott are misplaced or should we just take the view that such 'casualties' are a 'fact of life' in business?
5. Were Holt's policies on recruitment and payment of staff really suited to the firm's best interests (a) in the past when the firm was smaller and (b) now at its current stage of development?
6. Why does it appear that unionisation is increasingly likely to occur in firms as they grow?
7. Holt had always wanted a son who could one day take over the business. In the event, he had several daughters who, he assumes, will not be interested in management. Should he automatically make such assumptions? If you feel he is right in so doing, what long-term plans might he make for himself and the firm?
8. Are people like Holt an asset or a liability to a modern-day economy such as Britain?

CHAPTER 7

Franchising

Colin Barrow

1. Introduction

The term 'franchise' covers a wide variety of arrangements under which the owner of a product, a process, a service or even just a name having certain connotations (for example, that of a sportsman) licenses another to make or use something in exchange for some form of payment. This can be either direct, in the form of a fee and/or a royalty, or indirect in the shape of an obligation to buy a service or product in which the licence-holder has some kind of commercial interest. In the UK the 'tied' public house, which has been around for over 150 years, is one example of this type of arrangement.

In the USA, franchising is reputed to have started with Singer Sewing Machines after the American Civil War, when the continent emerged as a vast market, but when communications were too poor across great distances to make centralised distribution effective. The concept was picked up by the motor-car industry, though their problem was more one of establishing outlets to provide display space, back-up service and, of course, to buy the cars. All the manufacturers' money was tied up in plant so they could not finance stock too.

The success of such forms of franchise encouraged numerous imitators from the 1920s to the 1950s, during which time the trend was to rationalise small, locally-based manufacture into national and even multinational entities. This did, however, cause problems of sales and distribution. Local industries, aware of local market conditions, were shown in many cases to have been rather more successful in this respect than 'faceless corporations' located a long way distant. The answer was to recreate, in some way, the virtues of local industry by franchised distribution and licences. From the point of view of the franchisor, these arrangements turned out to have other advantages also over the costly alternative of keeping total control by setting up national networks of salesmen and warehouses to cover a region – and in the post-Second

World War period, overseas countries too. The franchisee was usually more dedicated to the interests of the franchisor, in whose success he stood to share, than many a salaried employee would have been. This was true even when the franchisee was also trading in goods and services other than those for which he held a franchise – indeed, distributorship franchises were often arrangements which placed no great obligation on the franchisor and gave a corresponding amount of freedom to the franchisee.

There are five types of relationship between licensee and licensor which can be described as franchises.

A distributorship For a particular product, such as a make of car or whitegoods such as washing machines, cookers and refrigerators. A distributorship is sometimes confused with an 'agency', which is a quite different legal relationship. An agent, even though he is not employed by a principal, acts on his behalf, and what the agent does, says, or represents to third parties is as binding on the principal as if they were employer and employee. A distributorship, however, is an arrangement where both parties are legally independent, as vendor and purchaser, except that the purchaser, in exchange for certain exclusive territorial rights, backed up by the vendor's advertising, promotion and, possibly, training of his staff, will be expected to hold adequate stock and maintain his premises in a way that reflects well on the vendor's product or service.

A licence to manufacture Granted for a certain product within a certain territory and over a given period of time, including having access to any secret process this involves and using its brand name in exchange for a royalty on sales. This arrangement resembles a distributorship. Licensor and licensee are independent of one other, except that the licensor will no doubt insist that the licensee complies with certain specifications as regards content and quality in order to preserve the good name of his product. This arrangement is often found in industry and two well-known recent examples have been the Rank Organisation's licence to produce the photocopying devices pioneered by the Xerox Corporation, and the licences granted by Pilkington's for their revolutionary plate-glass manufacturing process.

The use of a celebrity name To enhance the sales appeal of a product and guarantee, at least by implication, its quality. The most common example is the endorsement, by a sports personality, of equipment associated with his activity and bearing his name, in return for a royalty payment by the manufacturer. Examples of this include Arnold Palmer golf clubs and Steve Davis snooker sets. (So lucrative can this activity be, that a company, Matchroom, has been floated on the Unlisted Securities Market, whose main asset is the rights to four snooker players' names.)

The use of a trade mark   Here a widely recognised product is exploited commercially for a fee and subject to certain licensing conditions, rather than the name of an individual. A recent instance is the advertising of various microcomputers as being IBM compatible, always shown with the symbol 'TM' (for 'trademark') beside it. Yet another example of licensing a trademark is that of the ubiquitous use of the Dolby system in most cassette tape recordings.

Business format franchising   Although all these forms of franchising continue to flourish, Business format franchising has emerged as the dominant and the most rapidly expanding mode. Business format franchising incorporates elements from all the earlier ideas and combines them in a way that is particularly suited to current circumstances and economic conditions. Its main features are:

1. It is a licence for a specific period of time to trade in a defined geographic area under the franchisor's name and to use any associated trade mark or logo.
2. What is franchised is an activity, usually some form of service, which has already been tried and tested to produce a formula of operating that has been found to work elsewhere.
3. The franchisor provides the entire business concept of that formula (usually called the 'blueprint') for the conduct of operations, and this must be followed by the franchisee. In fast foods, for example, the ingredients of any 'secret' recipes for the type of food being offered are strictly laid down, as are the specifications for the surroundings in which it is served. The blueprint is generally set out in an operating manual which is given to the franchisee when negotiations are completed.
4. The franchisor educates the franchisee in how to conduct the business according to the method laid down in the blueprint.
5. The franchisor also provides back-up services in order to ensure that the franchise operates successfully. This should certainly cover advertising and promotion of the franchise's name in general and may also cover promotion of the particular franchise in its locality. It can cover many other aspects: ongoing business advice, including help in raising finance, market research into the viability of a particular location for trading purposes, assistance with negotiating leases and obtaining planning permissions, site development, the provision of building plans and specifications, a standard accounting system – virtually anything connected with setting up a new business.

6. In exchange for the business blueprint and the services the franchisor provides, the franchisee is expected to make an initial investment in the business and to pay a royalty to the franchisor thereafter, based on turnover or profits. There may also be an obligation on the franchisee to buy some or all goods and equipment from sources nominated by the franchisor.
7. The participation of the franchisor in setting up the business does not mean that he owns it. It belongs to the franchisee and he is free to dispose of it, though he will probably have to give the franchisor first refusal and obtain his approval of the person the business is sold to, if the franchisor does not want to take it off his hands.

Pyramid selling   This is often confused with franchising in the minds of the uninitiated, a mistake that has done much to harm the reputation of franchising in general and business format franchising in particular. That both pyramid selling and franchising operations have been in the hands of unscrupulous owners whose main objective has been to defraud the 'franchisees', is not in dispute, but there the similarity ends.

Pyramid selling is a form of multi-level distributorship which typically involves the manufacture or sale by a company, under its own trade name, of a line or products through 'franchises' which appear to be regular franchise distributorships. The pyramid may include three to five levels of non-exclusive distributorships, and individuals may become 'franchisees' at any level of entry. Once in, the individual earns a commission by selling the company's products, but at higher levels in the pyramid it is made more attractive to introduce new members.

The product is sold down the chain at progressively higher prices, until the final person has to sell to the public. Since most people make a profit by merely being a link in the chain, the emphasis is placed on recruiting more investor/distributors, rather than on selling to end customers, so the schemes, like chain letters, are lucrative for those at the top of the pyramid. But inevitably the market becomes saturated, and no further participants can be recruited – and the system then collapses.

Contrary to popular opinion, pyramid selling is not illegal in the UK. It is, however, controlled by the Fair Trading Act 1973 (Section 118) and the provisions of the Consumer Credit Act 1974 and it is expressly excluded in the American Franchise Association's Code of Ethics.

2. The growth of franchising

The USA is the world's largest business format franchising market. In 1984, sales by the 1700+ franchisors exceeded $120 billion, compared with $100 billion in 1982 and $90 billion in 1981. Over 300 000 establishments existed compared with 260 000 in 1981. Large franchisors, those with 1000+ units dominate the business format market, with 57 companies accounting for 55 per cent of all outlets.

Although viewed as a safe way into business, a total of sixty franchisors, operating 2000 outlets, failed in 1982. However, their turnover of $244 million represented only a fraction of a per cent of all business format sales. There is also evidence that franchisees are in general, satisfied with their investment. Of the 11 515 franchise arrangements that came up for renewal, 89 per cent were renewed and 1237 were not. Of those, 245 were not renewed because of objections by the franchisor, 737 because the franchisee did not wish to renew, and 255 by mutual agreement.

The UK also has a large and growing business format franchising industry: in 1985 some 220 franchisors operated over 8000 outlets, generating sales in excess of £1 billion, and employing over 70 000 people. Three major markets account for two-thirds of all UK franchises: home improvements and maintenance companies represent 31 per cent; food and drink, 18 per cent; and business services, 17 per cent. The split by turnover reveals a somewhat different picture: food and drink accounts for 29 per cent; business services, 21 per cent; and home improvements, 10 per cent. In terms of concentration, 5 per cent of franchises account for 35 per cent of total franchise units and over 50 per cent of sales value.

Franchised outlets have trebled since 1980 and the growth in sales turnover has consistently out-performed the growth in both retail sales and consumer expenditure. By 1990, the forecasters estimate this market to be worth as much as £5 billion or as 'little' as £2 billion (see Table 7.1). The growing maturity of franchising in the UK was signalled by the Body Shop's successful float on the USM, on 16 April 1984.

The international growth league for franchising is headed by the USA, closely followed by Canada and Japan. In Europe, the UK is in close company with France, Belgium and Sweden in the rate of development of franchise networks, and France is second to the USA in the rate of penetration of the UK market by overseas franchisors. Other areas with a significant level of franchise activity include: the Caribbean; Asia (other than Japan); Australia; Mexico; South America; and the Middle East.

3.   The franchisors

From the franchisor's point of view, the advantages to forming a franchise chain are that he does not have any direct investment[1] in an

Table 7.1 Franchising – growth and forecast

Year	Turnover (£M)	% Annual change	Retail sales (£M)	% Annual change	Consumer Exp. (£M)	% Annual change
1980	390	–	57 400	–	137 300	–
1981	450	15.4	62 100	8.2	153 100	11.5
1982	515	14.4	67 100	8.0	168 400	10.0
1983	600	16.5	73 300	9.2	184 500	9.5
1984	750	25.0	79 200	8.0	201 000	9.0
1985 (Est.)	1000	33.3	85 900	8.5	218 200	8.5
1990	2000–5000					

outlet bearing his name (though if he does his job properly, there are indirect costs in training the franchisee and providing adequate promotional and other back-up to ensure the success of the franchise); that the franchisee, as the owner of the business, is more likely to be highly motivated than an employee and more responsive to local market needs and conditions; that he saves on personnel and administrative costs; and that, without direct financial involvement, he may in this way derive some of the benefits of expansion, inasmuch as franchising gives him economies of scale from centralised purchasing and, if he wishes it and it is feasible, some degree of centralised administrative facilities.

The disadvantages are that although the failure of an individual franchise may reflect badly on the franchise operation as a whole, all he can control is the format itself and he can only influence the running of individual operations by pulling the reins on this or that clause in the agreement – the broad terms of which we shall discuss shortly. In extreme cases he may terminate the agreement or at any rate not renew it, but he cannot throw the franchisee out as if he were an employee. He is, therefore, dependent on the willingness of the franchisee to observe the rules and 'play the game', whilst at the same time any failure to do so is equally and perhaps more damaging to the franchisor (and to other franchisees) than to the franchisee concerned, because of its adverse effects on the franchise as a whole.

Another disadvantage occasionally turns out to lie in the curious mixture of dependence and independence that franchising produces. The franchisee is encouraged to think of himself or herself as an independent business entity and to a large extent this is indeed the situation. Nevertheless he or she is operating the franchisor's business concept under a licence for which a fee is payable. There are cases where the franchisee identifies so closely with the particular business he or she is running that the payment of the fee is ultimately resented: the success is felt to be due to the franchisee's efforts, not to the franchise concept or to the franchisor. This is apt to be particularly so if the franchisor adopts a lower profile than he should, either in terms of direct help or in matters such as national advertising. Clearly, of course, the franchisee would be obliged to pay under the terms of the agreement, but a sour relationship is not good for either party, so it is up to the franchisor to maintain his part of the bargain both in letter and in spirit: franchises are a matter of mutual interest and obligation.

Successful franchisors

Unlike many other forms of new enterprise, franchising is predominantly full of success stories. Kentucky Fried Chicken (KFC), begun in 1952 by Colonel Hartland Sanders, has grown into one of the largest fast-food franchise chains, world-wide; McDonald's, started three years later, has overhauled KFC with around 7000 outlets and a presence in most overseas markets; Holiday Inn and McDonald's are both large enough to support their own 'universities' to train and develop their prospective franchisees.

In the UK, Anita and Gordon Roddick have taken their Body Shop venture from a leaky shop in Brighton via franchising, to a public company with an annual turnover of nearly £10 million in just eight years. Like all good ideas, the initial concept was so simple that one now wonders why nobody had previously thought of it. (See the Case Study following Chapter 3 for the full story.) In 1986 the Body Shop announced plans for full stock exchange[2] listing and by then there was a two-year waiting list for the 'privilege' of becoming a Body Shop franchisee. Apart from patience, prospective franchisees also needed $30 000 to invest in the venture.

An equally impressive performance has been turned in by Prontaprint, the North of England-based fast print chain launched in 1971, using a franchising formula that had been tried and tested by others in the USA. With 300 franchised outlets and a market capitalisation on the USM of £12 million, it is one of the largest UK franchisors.

It would be quite wrong to imply that all franchisors succeed; on average sixty franchisors a year fail in the USA, and a dozen or so have failed in the UK over the past couple of years. The two largest UK failures, Zeibart and the La Mama chain (launched by Edward Young of Pronuptia fame), involved well over 100 franchisees, who for the main part were able to continue trading under new owners or as independent operators.

Developing the franchise chain

The central economic benefit of franchising for the franchisor is the ability to expand rapidly, first cultivating and then dominating a chosen market segment, moving at a speed that a conventional firm would find nearly impossible to fund or to manage successfully. This combination of high market share and fast growth can be expected to deliver a good return on investment and a secure, even unassailable, market position.[3] All this depends on the franchisor's ability to develop a successful franchise chain, which in turn depends on getting a number of things right – consistently.

The blueprint must work

What the franchisor should be selling is a proven business concept that is *capable of being replicated*. This requires that the franchisor should set up a pilot unit, from which an operating manual to run future units can be devised and tested. The operating manual must set out how every aspect of the business should be run, from 'making' the product, through accounting and control systems, to recruiting and appraising staff, and to advertising and promotion. Ideally, this business format as set out in the operating manual should then be further tested on a small number of franchisees to confirm that the 'formula' developed in-house is transferable, and only then can the franchisor turn his attention to expanding his franchising chain. It is not surprising that the greatest number of failed franchisors omitted much of this key stage, either because of poor management within their own firm, or as a result of a wholly inadequate capital structure.

Recruiting and training franchisees

Franchising is nothing if not a 'people' business. Finding potentially successful franchisees goes way beyond just identifying people with the requisite amount of capital, and who are prepared to part with their money with the minimum of fuss. This was the practice of 'cowboy' operators; however, the European code of ethics on recruitment set out in Table 7.2 provides for a sounder approach.

Once recruited, the franchisee must be rigorously trained in every aspect of how the 'blueprint' works. McDonald's, for example, insist on a minimum of 200 hours training before they will take on a franchisee. Once accepted, they undergo a further 11 days of basic operations training and two weeks' management training at Hamburger University of Elk Grove, Illinois.

Table 7.2   European code of ethics on recruiting and selecting franchisees

---

Rules governing recruitment advertising

Recruitment advertising will be honest and genuine. It will not contain any ambiguity and should not be misleading in any way. All advertising will comply, both in form and in spirit, with the laws and regulations.

Any recruitment advertising which contains direct or indirect allusions to results, figures or data relating to the income or profits which can be anticipated by franchised firms, will be objective, complete and verifiable, especially with regard to the geographic area and the period to which it relates.

Any information relating to the financial aspects of the acquisition of the franchise will be detailed in all respects and will indicate the total amount of investment required.

Selection og franchise holders

The franchisor will select and accept only those franchise candidates who possess the qualifications required by the franchise. All discrimination on the grounds of politics, race, language, religion or sex, will be excluded from the qualifications.

Territory size and site location

In defining catchment areas, territories and locations it is vital to make sure that the franchisee has a market of sufficient size for him to prosper and expand, but not so generous that he cannot properly service it. This will involve the franchisor in some basic market research covering such aspects as traffic flows, access, population mix by age and class, and so on. In franchises that require a retail site, soundly based and proven criteria for locating those sites is essential. More scrupulous franchisors frequently keep prospective franchisees waiting for up to two years until the right site comes on to the market.

Controlling and motivating franchisees

To some extent, franchisees can be considered to be self-motivating; after all, they own the business. But however careful the selection process, problems are bound to arise and in any event the franchisor will want an efficient system of communicating details of new or improved products and processes. This means that the franchisor must maintain a controlling head-office function with some support staff, troubleshooters and a franchise management team. Their role must include that of making sure the 'blueprint' is being followed throughout the chain, and that it is being continuously updated in the light of experience.

Any failure to support the existing franchise chain is likely to result in a disgruntled and highly vocal group of franchisees making future recruitment difficult. In the USA, a National Franchise Association was formed in 1975 to provide a centre for the expression of franchisees' viewpoints. No such organisation currently exists in the UK, but the bush telegraph works well within individual franchise chains.

Creating a good secondhand market

As the franchise chain develops it is inevitable that some franchisees will want to sell up and move on. The franchisor will normally insist on first refusal – or at the very least the right to approve the prospective purchasers. This process requires careful and sensitive handling as every impediment to a smooth sale has the probable effect of reducing the value of the franchisee's equity in the venture. In much the same manner, the market for new cars is dependent on a vigorous market for used cars that can be seen to hold their value.

The mixed ownership chain

Occasionally, an established business, having made the decision to grow via the franchising route, will sell off some or all of their existing outlets. A recent example is Holland and Barrett. By 1984 they had 150 company-owned outlets but their market research indicated that the UK would be able to support around 2000 health food shops by 1990. To maintain their 20 per cent share of this market they would need a further 300 or so outlets. With three manufacturing subsidiaries to finance in this rapidly expanding market, Holland and Barrett opted for franchising as a way forward in the retail market and as a consequence, a number of 'quality' outlets were put on to the market. This situation can be viewed as a particularly good example of proving the blueprint.

Financing the franchisor

Business format franchising calls for a substantial investment of both capital and management time before the chain can be developed. Unethical franchisors have used franchisees' money to finance pilot operations, product and process proving, and even the writing of the very operating manual that they are supposed to be selling as the formula for success.

Established business ventures such as Holland and Barrett have access to the normal sources of development capital that are open to any growing business, but until 1985 there was no specific source of finance for prospective franchisors. Then Franchise Investors Ltd (FIL) was launched by Granville and Co., the corporate finance group, to provide finance and expertise for franchisors. Its initial capital of £1.25 million is intended to help companies that want to expand by franchising. FIL's backers include Causeway Development Capital, Post Tel Investment Management and Legal and General, which together own about 75 per cent of the equity; the rest is held by Granville & Co. and the founders. It plans to identify and take equity stakes in companies whose business is suitable for franchising. It also intends to buy master licences, probably from North American companies, and develop franchise networks in the UK. With this exception, the City has virtually ignored the franchise market, with the exception of the clearing banks who provide a ready source of funding for franchisees. Even the Body Shop's flotation on the USM only raised £100 000 for the company itself.

4.   The franchisees

From the point of view of the franchisee there are advantages and disadvantages which might perhaps be most clearly expressed in the form of a list.

Advantages

   (i) A business format or product which has already been market tested and, presumably, been found to work; consequently, major problems can be avoided in the start-up period.
  (ii) A recognized name of which the public is already aware and which has credibility with suppliers.
 (iii) Publicity, both direct in that the franchisor advertises his product or services, and indirect promotion through signage and other corporate image promotion in all the franchisor's outlets.
  (iv) Usually a smaller initial capital outlay than if the franchisee was starting up on his own – though franchises which have shown a very high profit record are correspondingly expensive and can run well into six figures.
   (v) Direct and close assistance during the start-up period.

(vi) A period of training on production and management aspects.

(vii) A set of standard management, accounting, sales and stock control procedures incorporated in an operating manual.

(viii) Better terms for centralised bulk purchase negotiated through the franchisor, though he may be looking to mark-ups in this area as a source of revenue from the franchisee.

(ix) Design of the premises to an established scheme saves on interior design fees and may eliminate these altogether where the franchisor has a set of specifications.

(x) The benefit of the franchisor's advice on equipment and initial inventory levels, though this may not be impartial where the franchisor is also the supplier.

(xi) Help with site selection, negotiating with planning officers and developers.

(xii) Possibly, though not universally, access to the franchisors' legal and financial advisers.

(xiii) The exclusive rights to the franchise within a given area.

Disadvantages

(i) Business format franchising is, of necessity, something of a cloning exercise. There is virtually no scope for individual initiative in matters of product, service or design. However, the franchisor will demand uniformly high standards of maintenance, appearance and packaging in whatever the franchise entails and these are usually monitored by regular inspections.

(ii) The fee paid to the franchisor may be a percentage on gross turnover or on profits. The problem here is that if the franchisor is not pulling his weight or if the franchisee does not feel this to be the case, the fee can be a subject of bitter dispute. The franchisee may then feel justified in withholding all or part of it on the grounds of non-performance by the franchisor, but this is always a difficult matter to prove in the courts. Furthermore, the franchisor's resources to conduct a long-drawn-out case will usually be greater than the franchisee's.

(iii) A further problem is that a high turnover does not necessarily imply a highly profitable operation. If the franchisor's fees are wholly or partially based on turnover, he may try to push for this at the expense of profitability.

(iv) The franchisee is not absolutely at liberty to sell the franchise even though he is in many respects operating the business independently: the sale has to be approved by the franchisor, who is also entitled to vet the purchaser and charge the cost of any investigations made to the existing franchisee. Furthermore, although the business would be valued as a going concern in trading terms, the goodwill remains the property of the franchisor. Again, the franchisee may feel that, at least to some extent, the goodwill has been built up by his own efforts. The resale of a franchise, in other words, is a process rich in those grey areas which can lead to expensive litigation.

(v) Exclusive territory agreements may be difficult to enforce in practice. For one thing, under EEC competition laws the franchisor cannot prevent one franchisee trading in another's 'exclusive' territory, though he may decline to licence a competitor within it.

(vi) The franchisee, as well as paying a fee to the franchisor, may be obliged to buy goods and services from him as well – possibly at disadvantageous rates.

(vii) Though the franchisor places all sorts of controls and obligations on the franchisee to maintain the quality of his image, the scope for doing the reverse is more limited. If the franchisor's product or service gets bad publicity, this is bound to affect the franchisee adversely, and there is very little he can do about it. Equally, the franchisor may engage in promotional activities – and involve the franchisee in them as well – which, though perfectly harmless, are, from the point of view of a particular outlet, an irrelevant waste of time.

Mutual dependence

From this list of advantages and disadvantages to both parties a more detailed picture emerges of the business format franchise as a relationship of mutual dependence which allows each party to realise his strength to mutual and, at best, equal advantage. The franchisor is able to expand without further investment and, though the return is obviously lower than from expansion by ownership, he does receive an income from the franchisee as well as getting both an outlet for his product and more muscle in negotiating the purchase of materials and equipment. The franchisee, on the other hand, is able to concentrate his entrepreneurial skills at the sharp end of sales and customer service, while the administrative headaches of setting up the business are mitigated by the uniform nature of the format. By the same token, he is saved, through feedback to the franchisor of the accumulated experience of other franchisees, from making the errors to which businesses are prone in their early, most vulnerable stages. This relationship is expressed in agreements; the purchase agreement and the franchise agreement. It naturally follows that a prospective franchisee must satisfy himself that the franchise on offer is a sound investment. Close questioning of both the franchisor and existing franchisees along the lines of the points raised in this section will help with this appreciation.

5. Popular franchises

Franchise operations fall into three main groups. The simplest form, and usually the cheapest to acquire, is a service which is run from home: an interior design consultancy, for example. Much the largest group of franchises, however, are those which entail acquiring premises, and often a substantial investment in equipment in addition to the initial fee payable to the franchisor: fast food restaurants and print shops are two of the most visible and widespread franchises of this type. At the top end of the market are investment franchises such as Holiday Inn, where the start-up costs run into six figures. There are also some franchises which overlap the second and third categories: a prime Wimpy bar franchise will now also run into six figures. Overall, the range of activities which can be franchised is very wide and some sixty-five have been identified in the USA, ranging from hotel ownership at the top end to a soft-drink bottling franchise with the unlikely name of Cock 'n Bull at the other. There are at the moment at least twenty types of franchise in Britain, covering a variety of fields from fast food to acupuncture.

In the UK, for which statistics are still hard to come by, the largest number of franchisees are in motor vehicles and associated services, food, hotels and restaurants, and the business and personal services sectors (see Table 7.3).

In the USA, much more detailed information on franchise activity by business category is available. There, restaurants are the most popular, followed by automobile products and services, followed by business aids and services. A number of categories such as recreation, entertainment and travel; real estate; employment services; accounting, credit collection and tax preparation; and educational services, are barely visible in markets outside the USA (see Table 7.4)

6. Financing the franchisee

In the USA, the full gamut of venture capital sources is open to franchisee and franchisor alike. This includes assistance from the Small Business Administration (SBA), founded in 1953 for the purpose of providing intermediate to long-term financing for small businesses which could not obtain money on reasonable terms from elsewhere.

In the UK, on the other hand, the City institutions have largely

Table 7.3   Franchising trends in the UK, 1983–84 (by number of outlets)

	1983	1984	Percentage growth
Beauty and health	47	62	32
Building and maintenance	175	244	39
Food, hotels and restaurants	816	949	16
Motor vehicle and associated services	879	999	14
Printing	336	422	26
General retailers	251	325	29
Business and personal services	638	763	20
Totals	3142	3764	20

* Prepared from survey data provided by about half of all UK franchisors.

Table 7.4   Franchising trends in the US, 1981–83 (by number of outlets)

	1981	1982	1983	Percentage growth over period
Restaurants	61 846	65 151	70 500	14
Convenience stores	15 524	16 256	17 231	11
Food retailing	16 171	17 106	18 429	14
Auto products and services	39 616	39 721	41 496	5
Hotels, motels and campgrounds	6 416	6 622	7 350	15
Recreation, entertainment and travel	5 293	5 625	6 000	13
Business aids and services	48 835	49 672	58 608	21
Employment services	4 719	4 772	5 299	
Printing and copying	2 839	3 808	4 352	
Real estate	15 636	16 165	17 698	
Accounting, credit, collection, tax preparation, etc.	22 641	24 927	28 259	
Car and truck rental	7 463	7 863	8 284	11
Equipment rentals	1 635	1 683	1 776	9
Construction, home improvement and cleaning services	14 732	15 600	17 400	18
Laundry and dry cleaning services	3 105	3 178	3 273	5
Educational services	3 914	4 381	5 022	28
Beauty salons	1 650	1 769	1 984	20

* From figures published by US Department of Commerce.

shunned involvement with the franchise industry. Governmental small business financing schemes such as the Loan Guarantee Scheme[4] and the Business Expansion Scheme[5] have at best played an insignificant role in financing franchising, and at worst appear to have been designed specifically to exclude them.

The exception has been the main clearing banks. Five of them: Barclays, National Westminster, Lloyds, Midland and Royal Bank of Scotland, have identified franchising as an important market for them to be in. As well as earmarking some tens of millions of pounds to lend to franchisees, they have appointed managers and special departments to offer both general and specific advice to help potential franchisees evaluate a franchise. The banks have found the market particularly attractive for two reasons. First, lending to franchisees is easier and less time-consuming than lending to individual small businesses: the banks have only to evaluate a specific franchising concept in detail once, to allow them to agree in principle to lend to dozens of franchisees; and the franchisor selects suitable candidates only, to put forward to the bank for financing. Second, much of the start-up finance required is to buy, lease or improve premises.[6] This meets the security criteria that is always high on the clearing bankers' shopping list, when viewing a lending proposition.

The banks have one more weapon in their protective armoury. Normally, a borrower's relationship with his bank is his business alone, but banks have been known to ask franchisees to sign a release when they advance a funding package. This allows the bank to tell the franchisor if they are exceeding their financial limit. Nevertheless this ready supply of funds from the banks has done much to encourage and facilitate the growth of franchising in the UK.

7. Developing the business

Once the potential franchisor has decided that franchising is right for him, has chosen a franchise, and found the money to finance it, what options then lie ahead to develop the business, apart, that is, from doing the present job better?

Extending the product or service range

The franchisee is usually in the hands of the franchisor in this respect. It is unlikely that the average pizza house franchisee would be encouraged to start up a new line in English cooked breakfasts, for example. Corporate identity is a great strength for a small firm, but it also inhibits flexibility, initiative and enterprise. When it comes to introducing new products, the initiative comes from the franchisor, and the chain is expected to march forward together.

Horizontal growth

Many franchisees take on neighbouring territories, once they have satisfied themselves that the business format works. Both the Body Shop and Servicemaster have several franchisees with between two and four shops/outlets each. This has the obvious benefit that the franchisee fully understands the business, but it can pose some problems with geography. Certain franchises, by the definition of the catchment area needed to support them, have to be many miles apart.

The town ownership concept

Not much in evidence in the UK, but popular in some parts of the USA. The concept requires a successful franchisee to take on several different types of franchise in the same town. For example, he could own franchises in fast food, car hire, office cleaning and a beauty salon. This would involve selling more products to much the same people, and reverses the benefits and problems of horizontal growth.

Trading up

This is a variation of the horizontal growth approach, in which a franchisee sells out a small outlet and trades up to a larger one that it is hoped, will generate more profit. Both Wimpy and Kentucky Fried Chicken have two main sizes of franchise outlets that lend themselves to this strategy.

7. Future developments

In the USA, the main growth in business format franchising is expected to come from the following activities: financial counselling services; home repair; insurance; legal service centres; accounting service centres; medical services; dental clinics; and business brokers. Also high on the list are: weight reduction centres; figure control centres; smoking control centres; exercise studios; computers (hardware, software and counselling); and safe-deposit locations. With maturing home markets,

Table 7.5   US franchisors operating overseas

Country or region	Number of franchisors	Number of units
Canada	209	7068
Japan	63	3999
Continental Europe	75	3393
United Kingdom	52	2113

American franchisors are looking for international market opportunities in increasing numbers. At present some 300 franchising companies are operating around 22 000 outlets abroad; Table 7.5 above shows the main geographic split of that activity. In 1986, a further 121 American franchisors indicated that they were looking for opportunities to set up overseas. The interest was expressed mostly by small and medium-sized franchisors, and 'business aids' was the largest market sector to be pioneered. This expansion of American franchisors outside the boundaries of North America will continue. In a mature franchise market such as the USA, exporting is one important way forward.

A look at what is going on currently in the USA reveals some interesting and sizeable gaps in the UK franchise market. (Compare Tables 7.3 and 7.4). In the USA, the new franchise areas are in professional services such as dental centres, insurance agents, lawyers, optical centres and real estate brokers. Obviously, some of these would not be transferable because of the differences in professional controls between countries. In the UK, the most immediate new opportunities look like being in the computerised services such as tax and business services related to the needs of the smaller business; fitness and health centres; specialist retailing; and perhaps even estate agents.

The British Franchise Association (BFA)

The existence of this organisation, formed in 1977 by a number of leading British and international companies[7] engaged in the distribution of goods and services through franchise networks, is expected to contribute to the improved respectability[8] of franchising (and hence marketability and growth) in the UK. Eighty or so of the 200 firms that operate franchise chains in the UK have registered with the BFA, and by implication have agreed to its code of practice, shown in Table 7.6.

The BFA owes at least some of its inspiration to the International Franchise Association based in Washington, DC. Formed in 1960, this organisation represents 350 franchising companies world-wide. There are now Franchise Associations in Belgium, Holland, France, Ger-

Table 7.6   The BFA code of practice

1. The BFA's Code of Advertising Practice shall be based on that established by the Advertising Standards Association and shall be modified from time to time in accordance with alterations notified by the ASA. The BFA will subscribe fully to the ASA Code unless, on some specific issue, it is resolved by a full meeting of the Council of the BFA that the ASA is acting against the best interests of the public and of franchising business in general on that specific issue, in this case the BFA will be required to formally notify the ASA, setting out the grounds for disagreement.

2. No member shall sell, offer for sale, or distribute any product or render any service, or promote the sale or distribution thereof, under any representation or condition (including the use of the name of a 'celebrity') which has the tendency, capacity or effect of misleading or deceiving purchasers or prospective purchasers.

3. No member shall imitate the trade mark, trade name, corporate identity, slogan or other mark or identification of another franchisor in any manner or form that would have the tendency or capacity to mislead or deceive.

4. Full and accurate written disclosure of all information material to the franchise relationship shall be given to prospective franchisees within a reasonable time prior to the execution of any binding document.

5. The franchise agreement shall set forth clearly the respective obligations and responsibilities of the parties and all other terms of the relationship, and be free from ambiguity.

6. The franchise agreement and all matters basic and material to the arrangement and relationship thereby created, shall be in writing and executed copies thereof given to the franchisee.

7. A franchisor shall select and accept only those franchisees who, upon reasonable investigation, possess the basic skills, education, personal qualities and adequate capital to succeed. There shall be no discrimination based on race, colour, religion, national origin or sex.

8. A franchisor shall exercise reasonable surveillance over the activities of his franchisees to the end that the contractual obligations of both parties are observed and the public interest safeguarded.

9. Fairness shall characterise all dealings between a franchisor and its franchisees. A franchisor shall give notice to its franchisee of any contractual breach and grant reasonable time to remedy default.

10. A franchisor shall make every effort to resolve complaints, grievances and disputes with its franchisees with good faith and good will through fair and reasonable direct communication and negotiation.

many, Italy, Norway, Sweden, Switzerland, Canada, Japan, South Africa and Australia.

Case Study 1:   Balloon, Bromley

Eva Loffsted and Diane Gallacher are the enthusiastic but not uncritical franchisees of Balloon's Bromley (Kent) shop, selling fashionable maternity wear and baby clothes. Eva qualified as a dentist and still practises one day a week, and her husband was already in the fashion business. He played a key role in researching the market and finding the site. He knew that Bromley was an ideal place with consumer spending 40 per cent above the national average – but for that reason finding a shop wasn't easy. The site they settled for, a stone's throw from Bromley station, commanded a premium of £30 000 for a £15 000 per annum lease. Diane's husband, a songwriter, managed to get an impressive number of personalities to attend the venture's celebrity launch.

Given Eva and Diane's obvious commitment, intelligence and family support, the question that clearly had to be asked is why they chose to take up a franchise rather than starting up on their own. Eva admits: 'Originally that was what we intended to do. We had an idea for a speciality shop for teenage fashions, but then one of the multiples came along with something very similar and we realised how vulnerable we would be in a small business on our own.' At that particular point she heard of franchising, and of its success rate in getting new businesses off the ground. She read everything she could about franchising and eventually she and Diane came to the conclusion that it was worth sacrificing a certain amount of independence for the know-how that would otherwise have to be picked up via the hard and expensive route of trial and error. The franchise they eventually plumped for was Balloon, a relative newcomer to the UK franchising scene.

The Balloon concept

Until Veronique Delachaux came on the scene on 1971, most fashion designers felt that glamour stopped when pregnancy began to show. Once it did, women were expected to go into full dress purdah cehind garments of indeterminate shape and vague floral pattern: that they were longing for something more flattering was demonstrated by the instant success of Madame Delachaux's first Balloon shop in Paris. Showing her own designs for expectant mothers, it made pregnancy chic with a whole range of dresses, shirts, skirts, trousers, underwear and even swimwear. Her secret lay not only with clever merchandising and the superb cut that gives Paris fashion its own unmistakable quality, but in fact that her designs kept their fashionable line throughout the whole period of pregnancy. This contrasted favourably with other maternity wear which tended to look like outsize versions of something bought in slimmer times.

Balloon itself is part of a huge French group, La Redoute, whose turnover is said to be as large as Marks and Spencer. They opened in the UK in 1981 in Walton Street, a quietly expensive Chelsea backwater where 'Sloane Rangers' do their shopping. By 1983 they were satisfied enough to plan a programme of rapid expansion in the UK – spurred, probably, by the fact that others have seen the potential of an annual market of 450 000 women, all willing to spend money on one of the most important phases of their lives. Mothercare, now owned by Conran, has announced a new range of maternity clothes designed by Jasper Conran. In franchising, Edward Young, who runs the highly successful bridal-wear network Pronuptia, has also moved in to the field with his new La Mama franchise. Balloon, however, feel that, 'When it comes to design there is no substitute for French fashions.'

In January 1984, Balloon began to franchise in the UK. Site location is clearly the key to success in retailing and so the company laid down the following broad guidelines: shops were to have a customer base of 200 000 people, an area of 1000–1200 sq ft including storage space and a minimum frontage of 13 feet. They expected potential franchisees to be able to commit £37 500 to the venture, made up as follows:

Initial Investment

Licence Fee	5 000
Inventory	14 000
Fixtures and fittings	8 000
Legal costs	1 000
Launch	2 000
Training costs	500
Working capital	7 000
	£37 500

Balloon proposed to help with selecting the opening stock and providing fairly generous credit terms: 50 per cent of the first shipment due in three months and the balance after six months. The licence fee would not be due until the contract was signed, which effectively means when a site has been found. The fee includes the services of an architect to prepare plans for layout and interior design. It also includes staff training.

At the time of writing (1984) a 2 per cent royalty was under consideration. Balloon did not propose charging their franchisees a royalty on sales: the almost universally recognised formula by which franchisors are rewarded for marketing and maintaining a successful franchise chain. Their main income was to come from the mark-up on goods, as indeed would their franchisees'. Balloon's projected operating statement for an average shop is set out below:

Balloon Projected Operating Statement

		£
Income:	Sales	90 000
	Cost of Sales	48 000
	Gross Margin	42 000
Expenditure:	Rent and Rates	12 000
	Insurance	800
	Services	1 200
	Repairs	800
	National advertising	3 600
	Local advertising	600
	General and travelling	1 500
	Professional charges	1 900
	Bank charges	700
		22 600
Operating Profit:		£19 400

The expectation on this basis is that the initial investment will be recovered in about eighteen months. Balloon justify ignoring in their calculations any premium that may have to be paid for the shop, arguing that the income from a prime site will be correspondingly greater.

Suggested questions

1. Should Eve and Diane have taken up a franchise or would they have been better advised to go their own way?
2. Does the Balloon concept have the ingredients to make a successful UK franchise chain?
3. Do their figures seem realistically based – both for the initial investment and operating profit?
4. What help and support do you think Eva and Diane should expect from Balloon?
   (a) Now and (b) in the future when a 2% royalty charge is made?

Case Study 2:   Holland and Barrett, Fulham

Getting in on the ground floor of a successful business idea can be very rewarding in every sense, as Paul Geoghegan has discovered. Still in his early thirties, he had had five years running his own business, a sauna and workout area in a hotel near Heathrow Airport, when he read that Holland and Barrett were planning to franchise some of their shops. His wife Susan has a degree in Nutrition, and so, of course, she knew all about Holland and Barrett's products. The fact that one of the shops on offer was in Fulham, an important West London shopping area, made the proposition doubly attractive.

The company and the concept

Holland and Barrett are a major force in the UK health food market with over 20 per cent of all retail sales. Back in 1967 the Company already had 64 outlets, but with their acquisition by Booker-McConnell, the £1000-million-a-year giant, their involvement in this market grew rapidly and by 1984 they had 150 company-owned outlets all over the country from Newcastle-upon-Tyne to Plymouth.

Their prominently-sited shops sell a comprehensive range of health foods, including wholefoods, vitamin and mineral supplements, natural herbal remedies and natural cosmetics. To-day, however, the competition is hotting up. Apart from other specialist shops, even supermarkets now carry shelves of health foods. This does not worry Holland and Barrett boss Ken Mullarkey: 'I think it merely makes people aware of the product. Shops like The Body Shop are complementary to Holland and Barrett since they carry mainly cosmetics and no food lines.' Mullarkey also believes they have another great strategic advantage: 'It's not only that our subsidiary, Associated Health Foods is a major supplier – we also own Brewhurst, the principal national wholesaler of health foods, with 60 per cent of the market. We even have a subsidiary, Newman Turner Ltd, which is the leading publisher of books and journals on natural living.'

Holland and Barrett believe that the UK can support at least 2000 health food shops and they aim to have between 400 and 600 of those by 1990. More immediately, they plan to have 200 shops by the end of 1985 and will be relying on franchising to generate most of their growth. Mullarkey says:

> There are some clear reasons why our form of retailing lends itself more to franchising than some others. There's a strong element of personal service – it isn't a supermarket operation. People come in asking for advice on what products they should buy to achieve a particular aim – like healthy ways of losing weight, for instance.

Beginning with a modest two franchises in 1982, they had 17 by 1984 and a further 25 scheduled to open in 1985. The package on offer to potential franchisees is as follows.

The package

One of the attractions of the Holland and Barrett franchise is that although the concept is an unusually well tested one – they have, after all, been around for a relatively long time – the initial costs are not particularly high. The average investment is said to be around £55 000, of which £5000 is the franchise fee. The royalty is $7\frac{1}{2}$ per cent of turnover paid weekly during the first two years of the agreement, and 10 per cent thereafter. This is naturally a proposition which banks find attractive from a lending point of view, so that up to 70 per cent of the start-up costs can be funded by bank borrowing. The typical deal is that 55 per cent of the money is made available as a term loan and the rest is provided in the form of overdraft facilities to even out cash flow variations.

The agreement runs for 5 years and is automatically renewable. 'It's a fairly standard franchise contract,' says Mullarkey. 'We charge a small percentage of the price when a franchisee sells the business and of course we reserve the right to vet the purchaser, but they don't have to pay a fresh premium for the franchise.'

Site selection

So far, however, no franchise has changed hands in this way and there is usually a wait of three to four months between the time the agreement is signed and the franchisee takes over his or her new outlet. Some of the interval is taken up with shopfitting based on a tried format which encourages customers to browse and then to buy.

The main reason for the wait is the very great importance Holland and Barrett attach to site selection. Mullarkey explains the process: 'We have our own property department which is in constant touch with estate agents who keep a lookout for sites for us. When one comes up it goes through an intensive assessment of its suitability to house a Holland and Barrett shop because not all locations have the kind of socioeconomic mix we are looking for.' An evaluation of that factor is accompanied by a systematic pedestrian traffic count, a check on parking and transport facilities and, of course, the viability and exposure of the site. All these elements are then fed into a computer to see if they combine to give the kind of sales volume projection over the period of the agreement which is necessary to reach profit projections.

Finally, the site is also visited personally by a team consisting of Mullarkey himself, key personnel from the property department and someone who has first-hand knowledge of operational aspects to ensure that nothing is left out of the reckoning.

The actual lease is acquired by Holland and Barrett and then sublet to the franchisee. This is where franchising, when it operates under a nationally recognized name, is so advantageous: 'Landlords are reluctant to let property to business newcomers and if they do they are apt to demand a high rental from them,' says Mullarkey. 'On the other hand, having an established name like ours on the tenant roll is a magnet to others and hence a plus point in initial and rent review negotiations.'

As far as the franchisee is concerned, at least part of this time is taken up with training. The core programme is a sandwich of theory and practice designed to develop product knowledge as well as operating methods: two weeks in the classroom, followed by a week in a shop, after which there is a further two-week spell of instruction. The timing of the training is geared to the opening date as far as possible, but if there are delays franchisees can undertake further periods of practical work at the franchisor's expense. They are also given a good deal of literature about the products, together with the usual operating manual. The actual shop-opening procedures reflect this careful preparation: there is, in fact, a 'shop opener' who takes the franchisee through the initial period and who is an experienced Holland and Barrett executive. 'The average shop stocks about 1100 lines and the "shop opener" will help the franchisee make the initial selection, as well as helping to choose and train staff,' Mullarkey explains.

Advertising and promotion

Equally important, however, is the launch of the shop itself. All advertising costs in the first year are devoted to the promotion of the individual outlet and this is indeed unusual in franchising: 'It's an intensive process of making potential customers aware of the outlet, not only through local press advertising but also through leafleting households and distributing our free newspaper *Health Express*. Even after the first year, 20 per cent of the royalty is still devoted to advertising and promotion, much of it to arouse local interest.'

In the end, however, it is setting up and monitoring financial controls that ensures that the strength of the franchise is also reflected on the bottom line.

Table 7.CS.1 Model forecast for the first two years of a Holland and Barrett franchise (on an average investment of £50 000)

Profit and loss account	Year 1	Year 2
SALES	182 000	227 500
Opening Stock	–	18 460
Purchases	147 679	166 140
Closing Stock	18 460	23 075
GROSS PROFIT	52 781	65 975
Discounts	14 768	16 614
GROSS INCOME	67 549	82 589
EXPENSES		
Royalty	13 651	17 063
Salaries and NI	11 340	12 012
Rent, rates, utilities	19 424	19 944
Repairs and maintenance	600	750
Insurance	400	500
Telephone, stationery and postage	869	933
Miscellaneous	2 665	1 706
Legal and audit	1 500	500
Depreciation	5 500	5 500
TOTAL	55 949	58 908
OPERATING PROFIT	11 600	23 681
Loan Interest Repaid	-4 147	-3 863
Overdraft Interest	-927	-912
PRE-TAX PROFIT	6 526	18 906

Cash flow projection	Year 1	Year 2
OUTFLOW		
Franchise fee	5 000	–
Initial investment	50 000	–
Stock movement	18 460	4 615
Creditors investment	-7 591	-1 898
Loan capital repayments	2 171	2 465
Drawings	7 800	*
VAT payments/receipts	-259	-128
Total Outflow	75 581	5 054
INFLOW		
Bank Loan	34 000	–
Own money	23 201	–
Pre tax profit	6 526	18 906
Depreciation	5 500	5 500
Total Inflow	69 227	24 406
NET IN (OUT) FLOW	-6 355	19 352

Balance sheet	Year 1	Year 2
Investment	55 000	49 500
Depreciation	-5 500	-5 500
Net investment	49 500	44 000
Stock	18 460	23 075
Creditors	7 591	9 489
Current trading assets	10 869	13 586
VAT net	-259	-387
Net operating	60 110	57 199
Financed by:		
Accumulated profits	6 526	17 632
Fixed loan	31 829	29 364
Overdraft	6 355	–
Own capital	23 201	23 201
Drawings	7 000	*
Surplus	–	12 997
TOTAL FINANCE	60 110	57 199

*It is left to the franchisee's discretion how much of the year 2 surplus of £12 997 he or she wishes to draw out

The shop opener gradually recedes from the scene – though help is always available on the telephone – but before this happens the shop will have been seen through the first few weeks of the financial reporting that Mullarkey requires. 'I look for key ratios to make sure things are on track,' he says, giving as examples wage costs, drawings and general expenses to sales. These are measured against Holland and Barrett's profit and loss and cash flow predictions for each outlet. The model of the first two years of an investment of £50 000 appears in Table 7.CS.1.

Although Holland and Barrett stress that these figures – which show a pre-tax profit of over £38 000 at the end of the fifth year and a positive cash flow of very nearly that amount – are only for guidance and are not a binding forecast, Mullarkey says that existing franchisees are exceeding this handsomely. 'One thing that means is that we have selected the right franchisees,' he says. 'But we can also claim justifiably that they've chosen the right franchise.'

Suggested questions

1. Would you recommend Geoghegan to take out the Fulham Road franchise?
2. Do you think taking over an existing outlet has any special advantages or disadvantages compared with opening up a new franchised outlet?
3. What do you think of Holland and Barrett's growth strategy? Specifically, do you believe the UK market can support 2000 health food shops? (By contrast, there are around 12 000 chemist shops).
4. Do you think that a company can run its own outlets and a franchise chain successfully side by side?
5. Given sufficient resources and a fair degree of personal indifference, would you choose a Balloon or a Holland and Barrett franchise?

CHAPTER 8

Equity Financing in Small Firms

Lister Vickery

Behind the innocent term 'equity', with its impression of 'fairness' and 'equality', lie two emotive subjects – wealth and control. Wealth is always a delicate subject in small businesses, because of the potential confusion between corporate and personal wealth. In addition, there are strong social pressures (certainly in Europe and in Japan, though not in North America) against acquiring wealth, which lead many owner-managers to neglect the importance of building a substantial equity base for their company. These same pressures cause them to neglect the provision of satisfactory financial returns (remuneration and dividends) to the risk-takers. Control is also an emotionally-charged subject, since the majority of owner-managers are highly motivated by a desire for independence, often accompanied by a deep sense of insecurity relative to their environment. As a result, discussion of equity in small firms is virtually taboo – both amongst businessmen and amongst researchers – and there are neither adequate data nor appropriate concepts for the subject. The purpose of this chapter is to review a number of the major issues and to highlight the areas in which 'popular belief' is at odds with the limited data.

First, however, we must examine why equity is necessary in business. It is often thought of statistically as merely the (residual) balancing figure on the balance sheet, although a dynamic view shows that it is vital to absorb the uncertainties in business financing.

By its very nature, business deals with uncertainty. Future sales as well as future costs are uncertain; and earnings, being the difference between these two, may thus be fairly said to be 'doubly uncertain'. The financing of the business must take account of these inherent uncertainties: if there is no flow of cash through the business, the firm becomes insolvent and trading ceases.

Short-term fluctuations in the movement of cash can generally be handled by using suppliers' credit or drawing short-term debt. If the cash flow is plentiful, cash discounts may be obtained from suppliers or the funds may be placed on short-term deposit. The dividing line between short-term and long-term fluctuations is difficult to draw: a useful rule of thumb used to be applied to overdrafts – the account was to be paid off fully for two separate months each year.

It is the long-term fluctuations which are much more difficult to handle, however, since the uncertainties are of a different nature. The success of a new product launch or an expansion involves many factors outside the firm's control and the longer time horizon means that the business environment may have changed radically by the time the product is launched or the expansion comes on stream. The simple response of being very prudent in a turbulent economy is insufficient, since many good opportunities may be missed and businesses need to adapt their financing so as to be able to cope with these uncertainties.

Loan finance best suits a certain world. When a company receives a loan, both the amount of the repayments (principal and interest) and their timing is fixed in advance. If the company is unable to pay the full amount on the due date, it is 'in default' and the financier may take immediate legal action. If the company performs better than expected and wishes to repay its loans in advance, there will usually be obstacles, as though the financier were dissatisfied with his client's performance.

Equity, on the other hand, is well-adapted to an uncertain world. Dividend payments are dependent on the realised earnings of the business and are fixed with regard to neither amount nor timing. The business is not under any obligation to repay the initial investor, who recovers his investment by selling his shares to another investor, thereby realising a capital gain or loss, depending on the performance of the business.

Equity is thus essential to business in order to allow it to continue to operate, despite uncertainty. Running a business with inadequate equity may be compared to driving a car with worn shock absorbers – not merely it is uncomfortable for the driver and wearing on the engine, it is also unsafe.

1. Owner attitudes to equity

Discussion of equity with a group of owner-managers rapidly shows that there are two basic attitudes, separated not by differing views of money, but by differing views of control. The majority view may be called 'patrimonial' and corresponds to a proprietor's view of his personal estate. The minority 'entrepreneurial' view is much less concerned by questions of control, and takes a more economic and less personal view of equity.

The patrimonial view: Established family businesses

The patrimonial attitude may best be illustrated by reference to an apocryphal, but typical, family business which has passed to the grandson or great-grandson of the founder and the company is seen as part of the family estate. Although share ownership has become diffused, the company is still seen as the 'family business' and control is exercised by the senior member of the family, who is chairman of the board. Junior members of the family, and promising outsiders, grow in influence as they learn the business, but family shareholders who are not working in the business are only acknowledged by a (modest) dividend on their shares – they are expected to vote in support of the chairman. Should they wish to sell their shares, the sale will be arranged by the chairman.

Such attitudes, in which equity is not seen as an element of the financing of the business, so much as the pillar of control and perenniality, may be found in many countries and can be clearly seen to have their roots in the real-estate management of pre-industrial society.

Even for first-generation businesses, where there may be no intention of establishing a family firm, these attitudes are congruent with the overall personality of the 'craftsman entrepreneur' as depicted by Norman Smith.[1] Smith observed that the majority of small business owner-managers in his sample did not really conform to the 'opportunistic' model of aggressive wealth-creators, but showed more cautious attitudes, defending the status quo and preserving their independence. This has been confirmed by other researchers, for example Jacqueline Laufer,[2] who found that a majority of small-business owners were against the idea of growth and followed defensive, 'no-risk' strategies. More recently, Pompe, Bruyn and Koek[3] have analysed a substantial international survey of small firms and reported that dissatisfaction outweighed ambition by two to one in industrialised countries as the main motivation for starting a business.

To the extent that these businesses have already established satisfactory equity bases (through inherited capital and retained earnings) and that they can generate sufficient earnings both to finance inflationary expansion and to satisfy those family members who rely on their dividends, the patrimonial approach is adequate. However, it leads to substantial problems in two situations of critical current importance: first, inflation has forced growth on many companies and the post-inflationary positive real interest rates have changed the financial environment; and second, new businesses have neither inherited equity, nor retained earnings.

Inflation causes an increase in the working capital requirements, which may exceed the firm's retained earnings even if there is no real (volume) growth in the business. In the late 1970s, the relatively high levels of inflation and the unfavourable competitive climate combined to ensure that even the 'zero-growth' companies would be obliged to raise equity or to see their debt-to-equity ratio increase. This situation was not unique to small firms – a number of large companies were reported to be showing profits on a 'current cost' basis and a loss on an 'inflation-adjusted' basis. This situation is aggravated in the current, post-inflationary period, in which real (net of inflation) interest rates are high and companies are showing the reverse effects of leverage – that is, if the cost of borrowing is higher than the return on assets, the firm's borrowing depresses the return on equity. In addition, the inflationary period has made the public much more sensitive to financial returns, and traditionally 'passive' family shareholders have become more demanding in requiring a 'fair' dividend return on their shareholding.

These pressures have made the owner-managers of established businesses much more aware of the financial nature of equity, of both the desirability of raising capital and the importance of ensuring appropriate financial returns to the shareholders. While this does not necessarily conflict directly with the patrimonial attitudes – indeed, it helps to explain the enthusiasm for new, non-voting, equity instruments and for the secondary stock markets (with limited reporting and control, and reduced vulnerability to take-overs) – it encourages an explicit examination of such attitudes, and their appropriateness for the business.

These attitudes have led to much muddled thinking in the area of finance for new businesses. The patrimonial view-point can be justified by the concept of personal property, which the individual is free to manage as he wishes. There are strong sociological precedents for the idea that inherited family property is managed by the paterfamilias or by senior members of the family. But the new business creator – unless he is investing his personal wealth – has no such claim. Outside shareholders are understandably reluctant to invest in the equity of an entrepreneur who regards their money as his.

Recognising that patrimonial attitudes are widespread, various well-meaning attempts have been made to resolve the problem. The easiest approach, tried in several European countries, is to pretend that most businesses do not need equity, and to arrange for the government to guarantee bank loans. While this may be adequate for very small businesses, it is not clear how the new firms financed in this way will be able to generate retained earnings sufficient to build a future equity base, given the real cost of borrowing plus the cost of the guarantee.

A second approach is to experiment with non-voting equity instruments. The French Government created a very imaginative instrument – the 'prêt participatif' (participating loan) – in 1978. This was to have been an unsecured, long-term (10-year) loan with a variable interest rate linked to the borrower's performance. In addition, it was to count as 'quasi-equity' – that is, it would count as equity when calculating balance-sheet ratios in seeking loans from state-run institutions. Unfortunately, the mechanics proved to be far too complex for both entrepreneurs and the financial community, and the instrument, much-modified, is now only used for government-subsidised loans. This approach also underlined the fact that all financial instruments must have 'teeth' – terms which allow the financier to apply pressure on the entrepreneur in the event of non-performance – unless they are to be an open invitation to the unscrupulous.

A third approach is to provide 'prêts d'honneur' (integrity bonds) to either the company or the entrepreneur. Such loans are repayable if and when the company is sufficiently successful. The promoters of such loans generally look for public funds to cover the inevitable loan losses and the period during which the interest payments are below commercial rates, arguing that there is a multiplier effect on such a subsidy. If such a loan is made directly to the company, it may be difficult to show other creditors that it reinforces the equity. On the other hand, if the loan is made to the entrepreneur, it will be difficult for him to repay without incurring a substantial personal tax bill.

The entrepreneurial approach

In contrast to the patrimonial approach, a minority of small-business owners approach financing from a more entrepreneurial viewpoint. They are primarily concerned to obtain the use of the resources, rather than their ownership, and they consider that *de facto* managerial control is more important than financial control or legal ownership. They recognise that the creditors of a highly-leveraged business may severely restrict the independence of the owner-manager.

Such an approach recognises that there are different types of finance available, each with its own costs and advantages, and that returns to the financiers are the necessary compensation for obtaining the funds in the first place. This is not to say that the entrepreneur does not seek to minimise the total cost of the financing, but he sees an on-going relationship – in which he may well wish to raise further finance for expansion – rather than a static, inherited situation.

The sort of personality associated with this approach may also be seen in the studies referred to above. Smith (see note 1) contrasted the 'opportunist entrepreneur' to the 'craftsman entrepreneur', and showed that the former achieved significant growth; while Laufer (see note 2) observed that the 'achievement motivated' owners were not concerned by questions of legal control; were prepared to consider the sale of their business; and were to be found primarily in technological, rather than traditional sectors.

Dividends

Detoeuf[4] defines dividends as 'the way to use up profits, when all the other ways have been tried.' This view is clearly shared by most small-business owners, be they patrimonial or entrepreneurial. For the former, dividends are a wasteful expense, paid to people who are no longer contributing to the business; for the latter, financing growth has a higher priority than providing a current return to shareholders.

There is little research into the dividend practices of small firms. In France, the Crédit National[5] reported that only 40 per cent of small firms paid dividends and only distributed a small proportion of profits; while Tamari[6] surveyed data from the USA, the UK and Israel to conclude that 'the decision concerning . . . profit distribution depends primarily on the nature of the ownership of the firm and not on its financial structure or size.' He showed that unquoted firms paid relatively less dividends (as a percentage of profits), but relatively greater management compensation than quoted firms. In the UK, data from ICFC[7] show that their clients (average 1978/79 sales about £3 million) distributed about 15 per cent of earnings, compared with 30 per cent for all UK companies, large or small. Hay and Morris[8] studied nineteen unquoted companies in detail and found that only four paid more than 'minimal dividends.' Of the remainder, 'in four . . . cases the dividend would have been smaller still but for the need to consider fairly minority shareholders', while 'three companies felt less concerned about minority shareholders because the latter had inherited their shares rather than paid for them.'

Such negative attitudes towards dividends have been partly justified by the fiscal discouragement (double taxation effect, both on the company and on the recipient). The slow move towards fiscal neutrality (see below) and increasing shareholder pressures (see above) are making medium-sized firms at least more aware of the importance of a dividend policy as part of their financial strategy.

2. The environment's view

Throughout much of this century and until quite recently, there appears to have been a steady trend against equity investing in the European economies. It is difficult to know whether the total market value of corporations has declined as a percentage of national wealth, but it seems very clear that direct equity shareholding by private individuals has declined relative to personal real estate. This observation would probably hold true even if the indirect equity holdings through pension funds and life insurance policies were included. At a societal level, the aspiration of the private citizen for home ownership has been recognised and strongly encouraged, whereas the aspiration for share ownership has only appeared in the last few years. General Charles de Gaulle's intéressement (employee share ownership) projects in France in the 1960s met with considerably less enthusiasm than the British government's British Telecom and British Gas privatisations of twenty years later.

There would seem to be two underlying trends to account for this: first, the growing desire for security, leading to regulation of financial markets and the growth of fiduciary institutions; and second, the growth of central government, with an emphasis on economic planning and control.

From the investor's point of view, equity involves risk. However, the basic corporate risk may be compounded by speculative movements in the stock market and by the unjustified forecasts of unscrupulous issuers of shares. After the 1929 'crash', regulation was imposed on stock markets – notably through the 1933 and 1934 Securities Acts in the USA – in order to limit such risks and to make equity investments 'safer' for private investors. Although such legislation rightly limits certain risks, it introduces a high fixed cost (both for the initial prospectus and for on-going reporting) which significantly discourages small companies and new issues. It also encourages companies to pay more attention to presenting themselves as 'low-risk' rather than as 'high-opportunity' and 'attractive equity' has come to be associated with stable performance, regular dividends and regular growth.

The same search for security can be seen in the growth of pension funds and life insurance companies. Such financial institutions have become major actors in the world's equity markets, but their very nature imposes constraints on their operations. Since they have a fiduciary duty to the pension and insurance beneficiaries, they are much more sensitive to the 'downside risk' of their investments than to the 'upside potential'. This disturbing aspect of their attitude towards equity was already remarked upon forty years ago by Ralph (later Senator) Flanders, who was one of the moving spirits behind the creation of the first venture capital company (the American Research Development Corporation) in 1946:

> During the last year of my incumbency as President of the Federal Reserve Bank of Boston, I became seriously concerned with the increasing degree to which the liquid wealth of the nation is tending to concentrate in fiduciary hands. This in itself is a natural process, but it does make it more difficult as time goes on to finance new undertakings.

By its very nature, equity is much more difficult to control than loan capital: both the amount and the timing of dividend payments is uncertain and, for unquoted companies, the shareholders can rarely plan when and for how much they will sell out. This is in sharp contrast to loan capital, where the creditor can define all the terms from the start. From the viewpoint of government control of the economy, it is much easier to regulate loan capital than to regulate the flow of equity. The financial institutions are also biased in this direction, since their ability to manage their portfolio of future funds is much greater where loan and interest returns are concerned than with equity instruments. Those institutions, such as pension funds, which do invest essentially in equity, are very concerned about regular returns and liquid investments. It is also arguable that, if companies increase their indebtedness – often, as in France, state-controlled financial institutions offering subsidised loans – they become more subject to the direct control of economic planners in government.

Viewed in this way, the government's recent encouragement of equity finance represents a major reversal of thinking. It follows the demise of centralised economic planning in many European economies and the abandoning of credit controls as a way of managing the economy. Equally, financial institutions have become aware of the fact that some 'equity risk' is actually transferred to the loan creditor if the equity base of a business is insufficient.

One of the ways in which such trends are reinforced and given 'rational' economic backing is through fiscal policy. Owner-managers in many European countries have observed that it is fiscally advantageous to put their money into their company as a shareholder's loan, rather than as equity. For a start, there is no stamp duty on a loan (though stamp duties – usually about 1 per cent – are now being reduced or eliminated in several countries); more important, the interest may be charged as a business expense (at least up to a 'commercial' rate) and may be taxed at a beneficial rate in the hands of the recipient. It is interesting to note that the French government has diminished, but not eliminated, this fiscal imbalance over the last five years – the top personal income tax rate on interest has been raised from 26 per cent to 46 per cent (the top personal income tax rate on dividends can still reach

65 per cent) and dividends on new share issues can now be charged as a business expense for the first ten years after the issue of the shares. In the UK, since the introduction of the imputation system of Corporation Tax in 1973, the tax treatment of dividends has been neutral (that is, it is effectively taxed only in the hands of the recipient).

During the post-Second World War years, there have been many significant fiscal incentives to encourage private individuals to invest their savings in property (both the primary residence and rental property), in pension schemes and life insurance. Investment in equity has only received timid incentives, such as the 'Monory Law' in France which led to a minor stock market rally in the late 1970s. The first major fiscal incentive directed at stimulating the flow of private savings into equity investments was the British Business Expansion Scheme (BES), launched as the Business Start-up Scheme in 1981. Under the BES, which allows investors to deduct up to £40 000 a year of their equity investments from their taxable income, the new equity must be in an unquoted company and must be held for at least five years. Subsequently, other European countries have experimented with similar incentives both to attract direct investment into equity and to stimulate investment into venture capital funds.

3.   Equity and the company life cycle

If, as we have suggested earlier, the basic purpose of equity is to enable the firm to cope with business risks, then the prime determinant of the 'right' equity base is the 'riskiness' of its activities. Quite apart from the impact of changes in the external environment, these risks depend on the stage of development of the firm itself. Start-ups are inherently riskier than well-established companies; and high-growth firms run greater risks than those operating in a steady state.

Churchill and Lewis[9] have developed an attractive stage model of small business growth, including an examination of the changing financial needs at each stage and I have expanded on this approach in the context of fast-growing, venture capital-financed businesses.[10] Figure 8.1 illustrates the growth of a business through Churchill's five growth stages, plus one 'upstream' stage, and indicates the venture capital terminology for the appropriate equity financing.

Research & Development

At this stage, 'upstream' of commercial exploitation, financing is required for design and engineering work, prototype or pre-production manufacture. Such work is evidently subject to high risks, since the

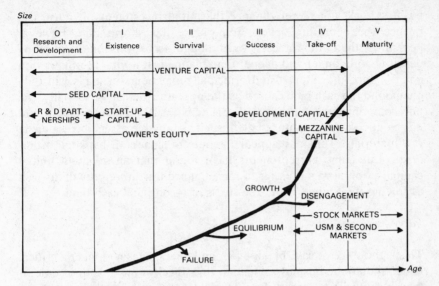

Figure 8.1   Financing the life cycle of a business

finished product may never be completed, or may fail to go into commercial production for a variety of reasons (the product's cost-performance may be unattractive or competition may have become too strong for example). In the event of failure, the financier will be generally unable to recover much of his investment, since most of the expense has been on 'brain-power' and there will be few resaleable assets. This stage calls for virtually 100 per cent equity financing and for new ventures, the owner-manager often has to find the whole of this investment from his own sources as the risks involved make it unattractive to many institutional financiers. Financiers generally require the promise of high returns in the event of success, in order to compensate for the likelihood of failure if they are involved at this stage. In many countries, government aid is available to carry part of the downside risk and thus to improve the risk–return ratio for the investor – in the USA, investments in 'R & D partnerships' receive favourable tax treatment; while in France, a government agency (ANVAR) can match equity funding – if sales materialise, ANVAR is reimbursed, at cost, through a royalty mechanism.

Existence

Cash is essential for a start-up, even if it may be minimised by the founder cutting his standard of living ('or moonlighting') and by the imaginative use of credit. Since this is the stage before break-even, the business must not merely finance the initial investments, it must also finance the operating deficit. Experience has shown that, however pessimistic the initial forecasts were thought to be, this initial operating deficit is both longer and deeper than planned. It is vital to fund it with equity, since the interest and principal repayments of loans will only compound the cash bind caused by the operating deficit. Essentially, the only loan financing which is appropriate is for those items which would not be at risk if the venture failed, such as tangible assets or resaleable raw materials. This may appear to some to smack of 'bankers' ortho-doxy', but many entrepreneurs have found that an adequate initial capitalisation makes it easier to raise finance for future growth, as well as freeing the founder from the stress of a continual cash bind.

Survival

This is the stage of cash break-even, and financing is no longer a critical issue. Should the business remain at this stage for any length of time, it may be difficult to renew loan funding – for new fixed assets or for working capital. However, this is probably the state of the vast majority of small retail outlets or services, in which the founder's equity receives no financial return and the founder earns only a modest personal income. In the long run, these businesses are believed to go into decline and to fail, but the process can take many years and may be as related to the physical ageing of the founder as to the economics of the business.

Success

The business which reaches this stage is earning enough to provide a satisfactory return on the equity, and thus provide a reward for the founder and the shareholders for the efforts and risks they have taken. If the founder has been unable to secure adequate capital for the earlier stages, this is the stage when the over-indebtedness can be paid off. After that, the business should be generating more funds than are needed for the long-term maintenance of the business (including re-newal of fixed assets and the development of new products or markets). The founder may either choose to 'disengage' – to launch a new business, to run for political office or simply to pursue a hobby – or he may choose to build the business further, into a medium or large-sized firm. In the former case, the profits will be distributed – not necessarily as dividends: a manager may be hired to run the business while the owner is developing his new activities; in the latter case, profits will need to be retained to ensure a strong equity base for the growth.

Take-off

Rapid growth always requires substantial equity financing, both because growth entails significant cash needs (working capital and fixed assets) which cannot be met by internally-generated cash, and because of the significant risks involved in launching new products, developing new markets, expanding production capacity, and so on. In absolute terms, the sums of money at this stage generally exceed the means of the founder, his family and the associates who have provided the bulk of the financing for the earlier stages. Even in the case of high-technology firms which have been funded by institutions from the beginning, this is the stage where the 'early stage' venture capitalists bring in the 'development capitalists' and investment bankers, with greater financial means to carry the firm through to a public quotation.

Maturity

At this stage, the company has probably outgrown the scope of this book and its financing concerns are well within the context of 'corporate finance'. Financial management must ensure that the company has a sufficient equity base to meet the ongoing business fluctuations and that the profitability is sufficient both for internal retentions and for shareholder distribution – insufficiency of one or the other leading to stagnation and decline, or to the ever-present threat of being taken over.

There have been regrettably few attempts to follow the financing of small firms over any length of time in order to investigate their equity requirements. Benoun and Sénicourt[11] studied the first four years of 100 French companies established in 1970. In order to obtain the financial data, they had to limit themselves to 'Sociétés Anonymes', so that their sample is biased to rather large start-ups (as will be seen from the average turnover in the first year – approximately £200 000).

The comparison of the 1970 and 1973 balance sheets (see Table 8.1) shows that the businesses have grown quite rapidly on average, even allowing for inflation – doubling their annual turnover in four years. Their asset rotation has improved slightly, so that the total financing required has grown by approximately 90 per cent over the period. Although the relative proportion of the major items of assets (net fixed assets, inventories and trade receivables) has remained constant, detailed analysis showed that the inventory rotation had improved from 130 days to 104 days, while customer credit was fairly constant at about 35 days. The financing of these assets has, however, changed substantially. Share capital and shareholders' loans were unable to keep pace with the growth and retained earnings were inadequate to make up the shortfall. Shareholders' funds (including reserves) fell from 26 per cent

Table 8.1   The financial requirements of growth (data on 100 French companies established in 1970)

	1970 KF	1970 (Percentage)	1973 KF	1973 (Percentage)	Percentage Change
Annual turnover	2542	(250)	5155	(268)	+103
Total assets	1021	(100)	1920	(100)	+ 88
Net fixed assets	287	(28)	530	(28)	
Inventories	257	(25)	490	(25)	
Receivables	254	(25)	493	(26)	+ 94
Share capital	168	(16)	217	(11)	+ 31
Shareholders' loans	103	(10)	138	(7)	
Retained earnings	–3	–	59	(3)	
Trade credit	325	(32)	753	(39)	+132
Banks and LTD	210	(21)	370	(19)	+ 76
Cash flow	58	(6)	174	(9)	

Source: Derived from Benoun and Sénicourt (see Note 11).

of total assets to 21 per cent. Banks and long-term debt have also failed to finance the expansion (falling from 21 per cent to 19 per cent), leaving trade credit to carry the brunt of the financing. Detailed analysis showed that trade credit increased from 73 days to 91 days over the period. If this is compared with the credit given, it is clear that trade credit was the primary source of finance for these new companies. This pattern may, of course, have changed, since it is arguable that trade credit is no longer available as abundantly or as flexibly as in the early 1970s, and banks and credit institutions have been encouraged to provide greater support for small firms.

4.   Some statistics on equity in small firms

It is well-known that there is a dearth of reliable statistical information on small firms, and it is not surprising that the financial data are both rarer and less consistent than 'demographics' (company births and deaths) or data on numbers employed. There are virtually no data-bases which permit compilation of country-wide data on the issuance of new equity in small firms, and few studies have been carried out to check the widely-held view that small firms are undercapitalised.

The volume of new equity for small firms

One of the few estimates of total new equity funding can be obtained from the US reports of 1984 and 1986 entitled *The State of Small*

Business: A Report of the President.[12] Using averaged data for 1978–80, they found that small corporations (non-farm, non-financial businesses with assets of less than US$10 million) raised US$1.9 billion of new equity annually and US$4.8 billion of shareholders' loans, representing together about 8 per cent of total sources of fund. While these figures are puny beside the US$40 billion of new capital being raised by large firms, they are none the less substantial in absolute terms, particularly as they are likely to have come predominantly from personal, rather than from institutional, shareholders. For comparison, American venture capitalists invested an annual average of US$0.9 billion over the same period, with a significant proportion going into growing companies that had already crossed the US$10 million asset threshold.

For the United Kingdom, the *Business Monitor* statistics do not differentiate between equity and long-term loans when they provide the sources and uses of funds data for small, medium and large companies. Although the data are rather old, the Wilson Committee's Research Report[13] showed that small firms (firms with capital employed of less than £4 million, and excluding subsidiaries of large firms) raised an annual average of £158 million of new equity in 1973–1975 and a further £231 million of directors' loans. Taken together, they represent about 13 per cent of total sources of funds. Although these figures may appear quite modest, it must be remembered that the economic climate was scarcely propitious for raising equity and very little of this money can have come from institutional sources. For comparison, large firms were unable to average more than £300 million of new equity during this period.

Relative capitalisation of small and large firms

Tamari[14] gathered data from the UK, the USA, Japan, France and Israel to test the notion that small firms are relatively undercapitalised. He concluded that in all countries, small firms operate with ratios of equity to total funds similar to, or higher than, large firms'. He observed that small firms had a greater dependence on short-term, rather than long-term, credit for their external financing, with trade credit being significantly more important than institutional credit. His data are now rather old – depending on the countries, the statistics vary from 1964 to 1973 – and the definitions of small and large firms are country-dependent (the data on medium-sized firms has been omitted here for clarity), but they appear to be confirmed by more recent statistics (UK – Wilson Committee (1979); USA – The State of Small Business (1986)).

It will be seen from Table 8.2 that shareholders' loans are a significant component of the 'equity' of small firms. Although legally distinct from

Table 8.2   Equity to assets ratios in small and large firms

Country and Period		Share capital and Retained earnings	Shareholder loans	Total equity
		←(as a percentage of Total Assets)→		
USA	(1964–68)	Small 46	11	57
		Large 57	–	57
	(1974)	Small 48	n.a.	n.a.
		Large 54	n.a.	n.a.
	(1985)	Small 44	n.a.	n.a.
		Large 47	n.a.	n.a.
UK	(1964–68)	Small 53	3	56
		Large 52	–	52
	(1972)	Small 34	10	44
		Large 45	–	45
	(1975)	Small 30	11	41
		Large 39	–	39
	(1980)	Small 20	n.a.	n.a.
		Large 44	n.a.	n.a.
France	(1973)	Small 16	18	34
		Large 32	6	34
Japan	(1970)	Small 16	6	22
		Large 18	4	22
Israel	(1964–68)	Small 23	22	45
		Large 27	9	36

Sources: Tamari (1980), except USA 1974 & 1985 – The State of Small Business, 1986; UK 1972 & 1975 – Wilson Committee, 1979; UK 1980 – Burns, 1985.

the shareholding, most observers agree that they must be considered as part of the owners' equity in the business, since these loans share fully in the risks of the company and interest payments (and, indeed, repayment) being dependent on its varying fortunes. Aside from their flexibility, such loans have also been fiscally more efficient than shares.

Table 8.2 also demonstrates the dramatic erosion of the corporate equity base in the USA and the UK over the past two decades. However, data cited by Burns[15] suggests that this decline may have been stemmed, at least as regards large UK companies. The very sharp drop in UK small firms' capital to assets ratio, from 30 per cent in 1975 to 20 per cent by 1980, may be due to the fact that the size definition appears to have been more restrictive in 1980 than in 1975 – it is known that the smallest companies have relatively less capital and relatively more shareholders' loans.

5. Sources of equity, informal and institutional

Despite the attention that has been paid to small firms in recent years, it remains difficult to identify the appropriate sources of equity finance. In many ways, the problem is analogous to that of the iceberg – only the tip is visible. Various 'Guides' are now published, but they tend to concentrate on the highly visible institutions, particularly on the venture capital funds. Although these institutions may be investing significant sums of money, it is generally in sizeable 'packages' (£100 000-plus, generally implying a total equity valuation of over £1 million).

The statistics quoted previously imply that institutional equity may indeed be in a minority, relative to 'private' or informal sources. While the bulk of this private financing may be from the owner-manager himself, or from the immediate family, little attention has so far been paid to the way in which individuals outside management invest in small firms.

Two recent studies in the USA (Wetzel and Seymour[16] and Tymes and Krasner[17]) have focused on the profile of private individuals investing in new, technology-based ventures. Both studies identified broadly similar 'typical' investors – executives in their forties who were financially well-established, though hardly 'rich' (salaries of US$50 000-plus and net worths of US$250 000-plus). They indicated a general preference for start-up or early stage investments with high growth prospects, rather than more mature ventures with less risk and lower growth. Their investments would be in the US$10 000 to 100 000 range, typically in combination with other private investors or venture capital funds. They planned to play an active, advisory role in the business and to sell out within about 5 years, aiming for an annualised rate of return between about 20 per cent and 50 per cent, depending on the perceived risks and duration of the investment. Interestingly, they did not appear to be investing to take fiscal incentives, nor were they explicitly diversifying their personal investment portfolio. Contact with the businesses came through their 'personal grapevine', which the Californians (who would typically make several investments a year) felt was adequate, while the New Englanders (making only one investment a year) sought better channels of communication between investors and entrepreneurs.

The results achieved in the UK by the *Venture Capital Report* in stimulating informal venture capital activity are noteworthy: this publication carries at least ten business proposals a month; in each case, the entrepreneur indicates what finance he is seeking, the percentage of equity he will sell and whether he is looking for a managing or a passive partner. The publisher of the journal imposes a certain level of disclosure, and carries out some screening to ensure a satisfactory quality of proposals. Between 1979 and 1984, some 600 proposals were published.

A survey of 90 per cent of these revealed that 16 per cent had raised the required funds through the *Venture Capital Report*, 11 per cent had raised the money through other contacts, and a further 8 per cent had raised 'some' of the needed funds. The total informal venture capital raised was in excess of £20 million.

The BES has also illustrated that there are substantial private funds available for investment in equity. Stimulated by attractive fiscal incentives, about £240 million was raised from private investors in the two fiscal years 1983–84 and 1984–85 for investment in over 1400 companies. Both because of the importance of respecting administrative procedures and because of the need to 'pool' appraisal costs between investors, most of the investments are channelled through specialised funds ('BES funds'), but a growing number of companies are issuing private prospectuses and seeking investors directly. With an average investment size of £170 000 per company, it will be seen that the scheme caters more for medium-sized companies than for the smaller firms.

With a few notable exceptions, institutional investors are seeking to make substantial capital gains with a medium-term horizon (ideally three to five years, though the reality is often somewhat longer). Although there has been a significant increase in the number of institutions offering venture capital in the UK (well over 100 at the end of 1986) they all complain of the shortage of 'good' projects – since they are all targeting that very small number of firms which are reasonably well-established, which aim to go public within five years and which can yield a 30 per cent-plus annualised capital gain. For the entrepreneur running such a business, raising capital is definitely a 'seller's market'.

The excesses are well-illustrated in Sahlman and Stevenson's recent study of the US venture capital market.[18] Between 1977 and 1984, some forty-odd Winchester disk drive manufacturers raised US$390 million from venture capitalists, followed by a further US$670 million when twelve of them went public in 1981–83. Such was the excitement surrounding this industry, that the twelve public companies had a combined stock market valuation in mid-1983 in excess of US$5 billion – corresponding to four times annual sales and fifty times earnings, compared with stock prices of established electronics or computer companies at 50 per cent of annual sales or ten to twelve times earnings. The stock market realised these companies were seriously overvalued when the growth in computer demand slackened in 1983–84 and the competition between disk drive manufacturers became tougher – the valuation of the twelve public companies fell by 75 per cent by the end of 1984, only one of them raised any new equity in that year, and venture capitalists cut their funding of the other (private) companies by over half from the 1983 level.

It should be observed that there are a small number of experienced venture capitalists who can provide significant advice and support for the small firm with growth potential, and who thereby 'add value' over and above their financing. Generally, this 'added value' is less institutional than personal and relational. It stems from the quality of the individual venture capitalist, his personality, his experience and his network of contacts, rather than from the size of the venture capital organisation or the institutional resources.

Over the last forty years, one institution has specialised in investing in the stable small or medium-sized firm. Investors in industry is probably the largest institution in the world of its kind: as of March 1986, it held long-term investments in some 4800 unquoted companies. The difference in scale between the investment opportunities in such businesses and those in high-growth venture capital may be judged from the 3i Group's 1986 Annual Report: during the previous five years, 3i averaged some 900 financings annually, with only 1 per cent being made by its Venture Capital Division (and half of these in the USA); in money terms, 3i averaged over £200 million annually in new loans and equity investments (the latter cumulatively represent 27 per cent of 3i's portfolio), compared with under £6 million in venture capital. The venture capital investments are, as might be expected, significantly larger than their equity investments in stable smaller firms, averaging about £600 000 compared with £60 000.

6. Financial structuring

'Packaging the deal' is often looked upon by non-financiers as a sort of magic trick designed to make the numbers look more attractive than they really are. As with all products, packaging can be used to hide defects, but good packaging is part of good product design, and financial packaging aims to give each party to a transaction an appropriate part of the deal – appropriate in terms of each party's 'risk–reward' requirements.

An unusually clear example may be found in the financing package put together for the management buy-out (MBO) of Ripolin UK in 1981. This financing was arranged before the current 'boom' in MBOs in the UK, and it involves the creative use of various types of shares in order to satisfy the requirements of each party to the deal. The total valuation agreed for the company was £4.8 million, with the selling shareholders realising 76 per cent.

The acquiring parties, who were to buy the totality of Ripolin UK through a new holding company (JACOA Ltd) were:

Management

Four key executives were prepared to invest up to £250 000, but required to be able to maintain control in all circumstances. In particular, they wished to be sure that the company would not be vulnerable to a takeover. They were quite prepared to see virtually no financial return on their investment for several years to come.

The minority shareholders (previously owning 24 per cent of Ripolin UK)

They were prepared to exchange their holdings in Ripolin UK for shares in JACOA of the same face value (that is, £1.15 million). In the main, these were family shareholdings, held since the 1930s. The shareholders were primarily concerned to see satisfactory, stable dividends as an important complement to their retirement income. Their relationship to current management was ambivalent, since the company had been close to failing in 1977 and a number of shareholders had lost their jobs in the reorganisation – at the same time, these shareholders recognised that the company's present value was due to the current management's efforts.

A development capital institution

Acting as financial advisers to the management, they were seeking high returns on their investment and/or fee revenues to cover their staff costs and their 'risk exposure' in appraising the company and arranging the deal. They were thus highly sensitive both to the amount of their investment and to its timing. They also wished to be able to monitor progress from within – through the board of directors.

A commercial bank

Encouraged by the appraisal of the development capitalists, they were prepared to provide substantial long-term loans for the acquisition. However, UK legislation in 1981 prevented them from taking any security in the underlying assets of Ripolin UK – as a creditor in JACOA (the new holding company), they would rank after all Ripolin's other creditors. The bank needed to be assured that their credit risk was low and that their return would be higher than usual.

The financing structure proposed was as shown in Table 8.3. It should be noted that share redemptions can only be made out of 'distributable reserves' – i.e. out of after-tax profits earned after the acquisition.

It will be seen that this arrangement endeavours to satisfy the require-

Table 8.3 Proposed financing structure of JACOA (Ripolin UK)

Description	Subscriber	Amount (£000)	
Ordinary Shares	Management	250	(75%)
Preferred Ordinary Shares[a]	Development Capital	83	(25%)
Total Ordinary Shares		333	(100%)
12% Redeemable Preference Shares[b]	Development Capital	417	
12% Redeemable Preference Shares[c]	Minority	383	
6% Convert. Redeemable Preference Shares[d]	Minority	767	
Total Share Capital (Ordinary & Preference)		1900	
7-year loan with Share option[e]	Commercial Bank	1500	
Short-term loan	Commercial Bank	1400	
TOTAL FINANCING		4800	

Notes:

[a] These shares are convertible one-for-one into Ordinary Shares, at the holder's option. Preferred dividends are equal to the greater of 12 per cent net or 1 per cent of the Company's pre-tax profit.

[b] These shares are to be redeemed before 31.12.82, otherwise £41000 of them are convertible into Preferred Ordinary Shares (note [a]).

[c] These shares are to be redeemed in ten half-yearly instalments from 31.3.86.

[d] These shares may be converted, at the holder's option, into Ordinary Shares at par equal to a total of 10 per cent of the issued share capital at the time of conversion. Any shares which have not been so converted at 31.3.86 will be redeemed in ten half-yearly instalments.

[e] The loan is at 2.5 per cent over Base Rate, and the Bank received an option to subscribe for Ordinary Shares at par equal to 10 per cent of the issued share capital at the time of conversion.

ments of each of the parties to the financing. Management can expect to retain 60 per cent control (after allowing for the dilution caused by the two 10 per cent options to the minority shareholders and to the commercial bank), and should maintain 53 per cent control even if they are unable to redeem the development capitalist's Preference Shares at the end of 1982. They would only lose control if they were unable to meet the long-term redemption schedule or were obliged to raise new equity, forcing their dilution. On the other hand, they are unlikely to see any dividend return on their investment for several years.

The minority shareholders get their steady dividend returns and a promise of capital repayment (which may appear attractive to some pensioners, though it would prove a poor choice in the event of continued high inflation). They also have an option on 10 per cent of the equity, to compensate their loss of liquidity (they could have insisted on selling out at the same time as the majority partner) and to maintain their long-term interest in the company. This five-year option would be attractive if the value of the company appreciates by about 55 per cent.

The development capitalist's attention to timing may be seen from the penalty conditions attached to the non-redemption of his Preference Shares. The relatively high dividend rate on the Ordinary Shares also provides for an attractive percentage return, while the absolute charge to the company is fairly modest.

The commercial bank's role is important in two respects, both of which provide the leverage without which this MBO would not have been possible. The 'equity risk' nature of the £1.5 million 7-year loan may be seen from the high interest rate and the 10 per cent equity option taken by the bank. As was noted above, in the event of the underlying business being unsuccessful, the bank would not hold any security in the assets, and would rank after all the ordinary creditors. The fact that recent legislation has made it possible for such long-term loans to take security in the underlying assets merely means that the other creditors of the business are now obliged to accept a dilution of their security and an increased share of the 'equity risk'. The second role of the bank loans is to provide a mechanism for the underlying business to finance part of the deal – immediately after JACOA's acquisition of Ripolin UK, the latter paid an exceptional dividend of £1.4 million, which was used to repay the short-term loan.

This illustrates explicitly the way in which an MBO corresponds to a reduction of the capital of the acquired business. A comparison of the consolidated accounts of JACOA and Ripolin UK immediately after the acquisition with Ripolin UK's accounts just before, would show that the corporate net worth has been reduced by £2.9 million (£1.5 million of new debt plus £1.4 million of exceptional dividends) – and £1.9 million of this reduced net worth is now redeemable (provided there are sufficient profits).

Subsequent to this MBO, JACOA developed sucessfully, despite difficult trading conditions in the home decoration and 'do-it-yourself markets'. From the MBO, concluded in mid-1981, to the end of 1983, JACOA earned over £3 million after tax (approx. 6 per cent on sales). This allowed it to pay out nearly £300 000 in preferred dividends, to redeem over £600 000 (including early redemption of some minority shareholders) and to retain over £2 million as reserves to rebuild the reduced equity base referred to above.

Case Study: Kara Foods Limited

'With a balance sheet like ours, how can we raise money for another acquisition?' Richard Stuart knew that his partner, Mike Philipp, had a flair for financial deal-making, but he was sceptical that their company could borrow more money from the City. With a minimal capital and no record of profits, they had been able to borrow £550 000 in June 1981 to buy a couple of companies in the frozen food business. Now, barely nine months later, they had an opportunity to acquire a business with a turnover of around £1 million, but they needed £300 000. The County Bank director who had sanctioned their first acquisition told them, 'It is obvious you have to do the deal if only you can find a way of financing it.'

Background

Richard and Mike had originally started in business together by designing a new frozen 'hamburger-in-a-bun' for the British 'pub' market (see page 233). Prior to setting up Hunky, Richard (who was twenty-nine at the time of this case study) had spent five years with Turner and Newall, a major British industrial group, first as a management trainee and then as a sales manager. Mike, eight years his senior, had worked principally in the property business since graduating from Oxford and also had some limited factory management experience. They had first met while taking their MBAs at INSEAD in 1977–8, but a chance meeting on holiday had led to their joint venture together.

Over an eighteen-month period from mid-1979, the two partners had put all their energies into establishing this business. Although part of their difficulties was due to the fact that they were creating a completely new market, they had also learned about the limitations and frustrations of personal selling to small customers. Late in 1980, they chose to distribute Hunky through frozen food wholesalers, first using one for the London area and subsequently gaining national distribution. The wisdom of this move was very rapidly evident, the sales volume rising from £70 000 to £350 000 annually. Part of the reason for this expansion was that the wholesalers were part of the 'established' supply network to pubs – and thus could generate regular sales – and part of the reason was that the wholesalers were also supplying many other types of customer – particularly the growing number of small, independent fast-food outlets.

Although they had previously subcontracted out the production side, Richard and Mike were looking for an opportunity to integrate vertically. They were concerned that the poor level of repeat orders for Hunky was due to problems of quality control. They were reluctant to get into the meat-processing business, with its heavy investments and complex sanitary arrangements, but they saw considerable growth potential for 'American-style' frozen hamburger buns. The longer shelf-life of the frozen relative to the fresh product was advantageous both to the distributor and to the fast-food outlet. By making an 'American-style' bun (that is, topped with sesame seeds and using a special dough) rather than the traditional British baker's 'bap', the partners hoped to offer a product which would appeal to those outlets seeking to be distinctive.

The Valecom acquisition

Early in 1981, Mike heard from the hamburger supplier that Bejam were planning to sell off their production of hamburger buns. The Bejam group operated the largest chain of retail frozen foods in Britain and had grown extremely rapidly during the late 1970s to around £120 million annual sales. Although publicly-quoted, it was still forcefully controlled by its founder, John Abthorpe. He had established bun manufacture to support the launch of a hamburger chain which had not been successful and which had been sold to the Grand Metropolitan Hotel group. Although Bejam were selling the frozen hamburger buns in their retail stores, John Abthorpe was keen to sell the production unit in order to use the cash for other expansion opportunities.

The 'package' for sale comprised three companies – Valecom, Springmoss and Kara. The first two companies were manufacturing units which had been set up for Bejam by an independent entrepreneur, Tony Fachino, and were jointly owned on a 50–50 basis by Bejam and Fachino (the latter through his holding company, Zephyr Investments). Kara was a marketing and distribution agency, acting for Valecom (who owned 51 per cent of Kara) and Springmoss as well as for Chic-O-Roll Ltd (a producer of frozen Chinese meals, holding the remaining 49 per cent of Kara).

Valecom, the manufacturing plant, was located at Iver, Bucks (west of London and about two miles north of Heathrow Airport). With a workforce of about forty, it was producing about 40 000 buns a day and operating at about 50 per cent of capacity. Direct sales to Bejam retail stores accounted for about 50 per cent of production, while deliveries to Springmoss accounted for a further 20 per cent. The balance was distributed through wholesalers (and through Kara) to a number of hamburger outlets in the London area.

Springmoss produced 'pizza buns' – consisting of a pizza topping on a Valecom bun – of which about 90 per cent were retailed through the Bejam group. Kara was operated on a break-even basis, costs being shared proportionately to turnover between Valecom, Springmoss and Chic-O-Roll. Chic-O-Roll supported about 70 per cent of Kara's costs, since its products were of much higher value than the buns.

Mike and Richard were very attracted by the package. They felt that their active presence in the business would enable them to find additional outlets and to rationalise the two production operations. The retail strength of Bejam would ensure sales growth for the frozen hamburger buns, the pizza buns and the Chinese meals. Although the partners were unable to obtain any specific agreement from Bejam, they did have the assurance that Chic-O-Roll would continue to market its products indefinitely through Kara, thus maintaining the effective subsidy of Kara's marketing operations.

There was also useful synergy to be obtained with the Hunky activities. Mike and Richard could bring Hunky production under their own control and Hunky clients would be interested in the range of products being made by Valecom and Springmoss.

The sellers offered the 'package' for £550 000 and declined to negotiate the price. Interpretation of the past accounts of the companies was somewhat difficult, since the owners had taken earnings 'above the line' and had minimised the tax liability. Looking in detail at the operating results for the first quarter of 1981, the partners were satisfied that operating profits (pre-interest and tax) were around £90 000 on combined sales of £380 000. The book value of the assets (both fixed and current) was about £220 000.

Financing the acquisition

At the time, Frolward Ltd (the company Mike and Richard had established to carry out the Hunky project) had a share capital of £200, directors' loans of £10 000 and accumulated losses. Mike had put up all the money, but the share capital was split 75–75, since Mike felt that 'the money and the idea should have 50 per cent and the work (himself and Richard) 50 per cent'.

Mike was in a position to realise personal assets for about half the required amount of financing, but Richard did not have any significant financial resources of his own. Mike proposed that Richard should continue to run Frolward, while the Valecom deal would be handled by himself and another business friend. Richard felt this was a 'non-starter' and was encouraged by an INSEAD friend to seek external financing in order to stay in the deal.

After some fruitless contacts with rich individuals, Richard met the County Bank, the merchant banking subsidiary of National Westminster Bank (one of the major British commercial banks), who were prepared to put up loan finance provided they also got an attractive equity stake. Since there was a potential disparity in the way Mike and Richard were providing the financing, and in the 'money/work' division, further negotiation was needed between the two partners before a deal could be worked out with County Bank.

They finally decided to raise the full £550 000 as a loan from County Bank, 'sweetened' by a 20 per cent stake at par (that is, £40). Mike and Richard retained their 75–75 split of the remaining shares. Appendices A and B show the investment proposal written up by the partners for County Bank and the latter's proposed loan terms. The partners also persuaded Chris Harrison, who was effectively running the three companies, to join their venture, investing £7500 for a small stake in the equity. He became joint Managing Director with Richard, while Mike became Chairman.

Assimilating the companies

The legal and fiscal mechanics of the take-over were fairly straightforward, but it became rapidly apparent that the previous owners had been experienced 'window-dressers' and that Mike and Richard had let their enthusiasm guide their judgement.

Bejam delisted the pizza buns almost immediately after the take-over. This turned Springmoss immediately into a loss-maker and knocked 20 per cent off Valecom's sales. The pre-sale accounts had shown very rapid growth in the pizza bun sales: with hindsight, this looked very much a deliberate profit booster. The attractive profitability of the business evaporated overnight.

Immediately after the completion of the sale, Chic-O-Roll declared that they were unhappy about continuing to market through Kara. Within a year they had ceased selling through Kara, leaving the partners with £200 000 of marketing overheads to cover.

Initially, Mike and Richard let Chris Harrison continue to run the business. As problems accumulated, it appeared that Harrison was maintaining his power by limiting the information he passed on to the partners. Finally, they learned that the £7500 Harrison invested in the business had been put up by Tony Fachino. Harrison left the business and returned to work for Fachino.

Fortunately, the frozen hamburger bun market continued to grow very rapidly and Bejam continued to take 50 per cent of the production (at attractive prices) for their retail sales. Richard concentrated his efforts on sales and marketing, specifically handling the sales to major customers. Appendix C gives his analysis of the market early in 1982. Sales of hamburger buns to the catering trade through wholesalers were handled by Gerry Holdway, who had previously been selling Chinese meals and pizza buns for Kara. Gerry was forty, and had fifteen years' experience in the frozen food industry.

Mike concentrated on the financial side and also spent time in the factory at Iver, since various investments were needed to improve production to adequate levels. It should be noted that the Iver factory was cramped and had old-fashioned, inefficient equipment. Working conditions were hardly ideal and labour turnover was relatively high. The factory manager, John Gallagher, aged thirty-three, was an enthusiastic and capable baker of fifteen years' experience. To complete their management team, the partners hired Mukesh Thakrar as Chief Accountant, who proved to be as vigilant in conserving cash and limiting expenses as the partners themselves.

By the end of 1981, it was clear that the growth in the hamburger bun business was limited both by volume and by the relative inefficiency of the Iver plant. With the loss of the pizza buns and the withdrawal of Chic-O-Roll, the profit trend was downward. Mike felt that the only way out of the impasse was to acquire a competitor – even if they were not seeking to sell.

Warburton Fast Foods

The Warburton group was a well-established and well-managed bakery in the Manchester area. Sensing a new growth market for hamburger buns (and possibly for other bakery products) in the fast food business, they had created a new unit – Warburton Fast Foods (WFF) – with a special factory to cater to both the fresh and frozen markets.

When Mike investigated the company records, he discovered that separate accounts were filed for WFF. While Warburton was earning £2 million on sales of £40 million, WFF was losing £250 000 on sales of nearly £1 million. Armed with this information, he called on the directors in mid-February 1982. His visit report records the following contributory factors for the lack of profitability:

- Strategy aimed at volume regardless of price;
- Disregard for economics of delivery – WFF were making direct deliveries to all Asda cafeterias, whereas Valecom used distributors;
- Overheads were high, relative to Valecom – WFF used six office staff and a full-time accountant and spent £1000 a month on a computer bureau – relative to the business volume, WFF was spending £1000 per week more on staff than Valecom – WFF employed a sales director and two sales representatives – factory electricity costs per unit were 2.4 times those of Valecom;
- The gyro-freezer was giving major quality problems. It could only generate $-7°C$ ($-18°C$ is the acceptable temperature) and handle 50 per cent of the factory output;
- WFF were making fresh deliveries into the London area, at a cost of 0.5p to 1p per bun, compared to a cost of 0.15p per bun for Valecom. (The selling price of a fresh bun was about 3.5p); and
- WFF management lacked knowledge of the catering and retail markets for these new products.

Mike was able to convince the WFF Directors fairly rapidly of the attractions of selling their operations to Frolward and so he returned to Richard with an agreement to acquire the fixed assets in the factory for book value (see Appendix D). Frolward thus needed to find £200 000 for the cash payment to Warburton, plus about a further £100 000 for working capital, since they were effectively acquiring about £1 million in annual sales, split roughly 50–50 between fresh and frozen.

Two days after the visit to WFF, the partners called on County Bank to discuss how funding might be arranged. County Bank encouraged them to go ahead with the deal, but were unwilling to offer direct long-term financing. They suggested that Frolward should arrange 100 per cent lease financing for the fixed assets and that the working capital should be funded under the Government Loan Guarantee Scheme (costing a 2 per cent insurance premium). Mike and Richard wondered just how much leverage they could support (see Appendix E for the Frolward Balance Sheet at the end of 1981).

Appendix A: Investment Proposal – Acquisition of Valecom, Springmoss and Kara

The proposal

The investment proposal is in the rapidly-growing frozen fast-food sector. It involves the purchase of a subsidiary of a major British frozen food company (which is currently trading profitably) and its merger with a company in the same sector which is managed and co-owned by the proposers.

The companies

Valecom Ltd, Springmoss Ltd, and 51 per cent of Kara Ltd form the proposed acquisition. Kara is a marketing company which buys various frozen food products including those of Springmoss and Valecom and sells them to frozen-food wholesalers and major accounts. Kara is operated on a break-even basis, its expenses being charged to Valecom, Springmoss and other suppliers.

The sellers

Bejam and Zephyr Investments Ltd each own 50 per cent of Valecom and Springmoss. Kara is 51 per cent owned by Valecom.

Rationale for sale

Valecom was originally established to supply Bejam's venture into the Trumps hamburger chain. Trumps has recently been sold to Grand Metropolitan and so Bejam wish to dispose of their interest. The owner of Zephyr Investments specialises in making capital gains via the establishment and sale of food factories – and wishes to do so again.

Historical financial performance

Balance sheets and profit and loss accounts are attached. Actual performance for the quarter to 27.3. 81 was:

	Sales	Net Profit
Valecom	£227 000	£59 000
Springmoss	£159 000	£31 000
Total		£90 000

Purchase price

The Vendors have agreed a sale price of £550 000 for the assets and goodwill of the companies.

The Purchasers

The intending Purchasers are R. S. Stuart and M. P. Philipp, founder directors and shareholders (25 per cent and 75 per cent) in Hunky Products (the trading name of Frolward Ltd). Their objective is to merge the companies with Hunky Products, the rationale for which is outlined below.

Hunky Products

The company was established in 1979. It is a marketing company selling branded ('Hunky') packaged, speciality frozen products (mainly hamburgers). Manufacturing is subcontracted, as is the physical distribution to a network of frozen food wholesalers.

Hunky Products has just become profitable, having spent the first eighteen months of its existence investing in the introduction of a totally new type of product (pre-cooked hamburger and bun combination for microwave). The product is now well-established with Hunky as a clear brand leader in an extremely fast-growing market. The company plans to capitalise on this strong base by extending its current range of frozen food to packaged products.

Financial information on Hunky and its recent sales and profit record are attached.

Rationale for merger

There are several areas of synergy between Hunky Products and the companies in question:

(i) Hunky purchase hamburger buns. Switching these purchases to Valecom would increase Valecom turnover by 25 per cent and profitability by a greater percentage;

(ii) Valecom and Springmoss provide excellent production units for currently subcontracted production and planned new products in the Hunky range;

(iii) Kara and Hunky sell via the same channels of distribution to the same and similar customers. Linking the two will substantially increase joint sales with no additional selling expenses and provide distribution economies.

Projected earnings

A projection of earnings for the first twelve months following the merger is based on the following assumptions:

(i) Valecom performs with the same level of sales and profitability as in the last quarter, as does Springmoss, that is, zero growth.

(ii) Hunky continues its current expansion to a peak in the summer of 1981.

	Sales(£)	Net profits(£)
Valecom	900 000	235 000
Springmoss	520 000	120 000
Hunky Products	1 000 000	100 000
Additional Hunky/Kara products	500 000	50 000
Valecom sales to Hunky	500 000	75 000
Total net profit before interest and tax		£580 000

Cash flow by quarter

		£ 000s		
	Q1	Q2	Q3	Q4
Trading profit	125	140	150	165
plus depreciation	10	10	10	10
less Inc. in Working Capital	(10)	(30)	(20)	(30)
Cash available for taxation, interest, loan repayments, etc.	125	120	140	145

Note: These figures do not include interest receivable from reinvested cash flow.

Appendix B: Terms of proposed loans by County Bank

1. *Borrower*:   Frolward Limited

2. *Principal amounts*:

No. 1 Loan	£275 000
No. 2 Loan	£275 000
	£550 000

3. *Security:*

    Both Loans:

    Mortgage Debenture containing fixed and floating charges on the assets of Frolward supported by fixed charges on the share capitals of Valecom Limited ('Valecom') and Springmoss Limited ('Springmoss') and on the 51 per cent holding by Valecom in Kara Speciality Foods (1980) Limited ('Kara').

    N° 1 Loan:

    Guarantee by Mr M. P. Philipp supported by appropriate security.

    N° 2 Loan:

    Guarantee by Mr R. S. Stuart supported by appropriate security.

4. *Purpose*:

    To finance the acquisition of the share capitals of Valecom and Springmoss for £550 000 cash.

5. *Repayment*:

    A repayment programme is to be agreed over, say, 7 to 10 years in the light of the anticipated cash flow. Early repayments on quarterly rollover dates (see below) would be permitted without penalty.

6. *Interest*:

    Interest would be payable quarterly in arrears on the balance outstanding at a rate over three months London Inter-Bank Offered Rate plus an adjustment in respect of the reserve asset or other liquidity requirement on the Bank. This rate would be calculated on drawdown for the subsequent three months and thereafter in advance on quarterly rollover. If the loans being drawn down today the interest chargeable for the first quarter would be at the rate of: 2.5 per cent + 12.375 per cent + 0.125 per cent = 15 per cent per annum.

7. *Drawdown*:

The loans would be drawn in full simultaneously in one drawing not later than 30 June 1981.

8. *Pre-Conditions*:

The following principal conditions would apply:

1. The Bank and its solicitors to be satisfied with all the necessary documentation.
2. The Bank to be satisfied with all the businesses following one- or two-day visits to each operating premises, including subcontractors where appropriate.
3. The Bank to be satisfied with the nature and valuation of the security offered.
4. The Bank to be satisfied with the accounts of all the businesses and with the investigatory work carried out by the accountants.
5. The Bank to be satisfied with a forecast of the anticipated cash flow of the business for the first twelve months of the merger and of the profits for that period.
6. The Bank to acquire a shareholding in Frolward on satisfactory terms of between 15 per cent and 20 per cent.

9. *Principal Continuing Conditions:*

1. The Bank to receive periodic management accounts and audited accounts promptly.
2. The Bank to have the right to appoint a director (which right the Bank would not envisage exercising for the foreseeable future).
3. The Bank's consent would be required for all borrowings and finance (other than from trade creditors and intra-Group).
4. The Group not to incur a pre-tax loss.
5. No changes in the share capital or shareholding to take place without the Bank's consent.

NB A breach of Conditions 1, 3, 4 or 5 would result in the loans being placed on an 'on demand' basis.

10. These outline proposals do not constitute any form of commitment on the part of the Bank.

Appendix C: The UK market for hamburger buns

(Based on analysis by Richard Stuart, February 1982)

Market growth

The total UK market for hamburger buns has grown from zero in the mid-1970s to about £5 million in 1981. Approximately 40 per cent of this market is tied to in- house supply (For example, MacDonalds and Wimpy), leaving an available market of £3 million for independent suppliers.

Table 8.CS.1   The market for hamburger buns (weekly turnover in £)

	Winter	Summer
Frozen Retail		
Kara (Bejam)	5 500	7 500
Total	5 500	7 500
Frozen Catering		
Kara	8 500	12 000
Warburton	6 000	12 000
Total	14 500	24 000
Fresh Contract to Chains		
Warburton - London	8 000	11 000
Other	4 000	4 000
Battens	5 000	7 000
Kara	3 000	3 000
Total	20 000	25 000
Seasonal		
Butlin - Ladbroke - Warner		5 000
Other		5 000
Total	–	10 000
Total market in specified segment	40 000	66 500

Note: This list does not include MacDonald's [£1.2M p.a.] and Wimpy [£1M p.a.], nor regional or local bakers.

The market is projected to continue to grow by at least 20 per cent annually. MacDonald's are committed to doubling their sales over the next two years and this is expected to stimulate the growth of the overall market. Retail sales of American-style hamburgers are increasing at about 20 per cent annually and the proportion sold with buns is growing rapidly (the ratio of bun to hamburger sales is about 7 per cent in Bejam's retail outlets).

Market segments

The following segments have been identified (sales volume estimates are given in Table 8.(S.1):

• Frozen retail	100 per cent Kara (Group)
• Frozen catering	60 per cent Kara, 40 per cent Warburton
• Fresh contract to chains	50 per cent Warburton, 30 per cent Batten, 20 per cent Kara
• Local fresh daily	
• MacDonald's and Wimpy	Small or regional bakers
• Seasonal market	
• New business	Own bakery

Competitive position

Frozen   The critical importance of the frozen distribution and sales

network, plus the relatively high initial bakery plant investment
(£300 000) make it unlikely that any company other than an existing
frozen food manufacturer would wish to penetrate this market. Of the
three major frozen food companies in the UK, Bird's Eye have tried to
launch a hamburger bun and appear to have failed and Ross are using a
Kara product. Findus may choose to enter this market in due course.
The minor firms in this industry are likely to find the initial investment
too high.

Fresh   The growth in the fresh market is expected to be sufficient to
satisfy the existing, relatively small, bakery competitors. National distribution of fresh bakery products is only likely to be undertaken by one of
the major firms and they have shown no signs of being interested in this
market – largely because it is too small for them and the customers take
little of their existing products. RHM has run a small regional operation
in Leicester since late 1980 and ABF has a declared aversion to sesame
seeds. Batten, the only competitor to Kara and Warburton which
specialises in hamburger buns has no capacity to enter the frozen
market.

Related products

Alongside the growth of the market for hamburger buns, there are new oppor-
tunites for other frozen bakery products for catering outlets:

- Hot dog rolls – Lyons Maid have a requirement for about £200 000 annually.
- Wheatmeal rolls – for sandwich and hamburger bars.
- Speciality cobs – for pub lunches. Whitbread have a requirement for £200 000
  annually.
- French bread – entirely imported at present.

Appendix D: Outline of agreement between Warburton and Frolward

1. Frolward to purchase the assets of the Warburton unit at Droylesden for
   current book value, being £290 000 (less any discrepancy on inventory) in
   three instalments:
   (i) £200 000 on completion.
   (ii) £40 000 six months from completion date or before if the gyro-freezer is
   sold prior to six months. Interest at 17 per cent per annum.
   (iii) £50 000 over three years paid in three equal annual instalments, plus
   interest at 17 per cent per annum.
2. Frolward to rent the building at £1.50 per sq ft with a 10-year lease with rent
   review after 5 years. Frolward to have the first option to purchase the
   building at any time Warburton wish to sell and to have the firm option to
   purchase after 5 years.

3. Warburton to collect all outstanding trade debts.
4. Frolward to purchase usable stock on completion date at cost.
5. Warburton to facilitate the smooth handover of existing customers to Frolward. Joint visits to commence following agreement, but prior to completion.
6. Warburton to agree not to supply existing customers at the Droylesden plant with hamburger buns for the next three years.
7. Warburton to pay redundancy for any staff not hired by Frolward. Frolward to take over existing contracts of any staff hired. (Note: Plant was operated as a 'closed shop', thus all staff were members of a bakery union.)

Appendix E: Consolidated balance sheets – Frolward Ltd.

	27.6.81 (£000s)	26.12.81 (£000s)
Net fixed assets	218	197
Goodwill on acquisition	332	332
Current assets		
Stocks	70	85
Debtors	455	376
Cash	71	28
	596	489
Current Liabilities		
Creditors	537	373
Taxation	25	25
Bank Overdraft	12	19
	574	417
Net current assets	22	72
	572	601
Financed by		
Share capital	0.2	0.2
Reserves	(5)	52
Loans	567	540
Deferred taxation	9	9
	572	601

CHAPTER 9

Developing Small Firms Out of Large

Tony Lorenz

This chapter is concerned with three areas of small business or venture capital finance, where larger corporations interface the smaller company. All successful large companies build from one or more successful smaller companies, often over a long period of time. In recent years, however, the process of agglomeration and ever-increasing size in the most advanced industrial economies has shown signs of encouraging a reverse, or parallel process of divestment, demerger and privatisation.

In the three areas of *corporate venturing, management buy-outs and buy-ins*, small-company financing techniques (as well as certain smaller company growth risks) become relevant to the larger company.

Corporate venturing

This is a way in which large or medium-sized corporations can partner small (or new) companies in growing or diversifying their own long-term business, often with the participation of venture capitalists as investing partners and 'referees' between large and small corporate partners. *Corporate spin-offs* or *spin-outs* are a variant on the corporate venturing theme, which is covered in the first section of this chapter.

Management buy-outs

These are now a well-established way in which larger corporations can divest business units to those units' own management teams, as a way of shedding peripheral, non-performing or high-value subsidiaries (or divisions) to the benefit of mainstream earnings, management stretch or short-term cash flow pressure. The second section of this chapter deals with the management buy-out.

237

Buy-ins

These are mirrors of buy-outs, frequently having more in common with take-overs than with buy-outs. Turnaround or recovery investment is a regular feature of buy-ins, where a new management is financing the acquisition of a controlling position in an existing business. Buy-ins are generally applied to established, often quite sizeable companies and are a blend of venture capital techniques and large-scale corporate finance. The last section of this chapter addresses the buy-in as an important new aspect of small-business finance.

1.   Corporate venturing and the role for venture capital

Although corporate venturing can take place on a 'solo', *ad hoc* basis, the venture capitalist can play a key role in fostering and even creating successful corporate venturing relationships. This has been demonstrated clearly in the USA, where corporate venturing has grown more than fivefold since 1980 – frequently in partnership with venture capital firms. In essence, there are three ways in which a venture capitalist can become involved in developing an entrepreneurially-independent business alongside a corporate venturer:

(i)   bringing a corporation into an existing portfolio company;
(ii) investing in a business or project which is spun-off from a corporation, the corporation retaining a financial interest;
(iii) joining with a corporate venturer at the outset of an investment, the initiative usually originated by the venture capitalist.

For corporation and venture capitalist to join together in financing the development plans of an independent business does not require that business to be new or in a start-up phase. Expansion financings for established companies and even, occasionally, management buy-outs can benefit from a corporate venturer as minority partner – particularly if the corporation is a key supplier or customer.

In the *ménage à trois* between entrepreneur, corporate venturer and venture capitalist, it might be thought that the latter's prime role is that of umpire. The relationships are, however, more complex. For a generally satisfactory outcome to the three-way relationship, motivations must mesh – so that each party's effort can be harnessed toward a common goal, which is the financial success of the enterprise.

Here the venture capitalist's fundamental aim of maximising long-term capital gain clearly meshes with that of the entrepreneur. This should be the aim of a corporate venturer too, but often there are other aims for the corporation, such as:

(i)   access to new technology or to new markets for its own products;
(ii) additional products for its own distribution networks;
(iii) inside track on potential acquisitions;
(iv) competitive intelligence on markets and technology;
(v)   laying off some of its own R & D risks;
(vi) improving its return on investment in otherwise speculative projects.

These aims can all be accomodated, and indeed are often the very reasons the corporation is venturing at all, provided they do not side-track the enterprise from the ultimate goal of financial success.

A venture capital syndicate has usually as much (or more) cash at stake in a three-way enterprise as has the corporate venturer – in fact, it is inadvisable for the corporation to be permitted to invest more than the venture capitalist. This position, together with his initiating the investment, gives the venture capitalist a pivotal role in the 'triangle'. Provided he is well aware of the major positives and negatives, he can manage the relationship with the corporate venturer to the benefit of all three parties.

For the venture capitalist and entrepreneur the main *positives* are:

Distribution/market penetration

It may be possible for the investor to achieve an earlier and more effective market entry than could be achieved 'solo', by accessing the corporate partner's distribution network, particularly in international markets.

Technology source

The corporate venturer can play an important validating role, if the investment is in its area of competence. More, as the project develops, the venture capitalist and entrepreneur may have ready access to a second technology source of greater depth than the entrepreneur's own.

Trade credibility

By linking with a well-known corporate partner, the investee company can develop a higher profile in its sector, improving customer and supplier confidence and possibly also ensuring better terms from suppliers and banks.

Management underpin

From the corporation, experienced management advice will be available on a broader base than is usual in the investee; this is not always capable of being contributed by even a 'hands on' venture capitalist.

Exit options

There is the real attraction of a ready-made realisation route for both entrepreneur and venture capitalist, through the corporate partner eventually acquiring the business, from his original minority equity position. This does not always happen, however, and as referred to later, there can be problems in maximising exit values, from such a corporate relationship.

Also, for the venture capitalist, a specific *positive* may be:

Deal flow enhancement

Particularly if the investment is a corporate spin-off, where the corporate venturer is in effect the 'host' or 'mother' to the newly independent business.

The principal *negatives* in a corporate venturing which the venture capitalist (or other intermediary) must manage, to minimise the risks of failure, include:

Entrepreneur perceptions

Domination by a corporate partner will be an apprehension in most entrepreneurs, particularly if they have recently spun-out of a large company themselves. The venture capitalist often has to act as 'minder' to the entrepreneur, to guarantee him protection from (often exaggerated) fears of management interference by the corporate partner.

Technology leakage

Concerns about the corporate partner lifting the entrepreneur's ideas or specific technology have to be dealt with – usually through the signing of secrecy or confidentiality agreements and access to the entrepreneur's technology being routed via the venture capitalist.

Decision speed

Many large corporations suffer from extended bureaucracy in making decisions on cash spend, market launches, project work in R & D facilities, and so on. The venture capitalist should ensure that the corporate partner relationship is managed through the chief executive's office, rather than the finance, marketing or R & D functions. This is critically important in relation to the hurdles of 'not invented here' which have to be dismantled if the corporate venturing benefits are to be delivered to the investment.

Marketing pre-emption

Although access to new products may be the rationale for the corporate venturer's participation in the investment, a 'first refusal' on distribution may not always be in the best interest of the investee company. It may be difficult for the venture capitalist to introduce alternative sources of distribution despite these being possibly more directly relevant to the business's needs.

Narrowing of exit options

Although a 'captive' potential purchaser may often be attractive, a pre-emptive purchase option may be a limited blessing – the entrepreneur's and venture capitalist's realisation value is not always maximised, when compared with the alternatives of stock market listing or third-party sale. The venture capitalist should ensure that external offers for the business are not 'shut out' by the corporate partner.

Provided the venture capitalist can ensure the mutual squeezing of maximum benefit from the corporate partner's participation without the negatives being brought into play, he will have performed his pivotal role in a corporate venturing relationship.

For the corporate venturer there are five basic options by which to achieve the interface with the venture capitalist and his deal flows, and a sixth – the corporate spin-off activity, with the involvement of a venture capitalist or other third party as partner to the larger corporation's own projects.

First, the corporate venturer can establish his own specialist vehicle – either internally or externally – and recruit venture capital expertise to operate to his specific requirements. For the venture capitalists, a corporate employer is not always a happy prospect. Most experienced venture capitalists have left large corporations, precisely because they were self-motivated to the extent that few large organisations tolerate. The venture capitalist's deal flow may not always follow him into such a corporate position, as many small-business entrepreneurs will be intimidated by the prospect of direct equity participation in their fledgeling enterprise – solely from a large corporation with (to the entrepreneur) questionable motives, particularly where there is no 'neutral' investor such as an independent venture capital fund – to ensure a balance of interest. In-house corporate venturing has long been established in the USA where many large (and medium-sized) corporations have over a decade of corporate venturing experience.

Second, he can invest in one or more selected venture capital funds, which are prepared to satisfy at least part of his own objects – a non-monetary involvement is unlikely to prove effective in motivating the venture capitalist. Taking one or more corporate investors into the fund itself is less intimidating but can cause conflict. Whatever the stated interest at the outset, the corporate venturer in an independent fund is rarely, in the long-run, prepared to give the fund complete freedom: for example, to handle its own deal flow without some degree of looking over the venture capitalist's shoulders – or to leave the fund to carry out its hand on aftercare without some technology or market intelligence information flow-back to the corporate partner. This mode has developed to a greater extent in continental Europe than in the UK hitherto.

The third option is for a looser policy of coinvestment alongside one or several venture capitalists in specific deals, where sufficient mutual self-interest exists to fulfil all parties' objectives – including, most importantly, the entrepreneur's. This is perhaps the most commonly practised mode in the UK at present.

A fourth option is simply that of cultivating a number of venture capitalists, so as to be first in line to make acquisitions from their portfolios. Although this is not generally recognised as corporate venturing, it is a relatively painless way of letting the sweat equity of the venture capitalist and the endeavours of the entrepreneur create a business – for which the corporate venturer then pays, hopefully, a handsome price. It is a perfectly legitimate and time-honoured method of acquiring new technology at low risk.

A fifth option, the solo corporate venturer, can be carried out in parallel with one (or a combination) of the above coventuring options. Many successful models exist in the USA of larger corporations entering into a symbiotic relationship with smaller businesses. These one-off deals can develop from the centre of the larger corporations, but it is more likely for such one-off deals to be achieved within a divison or subsidiary which has a limited mission, and can relatively easily identify synergistic opportunities among the smaller companies in its general area of business. To carry out such *ad hoc* relationships from a large corporation's centre, can result in a diversified portfolio of (minority) investments which may have no real effect on the larger corporation's primary business activity. Carefully planned 'centralist' corporate venturing, alongside venture capital groups can, by contrast, be a more effective way of growing new business activities. Indeed, there is increasing evidence in the UK that large corporations have identified the benefits of 'plugging into' a venture capitalist's deal flow, rather than attempting a 'go it alone' corporate venturing strategy.

2.   Corporate spin-offs

In the USA, many venture capital investments result from a group of experienced executives leaving their employer, often with a product ready to go to market. This is good for them, good for the venture capitalist but not so good for their large corporate employer! In the UK, largely for cultural reasons, the US scale of spin-offs is unlikely to be repeated. Preferable from the corporation's viewpoint, and possibly equally attractive to venture capitalist and potential entrepreneur, would be the ability to spin out budding entrepreneurs from within the corporation, and not lose total benefit, by retaining a minority position in their business – alongside an experienced venture capitalist as the cofinancier, 'hands on' adviser and umpire to ensure entrepreneurial freedom.

It is possible to devise an effective means of achieving this – the Technology Venture Partnership (TVP). A tax-efficient mechanism, the TVP presents the 'host' corporation with the opportunity to spin off a project with its internal entrepreneurial champion – who would probably otherwise leave, taking the project with him – while retaining a meaningful stake in the project, sharing the financing of its development off balance sheet and being first in line to buy back the project later, if and when it develops into a successful business.

3.   Management buy-outs

The buy-out is a relatively recent, if increasingly significant, form of investment in the European venture capital industry. In essence, it involves the creation of independent businesses by separating them from their existing owners, which may be successful or unsuccessful corporations, or family-controlled businesses. A buy-out will involve the existing or a new management team and a set of assets which may simply be a trade name or a small group of people. In most cases it will

Table 9.1   UK buy-out statistics: total number and value of management buy-outs, 1967–86

Year	Number	Cumulative Number	Value (£m)	Cumulative Value (£m)	Average Value in Year (£m)
1967–76	43	43	n/a	n/a	n/a
1977	13	56	n/a	n/a	n/a
1978	23	79	n/a	n/a	n/a
1979	52	131	26	26	0.50
1980	107	238	50	76	0.47
1981	124	362	114	190	0.92
1982	170	532	265	455	1.56
1983	205	737	315	770	1.54
1984	210	947	415	1185	1.98
1985	229	1176	1150	2335	5.02
1986*	248	1424	1438	3773	5.80

* Estimation
Source: J. Coyne and M. Wright, Nottingham University Center for Buyout Research

also involve one or more new investors, although in some cases buy-outs can be financed from the management team's own resources and/or through bank debt alone.

There have been buy-outs in the United Kingdom on a sporadic basis since the early 1960s; these reached a consistent and high volume only in the early 1980s. The practice has been active in the United States, however, since the early 1950s. The first practitioners of buy-outs in the United Kingdom were not US banks, venture capital funds or institutions with experience of the US market, but rather domestic merchant banks and savings institutions.

As will be seen from Table 9.1, there was a rapid growth in management buy-outs in the UK between 1980 and 1983 resulting largely from the general economic problems experienced by major industrial groupings due to the UK recession and subsequently the world recession. These large groups have found it necessary or desirable to realise cash by disposal of peripheral activities in order to sustain the core of their business and to avoid management stretch into non- essential activities.

The stabilisation in the volume of buy-outs since 1984 is at least partially due to recovery by the larger corporations. Another factor is the corporate vendor's increasing awareness of the 'resale' value of the corporation's peripheral businesses. A significant comparative statistic, which highlights the importance of the buy-out trend, is that between 1980 and 1986 there were more buy-outs than acquisitions by other industrial companies of divested subsidiaries. As can be seen from Figure 9.1, in 1977, by contrast, acquisitions of divested subsidiaries were roughly ten times the number of buy-outs. It should also be noted

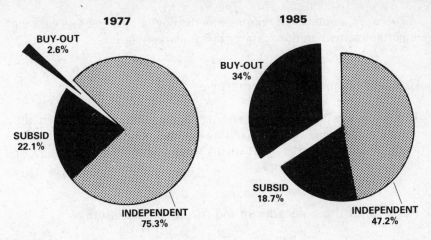

Figure 9.1   Acquisitions, divestments and buy-outs

that buy-outs are currently smaller, at about half the size of subsidiaries sold to new parents.

Indeed, a striking feature has been the small size of most buy-outs, with (until 1985) an average size of under £2 million consideration/ valuation and fewer than 200 employees. Many of these small buy-outs are mature businesses which have been in existence for a long time. It is difficult to predict how many will prosper and grow in time to become substantial businesses in their own right and how many will either fail in their now independent position or remain as they were when bought out – that is unexciting and without real growth prospects. A number, however, are businesses with real growth potential, often in high-technology areas but distinct from the main activity of their former parent. Larger buy-outs have been appearing more frequently since 1985, but as yet the sale of larger, particularly public market buy-outs, does not approach that experienced in the USA over the past decade.

The major hazard with many buy-outs is the high initial gearing (ratio of debt to equity) inherent in the buy-out funding structure, particularly where gearing is made up of bank lending rather than long-term prefer-ence or mezzanine capital. The use of equity-based syndications helps to keep the initial debt low and thus gives the company essential breathing space in its early years as an independent entity. However, most UK buy-outs include debt as a substantial proportion of the total funding, often where asset disposals or surplus cash flow from trading can be safely predicted to quickly reduce the initial level of debt. In smaller buy-outs (under £1 million) management teams can often achieve ulti-mate control of the equity, while typically subscribing only 10–20 per cent of the total funds. In larger buy-outs it is common for the managers to hold only a minority equity position.

There are a number of reasons why the buy-out has become such an important activity in the venture capital market-place.

Creation of smaller-scale enterpise

The buy-out is an additional and perhaps a more certain (from the investor's perspective) mechanism for the creation of small and medium-sized businesses, particularly when compared with start-ups or new technology-based firms.

Reversal of three decades of industrial concentration

The process of demerger and creation of smaller, more flexible profit centres is part of the divestment process of today's large industrial groups. These groups were built up after 1950 by uninterrupted merger and acquisition activity, and have generally shown themselves particularly ill-suited to today's conditions of rapid technological and economic change.

Remarriage of management and ownership

An unfortunate trend in the twentieth century has been the divorce of management of enterprises from their ownership. Efficiency has suffered through successful defence by inadequate management against the best interest of the owners. The buy-out provides the opportunity for common identification of goals by managers and owners, the managers in many cases having a substantial, even controlling, direct shareholding in the business.

Investor/banker common interest

Apart from the divorce of management and ownership, one of the major weaknesses of twentieth-century economic development has been the separation of interest between banker and investor, with the former concerned largely with security, that is, the absence of risk. The buy-out with its usually high initial gearing, often unsecured, provides an opportunity for banker and investor to agree on a common aim from the outset and proceed as partners with the management, throughout the good (and bad) early years of their buy-out's development.

Development of new entrepreneurs

After thirty years of growth of the 'organisation man' and the cult of the industrial bureaucrat, the buy-out presents a long-needed injection of new entrepreneurial skill by freeing the corporate manager from his umbilical cord to corporate headquarters. As we shall see later, however, there are risks involved in this.

Lower-risk investment than start-ups

Largely because of the established performance record of the business being bought out and of the management effecting the buy-out, and because of the established asset position, a buy-out represents a significantly lower degree of risk, in most cases, than does the new technology start-up. It should be noted, however, that many buy-outs do involve high-technology activities.

There are three basic types of buy-out:

 (i) Corporate disposals or 'hive-downs';
 (ii) Shareholder repurchases; and
(iii) Receivership acquisitions.

Corporate disposals or 'hive-downs'

This form of buy-out is by far the most frequent in the UK. It usually involves the sale of 100 per cent of the business, whether subsidiary, division or operating unit, through its assets alone, the business entity or only the product names, and so on. Occasionally, a partial divestment is carried out, with the parent retaining a minority stake in the new entity. This minority holding is often linked to deferred payment terms. The existing management team usually inititates the buy-out, but additional management is sometimes injected at, or after, the initiation of the independent enterprise.

The major reasons for this form of disposal are similar to those which would encourage the parent company to sell the same activity to another parent. However, there are often feelings of loyalty to the management team, which, if it has sufficient initiative, may be able to achieve first option before the parent proceeds to any sale within the trade. In addition, a strong subsidiary management team seeking independence may not make it easy to sell the subsidiary to another company. There is an element of moral and practical 'blackmail' available to the resident management team if it is sufficiently committed to independence.

There are many possible reasons for parental divestment. For example:

(i) The parent company is in difficulties;
(ii) The subsidiary is peripheral to core business strategy;
(iii) The subsidiary is unprofitable but overhead savings are available on buy-out;
(iv) Post-merger rationalisation of unwanted parts of an acquisition; and
(v) Difficult subsidiary/parent management relationships or parent management overstretch, where limited management resources are required elsewhere in the group, most probably in the main-stream activities.

There are particular advantages in this form of buy-out:

(i) Professional management is already in place;
(ii) An established track record is open to investigation;
(iii) Management disciplines and controls are established; and
(iv) There may be the opportunity to buy assets at a discount.

Inevitably, there are problems that may arise from this form of buy-out after independence:

(i) Professional, large-company management may not be able to withstand the harsh realities of entrepreneurial independence;
(ii) Vulnerability to markets and suppliers without parental 'protection';
(iii) It may be difficult to make a clean break with the parent: for example, if the latter is still a supplier, customer, lender or landlord;
(iv) Inclination to underestimate past contribution made by parent; and
(v) The parent may not be selling for the reasons stated.

These problems are often manifestations of the fact that membership of a group of companies does provide essential central services, insurance against poor decisions and market credibility, which may not be available to an independent unit. Sometimes, the management team and, indeed, its supporting investors/bankers do not take sufficient account of this fact beforehand.

Shareholder repurchases

An increasingly common buy-out is where the original founder(s) and current owner(s) wishes to retire but does not wish to sell to a trade buyer or seek a stock market listing. In this case the management team, which has often been in effective operating control of the business for a number of years, seeks outside finance to buy out the retiring owner and/or his or her family interest and thereby become the controlling shareholders themselves. Usually, this would involve gaining control of the ongoing business by purchasing the shares held by the current owner: it may be that the management already has a minority holding and seeks a majority holding through the purchase of this equity with the participation of new investors. In this type of buy-out there is rarely the need for a new banking relationship; the existing bankers remaining in their current position.

Variations on this theme occur when there is a division in family interest or objective, that is, part of the ownership of the family company wishes to sell out while others are prepared to continue in management. Here the investors would seek to repurchase the outgoing family shareholdings. It may also happen that the younger generation of a family business wishes to purchase the previous generation's holding and thereby gain control with the help of new investors. In the case of both these types of continuing family control, it is of critical importance for the outside investor that the remaining family management is competent to run the business in a professional manner. The *particular* advantages of this form of buy-out are the same as those for corporate disposals, except that asset discount is unlikely. However, a creative financial structure can be used to achieve a fiscal advantage for private vendors, while reducing the costs to managers/investors.

Specific problems of this type of buy-out are:

 (i) The price may not allow an adequate discount on assets;
 (ii) A collective vendor often presents difficulties in negotiations;
(iii) Management may covet the outgoing vendor's life-style; and
(iv) The personality of the vendor may be important to the customer and supplier, or in motivation of the management team.

Where a vendor involves more than one member of the family, there are often protracted negotiations over the terms acceptable to each vendor. The management team may simply wish to acquire the 'expensive life-style' enjoyed by the outgoing founder/entrepreneur(s), which is frequently the case in family-owned private companies. The potential investor must also be aware of the possible impact of retirement by the outgoing shareholder on the customer/supplier relationships of the company, which may not be as strong under the remaining management team.

Receivership acquisitions

This is probably the most difficult form of buy-out to achieve. It is a well-tried route by both management and supporting investors but is usually doomed to failure because of the urgency of the receiver's need to realise cash. Another reason is the obvious advantage to a trade buyer in being able to justify a pre-emptive offer to a detailed knowledge of the business unit for sale – knowledge that is not initially available to the investor. This form of buy-out is often pursued, however, because a 'good' part of an unattractive group may be available, and purchases by new management, (that is, 'outsiders') is possible.

The main advantages of receivership acquisitions include:

 (i) The opportunity of a 'clean' purchase, excluding liabilities;
 (ii) New management can be injected from the outset;
(iii) Special terms are often achievable; and
(iv) A choice of assets is available.

There are particular problems in this form of buy-out, however, which make it a greater risk than either of the two types:

 (i) Market standing/supplier relations may already be damaged;
 (ii) The better employees may have gone;
(iii) There are higher initial working capital needs; and
(iv) Trade buyers can often outbid managers/investors.

4.   Key factors in the success or failure of buy-outs

Some key factors in identifying or constructing a potentially successful buy-out are outlined below.

Management commitment/motivation critical

Apart from the need to ensure that the management team is financially committed and stands to lose a serious amount if the buy-out fails, a strong entrepreneurial drive is important to carry the team through any difficult times which lie ahead. Investors often mistake 'professionalism' in a management team for 'entrepreneurism'.

Need for outside experience on board

Non-executive directors of the right calibre will bring immeasurable benefit and essentially replace the advisory/protective role previously exercised by the parent company. The right outside directors can also bring a positive contribution through their industrial contacts, market knowledge or technological background, and are particularly relevant to strategy formulation – in which the team may be relative novices.

Personal relations must be good

The buy-out must be a tight-knit team of people who are unusually honest with each other while still remaining effective. This is not necessarily the case in a divisional or subsidiary relationship, where parent companies can make management changes at will if strains become apparent.

Balance of team essential, especially in finance

It is important that the team at senior level be in balance, covering each major business function. It may be necessary to hire extra senior management to fill any gaps in the buy-out team.

Cost of deal should allow cash generation from day one

The objective of purchasing assets at a discount is partly to provide future borrowing capacity and also to reduce initial debt through the sale of surplus assets. In trading terms, however, the buy-out should allow significant net cash generation from the outset beyond that required for major capital expenditure, product development or working capital funding.

Management performance incentive important

Although in many buy-outs it will not be possible for the management to have a majority stake from the outset, an important motivation is the willingness by the investors to allow their holdings to be reduced, possibly even into a minority position dependent upon performance. This can be achieved through the issue of extra shares to management or through a lower rate of conversion by the investor syndicate's preferred/preference shares, depending on whether projected profits or exit valuation targets are reached. An alternative type of incentive is for the management to start at its maximum share stake, with the venture capital investors allowed to convert sufficient preferred shares to dilute the management stake if management fails to achieve its own forecasts over an agreed period of years.

These arrangements are known as 'ratchets' or 'earn-outs' and are designed to give the management its desired equity holding – if their profit forecasts or eventual exit valuation are achieved – while maintaining the investor's rate of return requirement if forecasts or exit valuations are not achieved. Earn-outs are also used to structure other venture capital investments, particularly in early-stage financings.

In establishing the maximum management stake and consequently the minimum investor's stake, a rule-of-thumb approach has become common, known as the envy ratio. This is a simple formula by which the ratio of investor-to-management financial contribution is divided by the ratio of investor-to-management equity. If the management seeks too disproportionate an equity position in relation to its financial contribution, an investor syndicate may decline to support the buy-out on those terms.

Gearing must be realistic, especially to control early debt repayment/high servicing costs; bankers must be a partner

As already mentioned, excess initial debt is often the single major cause of failure in young companies. It is important when a buy-out is constructed, that any clearing bank lending be on more generous terms concerning security and repayment than is normally the case. To some extent the banker must be prepared to take a quasi-equity risk – not always a comfortable position for the traditional banker. Government grants may also be available to assist with the financing burden.

Tripartite negotiations make buy-outs unusually lengthy/complicated

Unlike the other forms of venture capital investment, where normally only two parties are involved, the investor and the investee, the buy-out includes an equally important party, the vendor. The interests of the management team and its investors are usually at one in achieving from the vendor the lowest possible price and the longest possible interest free deferred payment, but the investors are also keen to arrange a good deal for themselves. The real pressure in a buy-out falls on the management team which is negotiating a sale with the vendor and often simultaneously a funding package with investors. The management should certainly have its own financial advisers; a number of intermediaries specialising in buy-outs have become established in the UK, in addition to the major investment and merchant banks and the accounting firms that are becoming experienced in this new field of corporate advice.

Trade unions

The parent company's unions often resist a buy-out, as this will weaken their group membership. However, a poor management/union relationship is usually improved after a buy-out because of the closer liaison between operating unit management and shop-floor, in contrast to the tendency of large groups to manage their industrial relations from the centre.

At this stage, with the bulk of UK buy-outs having taken place only since 1980, there is little analytical material available on the reasons for any failures which have occurred. Indeed, from the published results of buy-outs which have been realised, the evidence suggests that the buy-out is a low risk/high return business sector – most unusual for equity investment!

It is inevitable, however, that the failure rate will increase as the weaknesses inherent in many buy-outs proved insuperable. The main causes of potential failure include the following.

Inadequate (or uncommitted) management team

Frequently a buy-out team goes 'into shock' for the first year or so. Weaknesses in the management team may not become apparent until some time after the buy-out, when external pressures may expose fragile areas which would have been covered by the previous parent company or where back-up management resources could have been made available by the parent.

Inaccurate pre-investment product/market evaluation

Just as with early-stage financings, the investors may well have misjudged or have been misled, and the rate of technological changes may not have been properly examined either. It is particularly important to ensure that the parent is not divesting because of a long-term declining trend in the health of the buy-out business.

Excessive initial debt gearing

This problem is equally applicable to start-ups, and although there are attractive arguments in favour of investors seeking a secured position in the initial funding, the major cause of failure in any young or high-growth company is the requirement to repay initial debt and particularly to service a high level of debt in the early years of development. Many venture capitalists find a way around this problem by seeking preference stock or 'mezzanine' loans (or other instruments) as part of the financial package, with preference stock having a low initial coupon but the right to participate in future profits once a satisfactory level of cash flow and profit generation is achieved. This preference stock would also be long-term with repayment possible over the extended period and usually not during the first years.

Insufficient cash contingency

It is important that the initial funding includes a substantial contingency against the management's projected cash flow; as much as 50 per cent additional provision may be required.

Disagreement between parties

If a buy-out runs into a difficult period, either through internal inadequacies or external circumstances, the first strains will appear between the management team and its investors. In such a case, it is important that the investor has the commitment and ability to provide 'hands on' support including, if necessary, the ability to replace members of the management team. Many buy-out investors are not staffed with this in mind and they will undoubtedly have problems with some of their buy-out investments in the years to come.

Equally, it may be that where a syndicate or a consortium of investors is involved, they do not share a common view as to the right solution in any problems that may occur. It is possible that because of this inability to agree, a buy-out may fail – although one of the investors is prepared in principle to provide further funds or accept a renegotiation of terms, but will not do so unless the partner investors agree.

5.   Buy-ins

Leveraged and management buy-outs, tagged LBOs and MBOs, are now part of the everyday corporate financing product range and have produced consistently sparkling returns for their investors, both in the USA and the UK. Now a variant on the buy-out, the buy-in, is appearing more frequently in the UK.

Superficially similar to the buy-out in form and structure, a buy-in is fundamentally different in both its origination and its inherently greater risks. A buy-in approach does not originate from the management team of the business unit subject to the transaction, in contrast to a buy-out. Typically, a buy-in is triggered by the approach of an external manager or group of managers to the owners of the business unit – which can be a publicly quoted company, a private business or even a previous management buy-out. The new management is usually a group acting as independent individuals but buy-ins can also be achieved by the reversal of an established smaller business, which the new managers control, into the target company.

A buy-in carries inherently higher risks than a buy-out due primarily to the incoming management team's (usual) unfamiliarity with the operating details of the buy-in target's business, by contrast with a buy-out team who are buying their own business. Buy-ins are also more likely to take place with businesses that are not performing satisfactorily – hence risks of overgearing, trading losses and substantial provisions being required. For these reasons, the buy-ins frequently require a venture capitalist's due diligence and investigative skills as well as the financial engineering skills which are adequate for most buy-outs. To attempt a buy-in while equipped solely with financial expertise is to amplify the already greater risks, than would be present in most buy-outs.

In the public markets to date, there have been few successfully completed buy-ins – these include Myson Group and Woolworth. A number of private company buy-ins have also been completed including venture-backed businesses whose investors have welcomed the external approach of proven managers to investments which have drifted seriously away from plan over a relatively long period of time. Another novel form of buy-in, which may be increasingly evident, is the introduction of new management into a previous buy-out. A recent buy-in of this nature is Melville Technology, where a group of managers resigned from Mowlem Technology to take over the management at Melville, which had itself been bought out from Alfred Herbert's receivership four years previously.

In the private arena, a buy-in is usually not possible to complete unless the present owners are willing sellers – the exceptions being where the company is in dire straits because of over-gearing or lack of profits. In the public arena also, it is likely that the target company's shareholders are disenchanted owners and thus willing sellers – as is the case with successful buy-ins in previous management buy-outs.

Hostile buy-ins are beginning to appear in the public share markets but, as is described later, a hostile buy-in carries with it some 'blind side' problems, as with any hostile take-over. A hostile buy-in can also result in the target's acquisition price being overvalued when compared with its near-term prospects, even allowing for the buy-in team's skills.

A buy-in is not unlike a take-over or merger, in that a new management group is gaining effective operating control over another company. In a buy-in, however, the acquirer is an individual or small group of individuals who usually have to structure a new vehicle to finance the transaction, and often have little direct knowledge of the details of the target company's business. In a take-over, by contrast, the acquirer is usually already well-financed, has in-depth management ability and often has day-to-day knowledge of the acquired company's business.

Perhaps the most important distinctions are the motivations of the principals and the financing structures. With a buy-in, the incoming management group is motivated by a significant personal capital gain, at least on paper, in the medium term (2–3 years) while they may also have ambitions to grow their own business from a flying start – compared with a standing start were they to form a new early-stage company of their own. As to structure, because a leveraged buy-in financing improves the management/investor group's equity return, a buy-in is usually significantly more highly geared than a conventional take-over. Notwithstanding the differences, a buy-in is in many ways more akin to a take-over transaction than to a buy-out.

6.   Key factors in the success or failure of buy-ins

Buy-ins are likely to be more successful given the following factors.

Strong entrepreneurial management

As evidenced by the incoming manager(s) backed by the buy-in syndicate. The incoming manager(s) do not always originate from the subject company's industry, although frequently they have some experience of the sector. Fundamental requirements are a clear vision of forward strategy together with a capability for hard-nosed operating efficiency.

Existing product market strengths

These usually have not been fully exploited by current management and are almost often found in fragmented markets where a 'niche strategy' can be highly profitable and where efficient major corporations are not in evidence.

Good cash flow potential

The buy-in target company must have this key factor even if it is not being optimised by the incumbent management, as is usually the case.

Availability of a pre-emptive equity holding

This must be adequate to exercise management control, which need not always require a 51 per cent or greater equity holding, dependent on the make-up of other voting blocks in the target company's equity structure. Ideally, the core equity holding should be available from a passive group of investors such as a dispersed family holding, or a group of indifferent institutions (in the public markets). Equally desirable would be a disenchanted, 'floating' block or blocks representing a family 'split' disappointed venture capital investors or a stalemated corporate minority (or a combination of these). The dangers in not ensuring an effective controlling position from the outset of the buy-in are third-party competition or current management counter-action resulting in either failure to complete the buy-in or success at a high price.

Turnaround symptoms

These are often the real trigger for a buy-in. Turnarounds can make high return buy-ins, provided the business has not reached terminal decline – defined as having finally lost customer credibility or long-term competitive advantage (possibly through technology obsolescence). Excessive present leverage may also argue against a successful buy-in, unless surplus assets can be realised quickly and senior debt radically restructured to reduce the load on operating cash flows from high interest costs and near term repayments.

As yet, too few buy-ins have been completed in the UK for enough evidence to be available to enable sound conclusions as to success ratios or the reasons for failure. No doubt researchers will investigate buy-ins in the years to come, but here are a few hazard areas:

(a) Buy-in attempts where a counter-offer from a trade buyer or any other serious party is likely can end up expensive to the victor. If the victor is the buy-in syndicate, potentially attractive returns can be reduced to a level below that commensurate with the risk. It is often possible to assign probabilities to a counter-offer, particularly if the current management under threat seek a 'white knight' acquirer.

(b) Management control in a buy-in means boardroom control from the outset, whatever the equity position of the buy-in syndicate. Often this is difficult to achieve from a minority equity position unless other existing investors support the buy-in initiative.

(c) A blind buy-in can be a dangerous move (just as with a standard public take-over) in that much of a subject company's affairs are unknown until after the buy-in takes place. The difference here is that the state of the subject company can wreck a buy-in syndicate's finances, whereas a standard trade acquirer usually has the substance to weather most, if not all, problems. Sound homework is, therefore, critical, and many buy-ins will only take place if there is the possibility of full due diligence by the incoming syndicate – the requirement being that the target business has controlling shareholdings which are friendly to the buy-in initiative. Because of public market procedures, friendly private company buy-ins with full access to the facts are easier than in the public markets.

(d) A buy-in can be too late if attempted, and has happened, after a new senior manager (or management) has been installed in the subject company, even if the change at the top appears not yet to be boosting the target company's results – the investors are likely to support the current management in such cases.

(e) Unless the target company is in trouble, a buy-in in the public markets is likely to fail if the existing investors are not offered the opportunity to join the buy-in syndicate and stay with the business under the incoming management, via the provision of a paper alternative into the buy-in sydicate's investment vehicle.

(f) It is always preferable for a buy-in team to include management with direct operating knowledge of the subject company's business, although a number of buy-ins have proved that the able managers can achieve buy-out success in industries where they have not previously operated. Experienced management with good operating records in the same, or a similar, industry sector will help to stabilise the customer, supplier and even banking (and hence working capital) bases of the target business.

As yet, there are only a few UK buy-ins, but it is likely that opportunities will increase over the next few years both in the public markets and among private companies – some of which will be previous management buy-outs or early-stage venture capital deals which have not fulfilled their original investors' expectations and may well be suitable 'friendly' subjects for another try, under a buy-in. The latter transactions will frequently involve new funding for the business as well as to buy out existing investors.

Although corporate finance skills are a key requirement for a buy-in syndicate, it will also take the venture capitalist's skills of product/market assessment, technology validation where relevant, and above all the ability to identify capable managers who can be persuaded to join their buy-in team – that is, if these managers are not the first to identify potential buy-ins and go out to seek their investors!

Case Study 1:   Types of buy-out

When a buy-out is based on the acquisition of a business from its parent company by its own management team, the transaction can take various forms. The share capital (and liabilities) of the business may be purchased, or solely the assets and trading rights. In either case, the structure of the deal will depend, among other issues, on the valuation of the assets being purchased and whether they are all required in the newly independent business. For example, if certain assets can be realised, or surplus operating cash flow generated within a relatively short period (say twelve months), then the deal structure can include a higher proportion of debt than where no asset realisation or surplus cash flow is possible. In the latter case, a highly geared deal structure is not ideal for the newly-independent business, since its initial gearing may well prevent financing flexibility if the growth of the business requires recourse to conventional sources

Table 9.CS.1   Debt-based small-scale buy-out (cost £1 million)
Assuming asset disposals possible:

Before asset disposals (£000s)		After asset disposals (£000s)
50	Management ordinary shares	50
100	Investors' convertible participating preferred ordinary shares (CPPOs)	100
100	Investors' redeemable preference shares	100
250	Total equity	250
500	Investors' loan stock	–
250	Bank debt	250
750	Borrowings	250
300	Debt: percentage equity	100

Table 9.CS.2   Equity-based small-scale buy-out (cost £1 million)
Assuming no asset disposals possible:

Equity buy-out (£000s)		Debt buy-out (£000s)
50 (40%)	Management ordinary shares	50 (55%)
50 (40%)	Investors' ordinary shares	50 (25%)
200 (20%)	Investors' CPPOs	50 (20%)
200	Investors' redeemable preference shares	100
500	Total equity	250
–	Investors' loan stock	250
500	Bank debt	500
500	Borrowings	750
100	Debt: percentage equity	300

of borrowing. It may also provide inadequate safety margins for new borrowings in the event that performance falls below the business plan expectations.

Another basic feature of buy-outs is the management's shareholding. In most cases where the purchase consideration exceeds £1 million, the management team is unlikely to be able to negotiate a controlling interest, at least not initially.

The deal structures illustrated in Tables 9.CS.1 and 9.CS.2 cover debt-financed or asset-leveraged buy-outs and also those where an equity-financed route is preferable. The illustrations do not embrace the complex issues of tax structures and methods of transferring assets from the vendor parent company to the new buy-out company.

In Table 9.CS.1 the investors have funded the short-term debt portion of the package in the expectation of their loan stock being repaid on the sale of surplus assets – which may take the form of a sale and leaseback to a savings institution. The management's equity holding will vary depending on its negotiating position and on the venture capitalists' philosophy. It is increasingly common for the management's eventual holding in a buy-out to vary according to its profit performance over a pre-set time period, say 3–5 years, or on the business valuation at a share listing or other exit. In the example above, with a commitment of £50 000 from a long-term equity requirement of £250 000, that is, 20 per cent of the total, it is possible that the management's initial holding would be a majority stake of, say, 55 per cent with an incentive to hit its profit or exit valuation targets – based on an increasing conversion rate by the investors' CPPOs, to the extent that management's targets are not met, which has the effect of reducing management's stake, on a 'ratchet' or 'earn-out' formula, down to, say, 30 per cent minimum.

The ratchet or earn-out means that the CPPO will convert into relatively more ordinary shares, the greater the shortfall of profit achievement or eventual valuation over a 2–5 year period – on a negotiated, pre-agreed scale. The ratchet often works in the opposite direction, where to the extent that the initial profit targets or pre-set 'exit' valuation are exceeded, the management team can achieve a higher equity stake.

In Table 9.CS.2 the investors have taken a position equal to management in ordinary shares to keep the equity base relatively unborrowed, to allow for further conventional (overdraft) borrowing as the company grows. It is likely that the investors will have a controlling shareholding, at least initially, by inclusion of their CPPO rights.

In the debt buy-out are no asset disposal possibilities, but the debt package includes a high gearing at the outset, which clearly has a depressive effect on profits due to the high servicing cost of the debt. The investors' shareholding position, however, is likely to be reduced to a minority participation as the investors have less equity at risk, at least in theory, with £200 000 as opposed to £450 000 in the equity buy-out example. In practice, of course, the investors' £250 000 loan stock is probably uncovered by disposal assets and thus amounts to an equity exposure – without the equity reward.

Where the vendors can be persuaded to defer part of their consideration, preferably at nil interest, for several years, the external debt element in the structure can be reduced. A deferred loan from the vendor may be guaranteed by the investors and this is illustrated in Table 9.CS.3.

In many ways similar to a small corporate sale (apart from size), the larger buy-outs (see Table 9.CS.4) are usually syndicated among several investors, whereas the smaller ones are often completed by one, or at most a pair of investors. Most large-scale buy-outs include investors' debt as well as equity, and the syndicate almost always has a controlling position throughout. The management stake can still be subject to a 'ratchet' arrangement, with an eventual equity position dependent upon profit performance, but rarely amounting to a controlling position.

In this case the investors are subscribing £2.8 million compared with the management's £0.2 million, that is, 56 per cent of the total commitment,

Table 9.CS.3   Deferred consideration buy-out

	£000s
Management's ordinary shares	60 (60%)
Investors' ordinary shares	40 (40%)
Investors' participating preference shares	100
Investors' redeemable preference shares	100
Total equity	300
Vendors' deferred loan	300
Bank debt	400
Total borrowings	700
Debt: percentage equity – gross	233
– net of deferred loan	133

Table 9.CS.4   Larger-scale buy-out (cost £5 million)

	£000s
Management's ordinary shares	200
Investors' preferred ordinary shares	300
Investors' convertible preference shares	500
Investors' redeemable preference shares	1000
Total equity	2000
Investors' subordinated loan stock	1000
Bank loans	2000
Borrowings	3000
Debt: percentage equity	150

compared with the management's 4 per cent and the bank's 40 per cent. It would be usual in such a deal for the management's shareholding to vary from 25–40 per cent, depending upon profit performance. In a £10 million buy-out, their stake would be correspondingly lower at 10–15 per cent of the eventual equity.

Where buy-outs are of an even larger scale, at £20 million–£50 million or more, it is frequently the case for three 'layers' of financing to be sourced from three distinct group of investors: the equity layer accounting for perhaps only 10 per cent of the total package; the mezzanine (or 'junk bond') layer of unsecured loan or preference stock with equity options or warrants and a high yield; and senior secured debt. Such packages are becoming increasingly common.

A less frequent form of buy-out or the more commonly found corporate disposal, the share repurchase (see Figure 9.CS.5) involves the existing management team – with the help of new external investors – buying out the (usually) controlling holdings of the original founders, who have retired from executive duties or are about to. The operation is usually designed to switch control to the present management team from the original, now 'sleeping', shareholders.

Table 9.CS.5   Share repurchase

Old company (£000s)		New company (£000s)
70 (70%)	Outgoing ordinary shareholdings	–
30 (30%)	Management ordinary shareholdings	60 (60%)
4900	Reserves	2250
–	Investors' ordinary shares	40 (40%)
–	Investors' convertible preference shares	2000
–	Investors' redeemable preference shares	650
5000	Total equity	5000
1000	Borrowings	1000
20	Debt: percentage equity	20

The outgoing shareholders have received part of the fruits of their early labours through an effective distribution of their retained profits, which have been replaced by an injection of new equity from the incoming investors. Simultaneously, the management team has switched from a 30 per cent minority to a 60 per cent controlling position.

The structure includes convertible preference shares for the investors, to avoid immediate change of control from the outgoing shareholdings to the incoming investors – which would leave management without its desired initial controlling position. There would usually be a 'ratchet' or 'earn-out' mechanism to adjust these initial shareholdings by enhanced conversion rights for the incoming investors, in the event that the management falls short of its own profits projection.

Case Study 2:   Melville Technology: A buy-in case study

Melville technology is one of the first cases of a management buy-in taking place with new investors in an underperforming previous buy-out, by another group of investors. The case study summarises the history of the transaction and illustrates the main relevant financial statements.

Background

The Sigma business was founded in 1919 and acquired by Alfred Herbert Limited in 1948. Alfred Herbert went into receivership in 1980 and Sigma became a receivership buy-out via a newly formed buy-out vehicle, Melville Technologies Limited, subsequently renamed Sigma Corporation Limited.

Between 1980 and 1984, Melville failed to live up to its investors' expectations and there were management changes. Despite these changes, one of the original buy-out financiers was reluctant to extend their debt repayment schedule and sought a purchaser for the company. An approach was made in late 1984 by the buy-in team.

The three-man buy-in team had worked together for three years at Mowlem Technology, the company established by John Mowlem to diversify from its construction-related activities. They had wide operating experiences in a range of industries and identified Melville as an appropriate target company for a buy-in.

Deal Structure

The transaction was structured as the acquisition for £3.3 million of the entire share capital of the existing business, which had net assets of £2.7 million. Leverage provided by the incoming investors was a £1.9 million ten-year redeemable unsecured loan stock, with an escalating coupon. Together with a £0.4 million subordinated bank loan facility, the total leverage was 2.7:1 (or 13.5:1 if goodwill on acquisition is written off). The £1 million equity investment was represented as £0.1 million by the management team and £0.9 million by the investor syndicate. The investor syndicate included two of the original buy-out syndicate – who reinvested from their cash consideration on the 100 per cent sale of Melville to the new team (see Table 9.CS.6).

Table 9.CS.6   Buy-in deal structure

Deal structure	Amount £000s	Percentage equity	Percentage of total finance
New management (Ordinary Shares)	100	15–35	
1985 buy-in investors[a]			
Hambros	245	23–17	
ECI	165	15–12	
County	165	15–12	
Candover	165	15–12	
Bank of Boston	15	2– 1	
1980 buy-out investors[a]			
3i	99	9– 7	
Sumit	66	6– 4	
Investor syndicate	905	85–65	
Total Ordinary Shares	1020	100–100	31
Investor 10-year loan stock[b]	1875		57 ⎫
Subordinated 5-year bank loan[c]	400		12 ⎬ 69
Total financing	3295		100

[a] Ordinary and Redeemable Ordinary shares with ratchet.
[b] Escalating interest rate, with eight months' holiday.
[c] Additional bank overdraft/currency facility of £1.4 million plus £0.4 million being balance of subordinated five-year bank loan, all arranged through Bank of Boston, London.

Table 9.CS.7   Post-buy-in balance sheet

	£000s	£000s	
Fixed assets	1209	1005	Issued capital
Stocks	1820	(771)	Goodwill
Debtors	1607	234	Shareholders' funds
Creditors	(1856)	1875	Subordinated loan stock
Overdraft	(279)	392	Bank loans
Net assets	2501	2501	

Table 9.CS.8   Profits performance (£000s)

Years ending 30th January	Pre-buy-in			Post-buy-in	
	1983	1984	1985	1986	1987
Turnover	6157	6735	7024	8100[a]	10000[a]
				8043[b]	11500[b]
Operating profit	245	235	462	695[a]	1160[a]
				661[b]	1500[b]
Interest	(238)	(235)	(315)	300)[a]	(300)[a]
				(114)[b]	(300)[b]
Pre-tax profit	7	–	147	300)[a]	860[a]
				547[b]	1200[b]

[a] Forecast at buy-in completion.
[b] Actual 1986, latest forecast for January 1987.

The management team's initial equity stake was 15 per cent increasing to 35 per cent – the application of the ratchet being related to the level of profits earned in each of the second and third years as discrete periods and the full redemption of the subordinated loan stock by the end of 1990. This earnout was tailored to a target 30 per cent IRR for the investors, a level which was considered adequate in view of the team's depth and quality of experience, the niche nature of the business and the growth potential in the markets served – all in all, this buy-in was regarded as (and has proven to be) a low risk deal when compared with many buy-ins, particularly those which are loss-making at the time of buy-in. The post buy-in balance sheet structure is summarised in Table 9.CS.7.

Post buy-in performance

Melville Technology is one of those rare business transactions where original forecasts were achieved and the figures given in Table 9.CS.8 clearly demonstrate the growth that has occurred from the pre-buy-in period of stagnation at around break-even.

Melville is itself now seeking to acquire other businesses in its appetite for growth as a specialist engineer. Its current products comprise precision meteorology systems for the aerospace industry and a range of gauges for wider application. Partly to be able to make acquisitions with quoted paper, Melville will be seeking a USM quotation at the earliest opportunity, at an indicated valuation which would show the buy-in investors a return substantially in excess of the 30 per cent IRR target at investment in April 1985.

The Business Plan

Paul Burns

1. The importance of the business plan

One of the most important steps in establishing any new business is the construction of a business plan. It can help the owner/manager crystallise and focus his ideas. It can help him set objectives and give him a yardstick against which to monitor performance. Perhaps of more immediate importance, it can also act as a vehicle to attract any external finance needed by the business. It can also convince investors that the owner/manager has identified high growth opportunities; that he has the entrepreneurial flair and managerial talent to exploit that opportunity effectively; and that he has a rational, coherent and believable programme for doing so.

The business plan entails taking a long-term view of the business and its environment. A good plan should emphasise the strengths and recognise the weaknesses of the proposed venture. Above all, it should convey a sincerity of purpose and analysis which lends credibility both to the plan and to the entrepreneur putting it forward. For an existing business, this process involves first coming to terms with the personal objectives of the owner/manager, and second, coming to terms with the strengths and weaknesses of the existing business and the opportunity and threats that it faces. This is often called a 'position audit' and once this is done the company is in a position to set the basic objectives. These fall into two parts: first a statement is needed describing the business. This sounds too simple, but it is needed if a business is to marshal its strengths and not waste its efforts going into areas where it has no experience. The statement should not be too restrictive to prevent development, or so broad as to be meaningless (for example, a coalman might say he is in the business of 'marketing and distributing home fuel requirements'). Second, a quantified primary long-term objective is needed which reflects what is wanted by the owner/manager(s) and what the business can achieve, given the prospects for

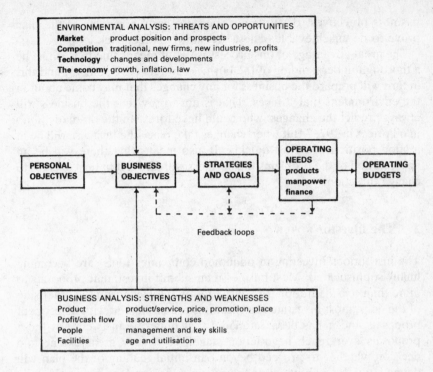

ENVIRONMENTAL ANALYSIS: THREATS AND OPPORTUNITIES
Market   product position and prospects
Competition traditional, new firms, new industries, profits
Technology   changes and developments
The economy growth, inflation, law

| PERSONAL OBJECTIVES | BUSINESS OBJECTIVES | STRATEGIES AND GOALS | OPERATING NEEDS products manpower finance | OPERATING BUDGETS |

Feedback loops

BUSINESS ANALYSIS: STRENGTHS AND WEAKNESSES
Product   product/service, price, promotion, place
Profit/cash flow its sources and uses
People   management and key skills
Facilities   age and utilisation

Figure A.1   The planning process

the environment it finds itself in. This will probably involve factors such as profitability, asset levels and growth (for example, an annual real growth in profit after tax of 10 per cent with minimum return on capital of 20 per cent). This objective achieves growth and maintains an asset base for the business.

Of course, setting the objectives is only the first stage, and possibly the easiest. How are these objectives to be achieved? Strategies need to be developed in four key areas of production, marketing, personnel and financing, and from strategies come some short-term goals, such as percentage market share, sales margins, number of customer complaints, and so on, which allows progress to be mentioned in these strategies towards achieving the objectives. Finally come operating needs in terms of products, manpower and finance to achieve these goals.

The final stage is the drawing up of long and short-term budgets. This is the translation of strategies and plans into detailed estimates of profit, asset investment and cash requirements. The whole process, including the position audit, is shown in Figure A.1. Of course, at each stage in the process, it is quite possible that changes will have to be made in the business objectives, or strategies, because certain aspects of the plan prove to be unachievable. These are shown as feedback loops.

The great advantage of this process is that it means that there must be a thorough understanding of the business and its environment, and this in turn will prepare the business for any changes that may come about in the environment that it faces. That is not to say that the business will always predict the changes: who could have foreseen the dramatic jump in oil prices in 1973? But when changes take place the business will be in a good position to adjust quickly. It also means that there will be an appreciation of the problems the business will face if it in turn decides to change direction.

2.   The investor's view

The institutions investing in unquoted companies today are becoming highly sophisticated. Most businessmen submit investment proposals to more than one institution for consideration. However, on the other side of the coin, most investment institutions are inundated with investment proposals and it has been estimated that only one in twenty of these proposals ever reach negotiation stage. To a very great extent, the decision whether to proceed beyond an initial reading of the plan will depend on the quality of the business plan used in supporting the investment proposals. The business plan is the first, and often the best, chance for an entrepreneur to impress prospective investors with the quality of his investment proposal.

An investor needs to be convinced of two things:

(i) That a business opportunity exists which has the potential to earn the investor the high return he demands; and

(ii) That the company proposing to exploit this opportunity can do so effectively.

Any business plan must, therefore, address both issues. This requires a careful balance between making the proposal sufficiently attractive on the one hand, whilst on the other realistically addressing the many risks inherent in any business venture and showing how they can be acceptably minimised. To do this, the business plan should emphasise the strengths of the company, particularly in comparison with its competitors. Behind all the plans and strategies, the business plan must demonstrate convincingly the determination and credibility of the owner/manager and other key personnel involved in the business venture. It has been said that the most important factor in the decision whether or not to invest is the credibility and quality of the firm's management.

The most difficult aspect of any deal is deciding upon the split in equity between the various partners involved in a deal. The simple answer is that there are no simple rules – the final result will depend on the attractiveness of the investment proposal and the negotiating ability of the individuals involved. However, the *Venture Capital Report*, a monthly publication of investment opportunities, suggest a starting point of 33 per cent each for the idea; for the management; and for the money. But it must be stressed that this is only a very rough guide. If an entrepreneur can provide no capital, he may receive less equity, but if the idea is a breakthrough, he may receive more, and so on.

It is also advisable to consider the objectives of the investing institution. It will be interested in generating income from its investment by way of dividends or interest and, over the long run, through capital gains. But will the institution take dividends or interest, and when will these be paid? A venture capitalist may require dividends, but it could be in the entrepreneur's interests not to take them because of tax problems. Indeed, it may not be in the interests of the company to pay dividends or interest in its early years. A further issue is how much of the control of the business the owner/manager is actually willing to surrender. Most entrepreneurs wish to part with as little as possible of their business and indeed, venture capitalists now rarely demand even a 50 per cent stake in the business. At the end of the day, a sensible financing package involving equity and deferred interest terms or convertible loans might be the answer.

The second question is: how will the institution realise its capital gain, and over what period? This issue is frequently called the problem of 'exit routes'. It is a major problem for many investing institutions, since it can often take quite a number of years before it can realise its investment. Related to this is the issue of further funding needs and their availability from the investing institution. Exit routes and their time scale need to be seriously considered and openly discussed. Is the business looking to go on the unlisted securities market (USM) or traded over the counter (OTC)? If not, the investing institution might be tempted to promote a merger with a larger company, once the business has taken off. Another possibility is for the owner/manager to 'buy out' the investing institution at a later date.

Also, investing institutions have very different ways of operating. Some prefer a 'hands off' approach whereby once they have invested they have little to do with the business – perhaps just meeting the owner/manager once a year to review the progress of the business. In contrast, some institutions prefer a 'hands on' approach, insisting on placing a non-executive director on the board and perhaps being in contact with the owner/manager up to eight times a month including at least one visit. They may require consultation on budgets and plans and even changes in senior management.

Finally, it must be realised that funds have different risk/reward profiles. Some specialise, either by size of business or industry sector. Frequently they have minimum investment levels. Certainly obtaining equity funding below £100 000 is still a problem in the UK. Many sound proposals are turned down by particular institutions simply because they do not fit the institution's investment profile, in which case other institutions should be approached. Undoubtedly, deciding upon the appropriate financial structure and choosing the right investors will be a major task for most entrepreneurs.

3.   The format of the business plan

Any format for a proposed business plan should be viewed as providing general guidance only. Every business is different and consequently a standard plan is totally inappropriate in every circumstance. Having said that, Figure A.2 attempts to outline the bare bones of a business plan. When looking at this it should be noted that it is unlikely that in every circumstance will all the items mentioned here be of sufficient importance or relevance to warrant inclusion in every plan. In particular there is one overriding principle with all business plans: *'keep it short!'* Any business plan should be sufficiently long to cover the subject adequately but short enough to maintain interest. Some business plans requiring a large amount of venture capital could be well over fifty pages long. However, more normal projects requiring less than, say, half a million pounds, should be restricted to 10–20 pages.

Clearly, then, Table A.1 is no more an outline, and an outline that will have to be judiciously precised. Nevertheless, it is an outline that is worth following.

Overview/summary

The executive summary must be brief – no longer than one or two pages. This should be treated as a stand-alone selling document and it is essential that the highlights of the entire business plan are contained in this summary. For many investors it will be the only part of the plan that they read. Indeed, some advisers recommend that investing institutions are only sent this summary initially and only if they show a further interest should the full business plan be sent.

Table A.1   Outline of business plan

1. **Overview/summary**
   Purpose of plan
   How much finance is required, and what it is for
   Brief description of business and its market
   Highlights of financial projections
2. **The company and its industry**
   Purpose of company
   History of company
   Past successes of company
   Discussion of industry
3. **The products/services**
   Description of products/services and applications
   Distinctive competences or uniqueness of product/service
   Technologies and skills required in the business
   Licence/patent rights
   Future potential
4. **Markets**
   Customers
   Competitors (strengths and weaknesses)
   Market segments
   Market size and growth
   Estimated market share
   Customer buying patterns
   Critical product/service characteristics or uniqueness
   Special market characteristics
   Competitor response
5. **Marketing**
   Market positioning – critical product/service characteristics or
       uniqueness in relation to competitors
   Pricing policy
   Selling/distribution policy
   Advertising and promotion
   Product/service support policy
   Interest shown by prospective customers
6. **Design and development** (if appropriate)
   Stage of development
   Difficulties and risks
   Product/service improvements
   Product/service developments in future
7. **Manufacturing and operations**
   Premises location
   Other facilities
   Production/service capacity
   Sources of supply of key materials or workforce
   Use of subcontractors
   Nature of productive process – machinery and critcal points
8. **Management**
   Owners/directors and other key management
   Expertise and track record (detailed CVs as an appendix)

Table A.1 cont.

Key management compensation
Summary of planned staff numbers and recruitment plans
Training policies
Consultants and advisers
 9. **Financing requirements**
Funds required and timing
Deal on offer
Anticipated gearing
Exit routes for investors
10. **Financial highlights, risks and assumptions**
Highlights of financial plan (sales, profit, return on capital,
   net worth, etc.)
Commentary on financial plan
Risks and how they will be tackled
11. **Detailed financial plan** (Quarterly for 3–5 years)
Profit and loss
Contribution and break-even analysis
Cash flow analysis (monthly in first year)
Sensitivity analysis
Balance sheets (annual only)
12. **Items frequently included in appendices**
Technical data on products
Details of patents, etc.
Consultants' reports on products or markets
Order and enquiry status
CVs of key managers
Organisation charts
Audited accounts
Names of accountants, solicitors and bankers

The company and its industry

This section attempts to establish the credibility of the owner/manager and his business in the eyes of potential investors. It is important because a common way of evaluating future potential is to look first at past performance. If, however, past performance is not a reliable indicator of future potential then it may be best to leave out this section entirely. Nevertheless, the owner/manager must display a thorough understanding of his own company and the industry in which it is seeking to compete.

The products/services

This section should define precisely the products and services to be marketed. Clearly it will vary according to the number and complexity of the products or services to be marketed. Whilst it is important to display a grasp of the technology involved, it is important that this section is written in clear, concise, laymen's language. Detailed information can be relegated to appendices. It is important that in this section and in others the distinctive competences or uniqueness of the product/service are emphasised. These can take many forms: new technology; product quality; low production cost; or the fit with customer needs. It is also important that the owner/manager demonstrates his ability to develop the product or service beyond its present form. Investors rarely participate in a one-product company without indications of future developments.

Markets

Markets and marketing are critical to all companies – even brilliant new technologies are useless without customers. Most institutional investors see this also as an area where major mistakes are made by new businesses. It is important to define precisely the market segments that the business hopes to attack, and estimates of market size, growth, share, and competitive reaction should be based on the market segment, not on some wider market definition. Having identified the market segment to be attacked, customer buying patterns need to be understood and, once more, the investor convinced that the product/service characteristics or uniqueness that the business is offering will meet a ready market. Investors are always interested in the reaction of competition. Any business, particularly one with a good product/service idea, will meet competition sooner or later. It is important to identify current competitors and their strengths and weaknesses. This is especially important in the case of small or new businesses entering markets dominated by larger and more powerful competitors. Every business must develop a strategy for dealing with its competitors.

Marketing

Marketing strategy can only be developed based upon a thorough understanding of the market. Often the exact details of the marketing strategy can be complex, covering such areas as market positioning, pricing policy, selling and distribution policy, advertising and promotion, product service support policy, and so on. Nevertheless, any business must analyse all these factors in detail when formulating sales projections and these projections should be built up in as much detail as possible to act as a cross-check against the sales targets developed from the market analysis process outlined previously. Sales estimates based simply on targets without the detailed 'nuts and bolts' of how these targets are to be achieved will inevitably prove unconvincing to a potential investor. Frequently this section can prove to be very lengthy. If this is the case it could be included as an appendix with only a summary in the main body of the plan.

Design and development

Many new businesses that are developing products which have not yet been marketed need to give a potential investor considerable information, not only on the stage of development the project has currently reached, but also on the difficulties and risks that it faces as well as the timescale involved in getting the product on to the market. Even existing products and services must look to improvements as well as new developments in the future.

Manufacturing and operations

In this section the manufacturing process should briefly be described. The section should highlight any potential problem areas such as new or untried technology or production facilities. It should highlight the intended use of subcontractors. Investors are very interested in how the business will control the quality of its product and in the case of a service operation it may be necessary to explain how the business is organised or controlled. Premises location and other facility needs should also be discussed. Finally, lead times in crucial supplies, how many sources there are, and how quickly output can be increased or decreased, should also be addressed.

Management

The importance of management cannot be overemphasised. In many ways, the development of a coherent business plan simply proves the ability of management. Investors invest in people, not in a business plan. This section is, therefore, vitally important, particularly for start-up companies. It is worth remembering that for a substantial business to emerge it will be necessary to talk, not about individuals, but about teams of people with complementary skills. Ideally these skills will cover all the functional areas of business, but it is unlikely that a start-up would be able to bring together a balanced team at such an early stage. It is, therefore, reasonable to mention areas of both strength and weakness for a start-up business, as weaknesses can often be addressed by using consultants. Key managers should be described in terms of their experience and abilities, together with a statement of their specific responsibilities. Detailed CVs may be included in the appendices. Investors are naturally interested in track record since this gives them some indication about the management's ability to meet the targets in the business plan. The summary contained in this section should, therefore, concentrate on the majority achievements and experience of each key manager. Investors will also be interested in the mechanism for retaining key managers and motivating them to achieve the target set in the business plan.

Financing requirements

The next three sections of the business plan focus on the translation of these plans and strategies into financial statements and financing requirements. The purpose of this section is to outline the funds that the owner/manager requires and the terms and conditions he is willing to offer to obtain those funds. Invariably, the precise nature of any financial deal will have to be negotiated with the investor. Indeed, investing institutions are frequently expert at constructing financial deals in such a way as to meet both their own objectives and those of the owner/manager. It is, therefore, appropriate to set down the skeleton of any deal (total funding required, timing, equity/debt structure, and so on) and leave the details for further negotiations. The key is to provide sufficient guidelines to indicate the main features of the financial structure of the business and indicate a fair price for the share of the business on offer, whilst allowing sufficient flexibility, particularly on minor points, to accommodate the wishes of investors. Remember that this is a negotiating situation.

Financial highlights, risks and assumptions

The purpose of this section is to pull out the highlights from the mass of financial data supplied in the detailed financial plan (see next section). For example, the possible worth of the company if forecast results are achieved should be highlighted, as indeed may sales, profit and return on capital targets. However, this section should concentrate not only on the rewards to potential investors but also on the problems and risks that the business may face. It may may be necessary to highlight the cyclical nature of sales or cash flow. It is important that the main risks

facing the business are stated simply and objectively: if the owner/
manager does not bring them out then it is certain that the potential
investor will. Such risks might be, for example, 'that the technology is
not protectable', or 'the meeting of sales targets is vitally dependent
upon the recruitment of a regional sales force'. However, it is no good
simply highlighting risks without stating how those risks will be minimised.

Detailed financial plan

A detailed financial plan for at least three years should be included with
the business plan. This will include profit and loss estimates on a
quarterly basis, cash flow analyses, monthly in the first year but quarterly thereafter, and annual balance sheets. Supplementary to the
forecasts should be the assumptions on which they are based, in particular the build-up of the sales forecast. Investors are particularly interested in contribution and break-even analysis, since the break-even
level is an indication of risk. Forecasts should also be treated to sensitivity analysis. This process involves different assumptions which would
vary the outcome of the financial plans. Typical variations would be
based upon changes in sales targets or, for example, timing of cash
flows. It is important to choose three or four main variables and to show
the effect a variation in these would have in the financial plan. Most
sensitivity analyses concentrate on timing, volume, gross margins and
credit given.

4.   Presenting a case for finance

The business plan is an essential element in presenting a case for finance
and as such it is important that it is well presented. This is not to say that
the business plan should be over-elaborate or expensively produced, but
simply that it should be functional, clearly set out and easy to use. It is
important that the plan has a table of contents. Tabulation should be
used in each section for easy reference and the frequent use of charts,
diagrams and graphs make detailed information more comprehensible.
Most business plans that contain financial projections use a double-page
layout for this information.

However, the business plan is a necessary but not a sufficient condition for obtaining finance for a business proposal. The single most
important factor in the eyes of any potential investor will be the
personal qualities of the owner/manager and the management team that

he brings along. Potential backers are looking for motivation, enthusiasm and integrity, but most of all the managerial ability and competence to make the plan actually happen.

To get a business to grow successfully requires a genuine desire to succeed, amounting almost to a need, and the owner/manager must be able to motivate his management team in such a way that they share that desire to succeed. Any entrepreneur must be willing to take risks – but only moderate risks that he believes he can overcome. The technical development engineer who has a good product idea but really only wants to build modified prototypes and is not interested in production and selling will not find any institutional investor willing to back him without teaming up with others who have the qualities that he lacks. Enthusiasm and drive must, however, be tinged with a strong sense of realism in taking a market view of the business and its potential. Sir Arnold Weinstock once said that all successful companies are run by people who understand the market.

Ability is important, and can be demonstrated to a potential backer by track record. Technical ability, along with patents, will protect the project from attempts by competitors to copy it. However, a crucial factor that will convince potential backers that the plan will succeed is the ability of the management team. It is important that the business plan conveys the competence of the management team, not only directly by the inclusion of CVs, and so on, but also directly through the competence of the plan itself.

Once the business plan gets through the initial sifting procedure, the presentation of the plan to backers will act as a further vehicle for demonstrating these qualities and convincing them of the competence of the team. First impressions are important, but demonstrated knowledge of the key areas in the business plan will go a long way towards generating the confidence that is needed. A leading venture capitalist once admitted that, whilst discussions with the owner/manager centred on the business plan, the final decision whether or not to invest in him really was the result of a 'gut feel', a personal 'chemistry' between the venture capitalist and the owner/manager. At the end of the day that chemistry must lay the foundation for a long-term working relationship; a working relationship based upon substance and trust.

Nevertheless, there are many ways of enhancing a presentation. It is always important to rehearse any presentation thoroughly. Among the elements of making the presentation successful it is often said that the owner/manager should manage the presentation with respect to his copresenters. He should always emphasise market and management team expertise. In terms of style it is important to demonstrate the product or service as far as possible and to maintain the eye contact with investors. Notwithstanding this it is vital that the owner/manager and his team demonstrate a thorough understanding, familiarity and competence with respect to the business plan. Investors will want to spend some time simply getting to know the team members informally, at further meetings or even over dinner. And if the investment looks attractive . . . well then it's down to haggling over the price.

Notes and References

Chapter 1 Introduction

1. *Bolton Report*: Report on the Commission of Enquiry on Small Firms 1971, Cmnd. 4811.

Chapter 2 The Start-up

1. Schumpeter, J. A. (1942) *Capitalism, Socialism, and Democracy* (New York: Harper and Brothers).
2. McLelland, D. (1961) *The Achieving Society* (Princeton, New Jersey: Van Nostrand).
3. Rotter, J. B. (1966) 'Generalized Expectancies for Internal Versus External Control of Reinforcement', *Psychological Monographs* vol. 80, no. 609.
4. Cooper, A. C. (1981) 'Strategic Management; New Ventures and Small Business', *Long Range Planning*, vol. 14, no. 5, pp. 39–45.
5. Birley, S. (1986) 'Succession in the Family Firm: The Inheritors' View', *Journal of Small Business Management*, vol. 24, no. 3, July.
6. Stanworth, M. J. K. and Curran, J. (1976) 'Growth and the Small Firm – An Alternative View', *Journal of Management Studies* vol. 13, no. 2, May, pp. 95–110.
7. Collins, O. F., Moore, D. G. and Unwalla, D. B. (1964) *The Enterprising Man* (East Lansing: Michigan State University Press).
8. Kent, C. A., Sexton, D. L., Van Auken, P. M. and Young, D. (1982) 'Lifetime Experiences of Managers and Entrepreneurs: A Comparative Analysis', Paper presented at the 42nd Annual Conference of the Academy of Management New York, August.
9. Gartner, W. B. (1984) 'Problems in Business Start-up: The Relationships Among Entrepreneurial Skills and Problem Identification for Different Types of New Ventures', *Entrepreneurship Research* (Babson College, Wellesley Park, Massachusetts; Centre for Entrepreneurial Studies).
10. Birley, S. and Norburn, D. (1986) 'Who are the High Flyers?', paper presented to the *Strategic Management Conference*, Singapore.
11. Teach, R. D., Tarpley, F. A. and Schwartz, R. G. (1985) 'Who are the Microcomputer Software Entrepreneurs?', Paper presented at the 1985 Entrepreneurship Research Conference, Philadelphia.
12. Dunkleberg, W. C. and Cooper, A. C. (1982) 'Entrepreneurial Typologies'

in K. H. Vesper (ed.) *Frontiers of Entrepreneurship Research* (Babson, Wellesley, Massachusetts: Centre for Entrepreneurial Studies).

13. Carland J. W., Hoy, F., Boulton W. R. and Carland J. A. C. (1984) 'Differentiating Entrepreneurs from Small Business Owners: A Conceptualization', *Academy of Management Review*, vol. 9, no. 2, pp. 354–9.

14. Birley, S. and Norburn, D. (1984) 'Small Versus Large Companies: The Entrepreneurial Conundrum', *Journal of Business Strategy*, vol. 6, no. 1, Summer.

15. Birley, S. (1985) 'The Role of Networks in the Entrepreneurial Process', *Journal of Business Venturing*, vol. 1, no. 1.

16. Aldrich, H. and Zimmer, C. (1986) 'Entrepreneurship through Social Networks', in Sexton, D. and Smilor, R. (eds) *The Art and Science of Entrepreneurship*, (Cambridge, Mass.: Ballinger).

17. This case was written by Professor Sue Birley, Cranfield School of Management, on the basis of information provided by Guy McClelland. The case is intended as a basis for classroom discussion, and not as an illustration of good or bad management.

Chapter 3   Strategies for Success and Routes for Failure

1. Burns, P. and Dewhurst, J. (1986) *Small Business in Europe* (London: Macmillan).

2. Stanworth, J. and Curran, J. (1976) 'Growth and the Small Firm – an Alternative View', *Journal of Management Studies*, vol. 13, no. 2.

3. See, for example, Hawkinson, A. (1984) 'Small Firms Investment – A Search for Motivations', *International Small Business Journal*, vol. 2, no. 2; and Scarse, R. and Goffee, R. (1982) *The Entrepreneurial Middle Class*, (London: Croom Helm). London, 1982.

4. See, for example, Bechefor, P., Ellios, B., Rushforth, M. and Bland, R. (1974) 'Small Shopkeepers: Matters of money and meaning', *The Sociology Review*, November; Boswelll J. (1972) *The Rise and Decline of Small Firms* (London: George Allen & Unwin); Bureau of Industry Economics (1979), 'The small business unit in non-manufacturing activities', *Journal of Commerce*, 21 December.

5. Ganguly, P. and Bannock, G. (1985) *UK Small Business Statistics and International Comparisons*, Small Business Research Trust (New York: Harper & Row).

6. Stewart, H. and Gallagher, C. (1985) 'Business Death and Firm Size in the UK', *International Small Business Journal*, vol. 4, no. 1.

7. Harris, C. (1984) 'Icebergs and Business Statistics', 1984 (unpublished Brookings Institution).

8. Barrow, C. (1986) *Routes to Success* (London: Kogan Page).

9. Porter, M. E. (1980) *Competitive Strategy* (New York: The Free Press).

10. Dewhurst J., and Burns P. (1983) *Small Business: Finance and Control* (London: Macmillan).

11. Shapero, A. (1975) 'The displaced uncomfortable entrepreneur', *Psychology Today*, November.

12. Goldstein, J. (1981) 'Shapero's Laws', *In Business*, May–June.

13. Churchill, N. C. and Lewis, V. L. (1983) 'The Five Stages of Small Business Growth', *Harvard Business Review*, May–June, pp. 30–50.

14. Ray, G. H. and Hutchinson, P. J. (1983) *The Financing and Financial Control of Small Enterprise Development* (London: Gower). 1983.
15. Perry, C. (1986–87) 'Growth Strategies for Small Firms: Principles and Case Studies', *International Small Business Journal*, vol. 5, no. 2.
16. See, for example, Glueck, W. F. (1980) *Business Policy and Strategic Management* (Tokyo: McGraw Hill); and Rumelt, R. P. (1979) 'Evaluation of Strategy: Theory and Models', in Schendel, D. and Hofer, C., *Strategic Management* (Boston, Mass.: Little, Brown).
17. Berryman, J. (1983) 'Small Business Failure and Bankruptcy: A Survey of the Literature', *European Small Business Journal*, vol. 1, no. 4.
18. De Carlo, J. F. and Lyons, P. R. (1980) 'Towards a Contingency Theory of Entrepreneurship', *Journal of Small Business Management*, vol. 18, no. 3, July.
19. Sadler, P. J. and Barry, B. A. (1970) *Organisational Development* (London: Longman).
20. Larson, C. and Clute, R. (1979) 'The Failure Syndrome', *American Journal of Small Business*, vol. IV, no. 2, October.
21. Argenti, J. (1976) *Corporate Collapse: The causes and symptoms* (Maidenhead: McGraw Hill).
22. Beaver, W. (1966) 'Financial Ratios as Predictors of Failure', *Empirical Research in Accounting, Selected Studies*, in supplement to vol. 5, *Journal of Accounting Research*.
23. Altman, E. (1968) 'Financial Ratios, Discriminant Analysis and the Prediction of Corporate Bankruptcy', *The Journal of Finance*, September.
24. Zavgren, C. (1983) 'The Prediction of Corporate Failure: The State of the Art', *Journal of Accounting Literature*, vol. 2.
25. Edmister, R. (1972) 'An Empirical Test of Financial Ratio Analysis for Small Business Failure Prediction', *Journal of Financial and Quantitative Analysis*, March.
26. This case was researched and written by Tony Kippenberger, MBA, of Case Writers Limited, 36 Shakespeare Road, Bedford, under the supervision of Professor Paul J. Burns. It is intended for classroom discussion only and is not an illustration of good or bad management practice. Copyright (c) 1987 — Cranfield School of Management

Chapter 4   The Entrepreneur

1. Bolton Report: *Report of the Committee of Enquiry on Small Firms* 1971, (Cmnd. 4811).
2. Economic Intelligence Unit (1983) *The European Climate for Small Businesses: A 10 Country Study*, (London: EIU).
3. Burns, P. and Dewhurst, J. (1986) *Small Business in Europe*, (London: Macmillan).
4. Wilson Report: *Report on Financing of Small Firms*, 1979, Cmnd. 7503.
5. Burns, P. (1985) 'Financial Characteristics of Small Companies in the UK' Paper presented to 8th National Small Firms Policy and Research Conference, 1985 and published as Strategy and Enterprise Working Paper 85.08. (Cranfield, Beds.: Cranfield School of Management).
6. du Toit, D. E. (1980) 'Confessions of a Successful Entrepreneur', *Harvard Business Review*, November–December, p. 44.

7. Kets de Vries, M. F. R. (1985) 'The Dark Side of Entrepreneurship', *Harvard Business Review*, November–December, p. 160.
8. Wiener, M. (1981) *English Culture and the Decline of the Industrial Spirit, 1850–1980*, Cambridge University Press.
9. Harper, M. (1985) 'Hardship, Discipline, Entrepreneurship', Cranfield Working Paper 85.1. (Cranfield, Beds.: Cranfield School of Management) May.

Chapter 5   The Entrepreneurial Process

2. This case was prepared by Associate Fellow Michael J. Roberts under the supervision of Professor Howard H. Stevenson as a basis for class discussion rather than to illustrate either effective or ineffective handling of an administrative situation. The history of Atlas up to 1975 is based, in part, on a case by Kenneth R. Davis, formerly of the Amos Tuck School of Business Administration.
1. See for example; Birch, D. (1983) *Share of Jobs vs Share of Job Creation – A Flow Analysis* (Cambridge, Massachusetts): Birch, D. (1983) *The Contribution of Small Enterprise to Growth and Employment (Cambridge*, Massachusetts); Birch, D. and MacCracken, S. (1983) *The Small Business Share of Job Creation: Lessons Learned from the Use of a Longitudinal File* (Cambridge, Massachusetts).

Chapter 6   Employment Relations in the Small Firm

1. Bolton Report (1971) *Report of the Committee of Inquiry on Small Firms, London*, Cmnd 4811, London, HMSO 1971, p. 21.
2. Schumacher, E. F. (1973) *Small is Beautiful* (London: Blond and Briggs).
3. Henderson, J. and Johnson, B. (1974) 'Labour Relations in the Smaller Firm', *Personnel Management*, December, p. 28.
4. The Bolton Report (1971) p. 23.
5. Kets de Vries, M. F. R. (1977) 'The Entrepreneurial Personality: A Person at Crossroads', *Journal of Management Studies*, vol. 14, no. 1, January, p. 53.
6. Kreckel, R. (1988) 'Unequal Opportunity and Labour Market Segmentation', *Sociology*, vol. 14, no. 4, pp. 525–50.
7. Curran, J. and Stanworth, J. (1981) 'A New Look at Job Satisfaction in the Small Firm', *Human Relations*, vol. 34, no. 5, pp. 343–65.
8. Ingham, G. K. (1970) *Size of Industrial Organisation and Worker Behaviour* (Cambridge University Press).
9. Blackburn, R. and Mann, M. (1979) *The Working Class in the Labour Market* (London: Macmillan).
10. Curran, J. and Stanworth, J. (1979) 'Worker Involvement and Social Relations in the Small Firm,' *Sociological Review*, vol. 27, no. 2. See also, Rainee, A. (1985) 'Is Small Beautiful? Industrial Relations in Small Clothing Firms', *Sociology*, vol. 19, no. 2, pp. 213–24.
11. Burns, T. and Stalker, G. M. (1961) *The Management of Innovation* (London: Tavistock).
12. Batstone, E. V. (1975) 'Deference and the Ethos of Small Town Capitalism'

in Bulmer, M. (ed.) *Working Class Images of Society* (London: Routledge & Kegan Paul).

13. Stanworth, J. and Curran, J. (1973) *Management Motivation in the Smaller Business* (Aldershot: Gower) ch. 8.

14. Watkins, D. S. (1983) 'Development, Training and Education for the Small Firm: A European Perspective', *European Small Business Journal*, vol. 1, no. 3, pp. 29–44.

15. Stanworth and Curran, (1973) *Management Motivation in the Smaller Business*, ch. 8.

16. Gouldner, A. W. (1969) 'Cosmopolitans and Locals' in Litterer, J. A. (ed.), *Organizations*, vol. 1, (London: John Wiley).

17. Commission on Industrial Relations (1974) *Small Firms and the Code of Industrial Relations Practice*, Report no. 69 (London: HMSO).

18. Rainnie, A. F. and Scott, M. G. (1986) 'Industrial Relations in the Small Firm' in Curran, J. *et al* (eds), *The Survival of the Small Firm*, vol. 2 (Aldershot: Gower).

19. Henderson and Johnson (1974) 'Labour Relations in the Smaller Firm', p. 29.

20. Curran, J. and Stanworth, J. (1978) 'Job Choice and the Manual Worker – Where the Theories Break Down', *Personnel Management*, September.

21. Westrip, A. (1968) 'Small Firms Policy: the Case of Employment Legislation' in Curran, *et al.* (eds) *The Survival of the Small Firm* vol. 2.

22. Dickens, L., Hart, M., Jones, M. and Weekes, B. (1984) 'The British Experience Under a Statute Prohibiting Unfair Dismissal', *Industrial and Labour Relations Review*, vol. 37, no. 4, July.

23. Henderson and Johnson (1974) 'Labour Relations in the Smaller Firm', p. 30.

24. Ibid., p. 31.

25. Curran, J. and Stanworth, J. (1981) 'Size of Workplace and Attitudes to Industrial Relations in the Printing and Electronics Industries', *British Journal of Industrial Relations*, vol. 19, no. 1, March, pp. 141–58.

26. Commission on Industrial Relations (1972) *Employers' Organisations and Industrial Relations*, Study 1 (London: HMSO).

27. Parliamentary Expenditure Committee (1978) *People and Work*, Prospects for Jobs and Training, 13th Report (London: HMSO) pp. 50 and 80.

28. Westrip, (1968) 'Small Firms Policy'.

29. Report of the Royal Commission on Trade Unions and Employers' Organisations, 1965–1968, Cmnd 3623 (London: HMSO).

30. Daniel, W. W. and Stilgoe, E. (1978) *The Impact of Employment Protection Laws* (London: Policy Studies Institute) June.

31. Clifton, R. and Tatton-Brown, C. (1979) *Impact of Employment Legislation on Small Firms*, Research Paper no. 6 (London: Department of Employment).

Chapter 7   Franchising

1. Some franchisors, such as Apollo Blinds, own the premises from which the franchisees operate, who in turn pay rent. In such cases the franchisor's investment is more akin to a portfolio of properties, rather than a direct investment in th franchisee's business.

2. Only ten companies graduated from the USM to a full listing in 1985.
3. Profit Impact of Market Strategies (PIMS) is a major research programme initiated in 1972 at the Marketing Science Institute at Cambridge, Mass., and now run by the Strategic Planning Institute, an independent, non-profit-making organization. The aim of the programme is to provide businessmen with information on what factors had the greatest impact on profitability under various competitive conditions. In effect, to uncover the 'laws of the market place'. The study embraces 57 corporations with 62 separate businesses. Profit performance was found to be related to at least 37 factors, including market share, research and development expenditure, marketing expenditure and corporate diversity.
4. Introduced in the UK in 1981, to allow the clearing banks to lend up to £75 000 over 2–7 years so small businesses that do not meet normal lending criteria. The government guarantees 70 per cent of the funds on loan.
5. Introduced in the UK in 1983, to make it attractive for higher rate tax payers to invest in certain categories of new or growing businesses. Each investor can get tax relief at their highest rate on up to £40 000 invested in any one year.
6. Newly-appointed franchisees have to find an average of £26 000 – just under £5000 for the franchise fee and £21 000 for premises, equipment and fittings. Recurring annual payments to the franchisor total nearly £9000, two-thirds of this being a $5\frac{1}{2}$ percent royalty on turnover, and two-thirds of the balance being a $4\frac{1}{2}$ percent mark-up on supplies.
7. The BFA's founder members were: Budget Rent-a-car, Dyno-Rod, Holiday Inns, Kentucky Fried Chicken, Prontaprint, Servicemaster, Wimpy International and Ziebart.
8. This respectability is proving hard to achieve. It has not been much helped by the recent failure of one of its founder members, and the BFA's 1982 Chairman's 70-outlet franchising chain going into receivership in 1985.

Chapter 8   Equity Financing in Small Firms

1. Smith, N. R. (1967) *The Entrepreneur and his Firm: the relationship between Type of Man and Type of Company* (Michigan State University).
2. Laufer, J. (1975) 'Comment on devient Entrepreneur,' *Revue Française de Gestion*, November.
3. Pompe, H., Bruyn, M. and Koek, J. (1986) 'Entrepreneurs in Small Business, an International Comparative Perspective'. (Paper presented at the 13th ISBC (London), Sociological Institute, University of Groningen, The Netherlands).
4. Detoeuf, A. (1965(*Propos de O. L. Barenton, Confiseur* (Paris: Editions du Tambourinaire).
5. Crédit National (1973) *Bulletin du Crédit National* (Paris) October.
6. Tamari, M. (1977) *Some International Comparisons of International Financing*, ch. 4 (London: Technicopy).
7. Industrial and Commercial Finance Corporation (ICFC) (1982) *The Small Firm Survey* (London: ICFC).
8. Hay, D. A. and Morris, D. J. (1984) *Unquoted Companies* (London: Macmillan).

9. Churchill, N. C. and Lewis, V. L. (1983) 'The five stages of small business growth', *Harvard Business Review*, vol. 61, no. 3, May–June.
10. Bertonèche, M. and Vickery, L. (1987) *Le Capital Risque*, (Paris: Presses Universitaires de Frances).
11. Benoun, M. and Sénicourt, P. (1975) *Approche Théorique et Pratique du Financement des Entreprises Naissantes* (Paris: CREFI).
12. United States Government (1984 and 1986) *The State of Small Business: A Report of the President* (Washington, DC: US Government Printing Office).
13. Wilson Committee to Review the Functioning of Financial Institutions (1979) *Studies of Small Firms' Financing*, (Research report no. 3 (London: HMSO).
14. Tamari, M. (1980) The Financial Structure of the Small Firm – An International Comparison of Corporate Accounts in the USA, France, UK, Israel and Japan, *American Journal of Small Business*, Baltimore, Md.
15. Burns, P. (1985) *Financial Characteristics of Small Companies in the UK*, Working Paper 85.8 (Cranfield: Cranfield School of Management).
16. Wetzel, W. E. and Seymour, C. R. (1981) *Informal Risk Capital in New England*, (Washington, DC: Office of Chief Counsel for Advocacy, US Small Business Administration).
17. Tymes, E. R. and Krasner, O. J. (1983) *Informal Risk Capital in California* (Wellesley, Mass.: Frontiers of Entrepreneurship Research, Babson College).
18. Sahlman, W. A. and Stevenson, H. H. (1985) 'Capital Market Myopia', *Journal of Business Venturing*, Winter.

Chapter 9   Developing Small Firms out of Large

References

Lorenz, J. A. (1985) *Venture Capital Today* (Woodhead-Faulkner).
National Economic Development Office (NEDO) (1987) *Corporate Venturing – A Strategy for Innovation and Growth* (London: NEDO).
Lorenz, J. A. (1985) 'Capture the Entrepreneurial Spirit in Corporate Venture Spin-Offs', *Accountancy Age*. 24.1.85.
Coyne, J. and Wright, M. (1986) Paper presented The Climate for Buy Outs to CFI Conference on 10.12.86. The Centre for Management Buy-Out Research, University of Nottingham.
Lorenz, J. A. (1986) 'Management Buy-Outs', *Acquisitions Monthly*.
Economist Intelligence Unit (Oct 86). 'Management Buy-Outs' (London: Economist Intelligence Unit).
Management Buy-Outs June 87. 3rd edition – Spicer & Pegler publication.
Lorenz, J. A. (1986) 'Management Buy-Ins', *Acquisitions Monthly*.

Index